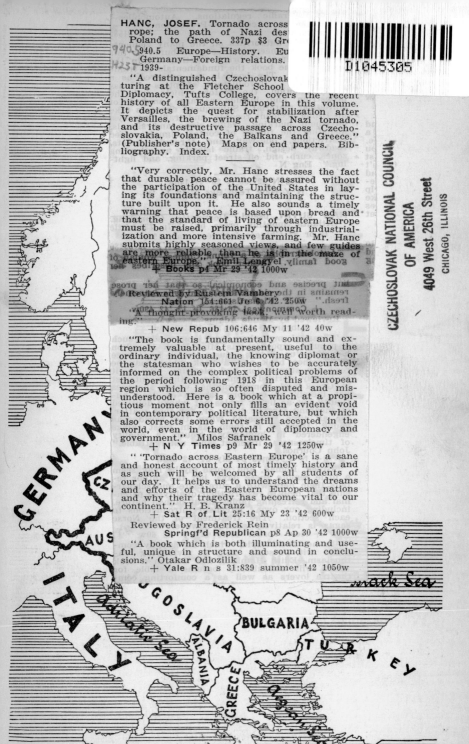

HANC, JOSEF. Tornado across [Eu]rope; the path of Nazi des[truction] Poland to Greece. 337p $3 Gr[eystone]

940.5 Europe—History. Eu[rope—] Germany—Foreign relations. [Europe] 1939-

"A distinguished Czechoslovak [lec]turing at the Fletcher School [of] Diplomacy, Tufts College, covers the recent history of all Eastern Europe in this volume. It depicts the quest for stabilization after Versailles, the brewing of the Nazi tornado, and its destructive passage across Czechoslovakia, Poland, the Balkans and Greece." (Publisher's note) Maps on end papers. Bibliography. Index.

"Very correctly, Mr. Hanc stresses the fact that durable peace cannot be assured without the participation of the United States in laying its foundations and maintaining the structure built upon it. He also sounds a timely warning that peace is based upon bread and that the standard of living of eastern Europe must be raised, primarily through industrialization and more intensive farming. Mr. Hanc submits highly seasoned views, and few guides are more reliable than he is in the maze of eastern Europe." Emil Lengyel
+ Books p4 Mr 29 '42 1000w

Reviewed by Rustem Vambery
Nation 154:661 Je 6 '42 250w

"Thought-provoking book worth reading."
+ New Repub 106:646 My 11 '42 40w

"The book is fundamentally sound and extremely valuable at present, useful to the ordinary individual, the knowing diplomat or the statesman who wishes to be accurately informed on the complex political problems of the period following 1918 in this European region which is so often disputed and misunderstood. Here is a book which at a propitious moment not only fills an evident void in contemporary political literature, but which also corrects some errors still accepted in the world, even in the world of diplomacy and government." Milos Safranek
+ N Y Times p9 Mr 29 '42 1250w

" 'Tornado across Eastern Europe' is a sane and honest account of most timely history and as such will be welcomed by all students of our day. It helps us to understand the dreams and efforts of the Eastern European nations and why their tragedy has become vital to our continent." H. B. Kranz
+ Sat R of Lit 25:16 My 23 '42 600w

Reviewed by Frederick Rein
Springf'd Republican p8 Ap 30 '42 1000w

"A book which is both illuminating and useful, unique in structure and sound in conclusions." Otakar Odlozilik
+ Yale R n s 31:839 summer '42 1050w

Tornado across Eastern Europe

TORNADO
across
EASTERN EUROPE

*The Path of Nazi Destruction
from Poland to Greece*

By

JOSEF HANČ

THE GREYSTONE PRESS
NEW YORK

Foreword

January First, 1942,
Year of the United Nations.

MY OLD FRIEND and collaborator Josef Hanč has devoted much
time to the study of the Central and Eastern European problems—
political, economic, national, etc.

This book contains a great deal of useful information and many
ideas which clarify the conditions in a hitherto undeservedly
neglected corner of the earth. I often hear, and partly agree, that
too many books on international affairs and recent history are
being written. "Tornado across Eastern Europe", in my estimation, is not one of the "too many". Though not necessarily pro-
fessing full agreement with all of the author's interpretations, I
heartily recommend the volume to all those who realize the
importance of the problems dealt with.

JAN MASARYK

New York, N. Y.

Preface

THE RAPID EXTENSION of World War II to all the continents is bound to draw the attention of the world to the geographical area from which the avalanche made its fateful start. As in the First World War the explosion was set off in Eastern Europe. On both occasions the contesting armies were drawn from nearly every part of the earth. After the military victory of the allies and revolutions in 1918 the face of Eastern Europe took on a new shape. Between Finland in the north and Greece in the south fourteen nations, numbering a hundred and twenty million, won a new lease on life and liberty. The destiny of these nations constitutes once again one of the primary stakes of the present struggle.

In reality the two decades between the wars gave little peace and no tranquility to Eastern Europe. They were filled with continual anxieties, efforts and counter-efforts, which revealed the inherent characteristics of this exposed region. Nowhere else have geography and history accumulated so imposing a variety of problems as in this area only four times the size of Texas. Throughout their long past the peoples of the Baltic-Danubian-Balkan lands have stood at the crossroads of opposite movements of population, currents of thought and political pressures. Their strategic location between the industrial peninsula of Europe and the vast Eurasian hinterland made them the carrier and the victim of economic and military struggle which acted as a factor of retardation and instability. In the early centuries the Eastern European zone of

vii

small nations was the pathway for the tribes marching from the east and north to Europe. More recently the region has become the route of a reverse movement from the west toward the Eurasian mainland.

The year 1939 showed that the last twenty years were only a fragile truce between two sanguinary periods which the future historian will treat as one continuous struggle of small nations for survival. Once again the face of Eastern Europe has been radically changed. Within a few months many peoples have been forced back into a position of servitude after enjoying barely twenty years of relative freedom—an infinitesimal fraction of their thousand years of history.

The circumstances under which Eastern Europe developed, was conquered, freed and reconquered, supply the unifying principle for treating as a unit an apparently heterogeneous territory. In the light of long-term history these variegated human groups have a common destiny. It is the purpose of this volume to contribute to an understanding of the factors involved in the political and economic reversals which have left indelible marks upon the peoples concerned. It may safely be predicted that without a reasonable and just solution of the Eastern European issues the peace of the whole continent will continue to be in suspension.

The first part of this volume gives a retrospective sketch of the ethnic groups of the area and their development down to the historical settlement of 1919. The subsequent three parts outline in chronological sequence the efforts to secure for the post-war order a title to permanence as well as the missed opportunities and the failures which accompanied the process. The final part is a venture into the future suggesting possible solutions in terms of desirability and practicability. This volume is an attempt to treat the very complex subject in its unity. It need hardly be added that no claim to finality is made at a time when history is still being forged by arms.

JOSEF HANČ

Contents

ix

Tornado across Eastern Europe

Part One

The Land and The Peoples

Early Migration and Settlement

It has been said that all reasonable hopes of the future depend on a sound understanding of the past. To no part of the world can this aphorism be applied with more justice than to Eastern Europe. Until the post-World War I years the culturally interesting and politically exposed area between the Baltic, Black and Mediterranean Seas was studied largely from the point of view of political strategy of the principal great powers. The histories paid fleeting attention to the various regions of the area when these were shifted from one sovereignty to another; except on rare occasions, however, the peoples of these provinces failed to come into the proper focus.

This general observation can be applied to each of the ethnic groups making Eastern Europe their permanent abode. Finland was known vaguely as an appendage first of Sweden and then of Russia. Estonia, Latvia and Lithuania were submerged in the Tsarist Empire. The general public in the west had only a faint knowledge that in the hinterland of the Russian seaports of Reval, Riga and Libava peoples with distinct individuality existed who cherished the ideal of independence. The partitions of Poland outraged men like Thomas Jefferson, but only a few readers of

Joseph Conrad suspected the Polish descent of the writer. Students of the Reformation knew the name of John Hus but only a handful realized that the Hussite movement was one of the earliest popular manifestations for religious, national and social democracy. The Slovaks lived in almost complete oblivion in Hungary, and hardly more was known about the Slovenes of Austria, the Rumanians of Transylvania, or the Croats. The Rumanian provinces of Wallachia and Moldavia entered the text-books chiefly after the Crimean Wars.

The progressive decay of the Ottoman Empire drew the attention of the European Powers to the problems of the Near East. In this connection the Greeks, Serbs, Montenegrians, Albanians and Bulgarians received some prominence. They aroused sentimental and active sympathies among the western liberals and in the diplomatic chancelleries because of their revolts against the Sultans and the massacres of the revolutionaries. Yet the history of the peoples as such remained closed. Historians absorbed in the problems of empires failed to impress upon the public that the Eastern European peoples, small though they were, had developed their own individuality and their own traditions which have not perished throughout the long centuries of wars, conquests and subjection.

To a degree postponement of general interest in Eastern Europe was natural and could be explained by the geographic, cultural and political circumstances under which this zone of varied ethnic groups was populated and developed. The Mediterranean coast-line and the Baltic seashore were successively opened up to world trade and to cultural penetration by enterprising Greeks, Venetians, and the Hanseatic League. But the mainland of the zone remained for a long time with only the scantiest channels of communication. There were several historic overland routes used by migrants, armies, traders and missionaries. Some of them were built by the Romans and continued their usefulness down to the age of railways. Such natural barriers as the Alps, Carpathians, or the Danube did interfere with freedom of traffic, but the obstacles they placed in the way of movement were not insurmountable. They were crossed by conquering armies on several occasions, and peaceful penetration had been going on almost without interruption.

However, none of these local conveniences and obstacles were decisive. What was of actual importance, both in terms of space and of time, was the distance which separated Eastern Europe from the western countries. Moreover, the peculiar local conditions which existed in Eastern Europe in the early period could hardly stimulate the interest of the western peoples. Forests and marshes prevailed in the larger part of the area. Aside from the fringes of land neighboring on the seas and the ancient routes, population was meagre, the primitive village type of community was general, and towns were few. There was usually enough food, and the inhabitants, mostly herders and peasants, managed to get along with simple methods of cultivation. There were none of the incentives toward greater activity that characterized developments in the west. The period of urbanization and industrialization was delayed, and has not yet reached the impetus equal to that which animated the social structure of western Europe. The Greeks and Albanians were practically the only local people, who engaged in overseas colonial activities, the kind of pursuit which made western Europe the most prosperous part of the world. Down to the nineteenth century Eastern Europe remained substantially isolated from the world highways of progress.

In the course of the Great Migration the various Germanic tribes pressed from their habitat in the Rhine, Main and Neckar basins against Roman Gaul. The Goths and Marcomanni penetrated farthest to the East, to the Eastern and Illyrian Prefectures of the Roman Empire. The Ostrogoths moved to the Balkans, the Lower Danube and the Save and Drave basins. The Marcomanni appeared for some time in Bohemia, Carinthia and Styria. In Bohemia they were presumably preceded by the Celtic Boii.

From the East, Asiatic tribes, "the scourges of God," were invading Eastern and Central Europe. The Huns led by their military leader Attila came to the Rhine in the fifth century. The Avars penetrated to the Eastern Alpine regions in the sixth, and the Magyars succeeded them in the ninth century.

Down to about 600 of the Christian Era the Germanic groups are believed to have occupied with sparse, loose and fluctuating settlements the area between the rivers Rhine, Vistula and Danube. Interspersed in these lands were to be found various Slav settlements, founded by tribes presumably driven out of their homes in Polesia, in the Pripet region. The Slavs came in partly as the vanguard of the Asiatic invaders, and partly in the train of the Avars. But between the sixth and seventh centuries the map of Eastern Europe must have undergone an important change. Instead of the Germanic peoples it was the Slavs who formed the bulk of the population between the Elbe and the Vistula rivers, and between the Baltic, Black and Adriatic Seas. Their settlements were also sparse and scattered, but in contrast to the nomadic Asiatic horsemen and to the restless Germanic tribes the Slavs settled down permanently as cultivators of land. Somewhat later their geographic continuity was broken up by two non-Slav peoples, the Magyars and the Daco-Rumans, who drove a wedge between the Slavs in the north and those in the Balkans.

By the end of the tenth century, when the task of building up the early political organizations of Eastern Europe began in earnest, the ethnic map was pretty well settled. The different groups who inhabited the area by that time have since, in general, lived in their present location for a thousand years. The political map of the zone, however, has been exposed to constant changes. The process of political crystallization has been repeatedly hampered by adverse influences. During the thirteenth century the early Germanic *Drang nach Osten* assumed the character of an organized mass movement. The Slavs were being systematically dislodged, exterminated, or Germanized. The borderline between these two major groups began to be shifted eastwards. At the same time the stream of Asiatic inroads continued through the Middle Ages. It was not until 1683 that the Ottoman Turks were repelled from Vienna, and even after their withdrawal from Central Europe they maintained their hold over the Balkans. There was also a movement of armies and migrants from the North, the Arctic and the Scandinavian peoples having made attempts to establish themselves in the Baltic basin and the surrounding plains.

Consequently each people happened to be in the way of some-one else. An unrelenting struggle went on for better military frontiers, natural resources, access to the seacoast, or for the satisfaction of the urge for more power. The Finns were exposed to the Swedes along their western border and to the Russians in the South and East. The Baltic peoples stood in the path of the Germans pushing eastwards along the coastline, while the Russians drove westwards to reach the sea. The Poles tried to secure more solid geographic features of support in all directions, but were in turn hemmed in by their neighbors. The Czechs were gradually surrounded by Germans on three sides. The Magyars took some time before they settled down in the new surroundings. Each of the Eastern European peoples developed its national psychology in the teeth of opposing forces and competing currents of civilization. Having encountered one another in an undeveloped region devoid of any compelling antecedent culture, the ethnically varied groups worked out their separate psychology which rendered the process of integration more difficult. The powerful movements of thought and action which changed the structure of Western society did eventually flow through the zone, often with a delay of centuries, but they only touched the upper strata leaving the bulk of the peasantry immune. Occasionally the Bulgarians, Serbs, Czechs, or Poles developed a high degree of culture and measured up to the best standards for the period. Each time, however, adverse factors, arising partly from the unsettled conditions at home, but more often from foreign conquests, cut short "the Golden Age" and made an end to a development which might have grown into an era of enduring prosperity.

The Imperial Idea and Nationalism

For two thousand years Europe was dominated by the imperial idea. In Eastern Europe this idea persisted longer than in the west, lasting indeed until World War I. At its best the medieval empire represented the political expression of Christian universalism. The Holy Roman Empire implied suzerainty over the whole known world, even if that ideal had never effectively materialized. The empires were supra-national organizations, within which sovereign authority radiated from the imperial centers over the provinces conquered by force or drawn to the empires by the attraction of their majesty. Their sway was marked by an element of brutal conquest, cruel subjugation of alien peoples and frequent warfare. Yet at the same time there was another element involved, that of the hierarchical distribution of central authority to maintain the integrity of the acquired territories by keeping peace and by ensuring the smooth functioning of the far-flung organization. This second element, as long as it lasted, gave the imperial concept a certain positive force by placing the empires above the ethnic differences of the subject groups.

Situated in the border zone between the Western and the Eastern Empires the peoples of Eastern Europe were exposed to the impact of both. The builders of the early states had to make their choice between the two. In the west Roman civilization and tradition took firm roots facilitating political consolidation. Yet the latent contest between the Emperor and the Pope for supremacy was taken advantage of by aspiring rulers for the furtherance of the particular interests. In the east no such contest existed. The Emperor was the bearer of both the temporal and spiritual authority. If the Western world manifested a tendency toward realism, the East was inclined toward mysticism.

The medieval history of the Eastern European zone was largely concerned with the struggle between these two conceptions of authority and between these two general outlooks. The attainment of the imperial crown marked the highest ambition of the rulers. In the shadow of the great imperial vision numerous lesser concepts arose which could be traced throughout the Middle Ages. In 917 Simeon of Bulgaria adopted the title of "the Tsar /Caesar/ and Autocrat of all Bulgarians and Greeks." In 1001 St. Stephen of Hungary received from Pope Silvester II the Holy Crown which to these days is kept as the greatest treasure. In 1346 Dushan the Great of Serbia assumed the title of "the Tsar of the Greek and the Serbs." His contemporary Charles the Great of Bohemia received the Holy Roman Crown and used the occasion to congratulate Dushan on holding "the second Imperial title." The power, authority and splendor of the Imperial crown had a magic spell which impelled the medieval rulers to divert their energies into Empire building.

The Reformation brought with it the weakening of the idea of imperial universalism. Western Europe embarked on the road of building national states. In Eastern Europe the existence of numerous small and ethnically different peoples still offered a field for the organization of larger supra-national political formations. The consideration of security induced several smaller states to enter into voluntary unions, and to combine their forces of defense against common enemy. The menace of the Turks, engaged in building an empire by conquest, induced the Austrians, Czechs and Hungarians in the sixteenth century to oppose it by an empire by consent. The concern for security played also an important part in the foundation of the Polish-Lithuanian Union. However, the same elements of diversity which imposed the policy of integration contained in themselves the danger of dissolution. Unless the imperial unions extended equal protection to all their members, unless they dispensed justice in a truly supra-national manner, they were doomed to disintegration. Indeed, the subsequent history of the surviving empires was marked by incessant conflicts between the imperial governments practicing conquest and the nationalities demanding justice and equality. Napoleon, one of the latest pretenders to the imperial heritage, witnessed the turning point when the imperial idea became an intolerable burden from which the subject peoples endeavored to deliver themselves.

At the time when diplomacy at the Congress of Vienna had produced in Eastern Europe a political order which in its territorial simplicity had no precedent, the national forces within the empires began the work of inner corrosion. In distinction from western Europe where modern states antedated modern nations, in Eastern Europe during the nineteenth and twentieth centuries national feeling preceded statehood. Nationalism began with a cultural revival, and gradually took the form of social and political struggle for equal rights and opportunities within the Empires. Earlier desire for autonomy grew into more definite demands for full independence. In a certain sense states were built in the minds of the people before they could be created in reality. Urged on by the inner dynamic of nationalism the people conceived the state as the only really effective juridical and political instrument for self-preservation.

The mere existence of national movements was not by itself sufficient to create national states. In Eastern Europe no people was powerful enough to achieve independence by wresting it from the conquerors by its own force. As long as the imperial regimes of the Turks, Habsburgs and Tsars functioned efficiently, the submerged nationalities were kept in check. The existence of national feeling was a vital prerequisite, however, and it had to reach sufficiently advanced form to take action. The decay of imperial organization to the point of impotence, and the connivance, support and eventual recognition by third powers had to act as coincidental elements. Empires did not break up easily. As a rule it needed wars and revolutions to loosen their cohesive forces. Many a small people looked forward to war as a lesser evil than a stabilized peace regarded as unjust. In his "Litany of Polish Pilgrims" Mickiewicz prayed for a universal war "which would bring deliverance of the peoples." But the third powers often abhorred "creating a vacuum" and feared chaos. The fear of one another and of the unpredictable led them to keep the Ottoman Empire alive by artificial injections. Not knowing what would take the place of the Habsburg Monarchy they hesitated long before sanctioning its dismemberment. Each of the great powers consulted primarily its own national interests.

Chronologically Greece was the first nation of the group to secure independence in 1832. The Baltic states were the last. Recognition was extended to them in 1920. The liberation of the subject nationalities proceeded thus from the extreme south to the extreme north. It followed the sequence in which the Turks, Habsburgs and Tsars were weakened as the result of the strain of their subject nationalisms and of the stress of wars with outside powers. The Ottoman Empire dwindled to the residual state of Turkey after World War I. The other Balkan nationalities reached autonomy first and full independence afterwards. Greece was followed by Serbia, Rumania and Bulgaria. The last of them, Albania, was established in 1913 after the Balkan Wars.

The dissolution of the Habsburg Monarchy in 1918 cleared the path for the subject nationalities of Danubian Europe to rise to statehood. Only a genuine and timely settlement with its rival subject national groups could have saved the Monarchy from dissolving into its ethnic parts. The dissolution started in fact in 1867, by the "compromise," which delivered ten million Rumanians, Croats, Slovaks, Ruthenes and Serbs to ten million Magyars, and twenty million Czechs, Poles, Ukrainians, Slovenes, Serbs, Croats, Italians and Rumanians to ten million Germans. In default of a federation of equals only a successful Germanization and Magyarization might have given the dual Monarchy a new lease of life. Yet not even reliance upon Germany could accomplish the impossible. The World War in which Austria-

Hungary with her Slav and Latin population stood against Russia and Serbia and against Rumania and Italy was bound to bring the process of disintegration to a head.

In Russia the cosmopolitan Panslavism of the nineteenth century developed into Russianism which in some ways resembled the political, social and cultural workings of Germanism. The Russification of the Estonians, Letts, Lithuanians, Poles and Finns provoked a strong reaction which led to the consolidation of the separate nationalisms of these submerged groups. The Bolshevik revolution of 1917 introduced an entirely different aspect, that of the struggle of the working class against international bourgeois capitalism. Its thesis was that racial, ethnic, linguistic, cultural and historical frontiers dividing peoples were the product of and cloak for the vested interests of the privileged classes, and that the real barriers dividing nations from one another lay in the fact that the holders of the monopoly of political power identified their class prerogatives with general national interests. The struggle was to be concentrated on the economic divides. Participation in World War I, which cost Russia more lives than any other belligerent, and the outbreak of the social revolution weakened that country to such an extent that it could no longer prevent the Baltic peoples from asserting their claims to separation and independence.

Lines of Division

In dealing with the complex ethnic structure of Eastern Europe confusion should be avoided that might arise from the inaccurate use of terms defining the varied distinctions between individual peoples. The following dividing factors should be given due consideration: historical, cultural, religious, linguistic, racial and social.

The cartographic simplification of the area brought about by the substitution of a few large empires for the numerous small states and principalities of the Middle Ages could not erase the memory of the earlier political systems. The historical boundaries continued to exist in the minds of the succeeding generations. The power of historical memory became a factor that could not be suppressed. This was doubly true whenever the new boundary entailed the deterioration of preceding conditions of life, or when it cut across the living ethnic organism. The Poles never stopped thinking of their nation as a unit divided into three parts by hostile powers. The virtual submergence of the Bohemian Kingdom within the centralized Habsburg Monarchy did not prevent the Czechs from refusing to admit the extinction of ancient statehood. Underneath the apparent imperial unity a great national diversity could be discerned nourished on reminiscences. It was not an accident that the postwar map of 1919 corresponded in rough outlines with the map of Eastern Europe as it had existed about 1000 A.D.

The cultural lines of demarcation were even more real. Particularly painful situations developed where and when cultural units were dissected by political boundaries. The Finns felt keenly that beyond their ethnic borders lay a different type of culture which they regarded as eastern. Considering the Asiatic origin of the Finns, the distinction they draw between themselves and the Russians was noteworthy. It demonstrated that the cultural influences conveyed through Swedish rule were more profound than the traces of racial origin. The Magyars, also of Asiatic descent, portrayed themselves as the forbears of western civilization in contrast to the Rumanians whom they regarded as culturally oriental. The Rumanians on the other hand, proud of their quasi-Roman associations, considered themselves as the easternmost outpost of western Latinism. The Croats of Hungary, enjoying a slightly higher level of culture than the isolated mountain Slavs of Serbia, looked down on the Serbs as inferior.

Often distinctions such as these lacked objectivity and were merely expressive of self-assumed conception of one's own superiority. Elsewhere they grew out of the complex of inferiority. The peoples who happened to be in political control or in a privileged economic position usually developed a strong superiority complex. "A Slovak was not a human being," even if he shared the same state with his Magyar master. As far as the Germans were concerned, their Slav neighbors were to remain hewers of wood and drawers of water. This attitude was partly due to the role which the medieval German colonists played in Eastern Europe. As artisans, miners and town folk they were granted privileges denied to the natives. They were permitted to settle in close communities and be governed by their own laws. No attempts were made to assimilate them either peacefully or by coercion. The feeling of superiority survived the ages and was stimulated by the nearness and the power of the German fatherland.

The cultural aspect of divisions could not be properly understood unless all component manifestations of life were considered. Each national society developed its own institutions and sets of values in the course of centuries. Only through careful selection, observation, comparison and interpretation could the various elements of culture be set in correct relationship, whether they derived from geography, climate, history, economy, national psychology or religion. In some regions two groups might, for instance, be closely related to one another through culture despite linguistic differences. In other regions cultural divisions would be important in defiance of the identity of language, for instance in Prussia and Austria.

The age-long struggle between churches added to the cultural differentiation quite conspicuously. Eastern Europe provided the maneuvering ground for the contest between Roman and the Orthodox Churches. Catholicism brought with it Latin civilization while the Orthodox Faith introduced the Byzantine concepts. Torn between these rival conceptions the peoples of Eastern Europe were compelled by economic and political pressure to align themselves either with the west or the east. The place of Roman commanders was taken by Catholic bishops, and the

Legions made room for Roman clergy. Monasteries replaced the abandoned imperial forts. Leaning upon a more efficient organization and imbued with a more aggressive spirit, Catholicism gained ground everywhere except in the Balkans where the tradition of Byzantium was strong. The Czechs, Poles, Lithuanians, Hungarians, Croats and Slovenes accepted Latinism, whereas Bulgarians, Greeks, Serbs, Russians and Rumanians chose the eastern Church. Thus religion divided the Slavs into two opposing camps with far-reaching consequences of disunity. To a lesser degree Protestantism added one more mark of distinction, as illustrated by the relationship between the Czechs and Slovaks. Old Slavonic, the language which Cyrill and Methodius attempted in the ninth century to introduce as the liturgical medium among all the Slavs, might have developed into an instrument of unity. However, according to Rome only Latin, Greek and Hebrew were proper languages for glorifying God. Most of the western Slavs became Catholics but Old Slavonic maintained its place in the Balkans and in Russia and was, after Latin, the most commonly used medium of Christian liturgy. The peoples who accepted Roman Christianity were saved for western civilization. Yet they often paid for that privilege by succumbing to the power of Germanism.

The religious schism complicated the picture of Eastern European diversity. It looms as one of the causes for repeated wars between the Poles and the Muscovite State; it hampered unity among the Southern Slavs; and it gave the Ukrainian peasant revolts the added stress of a struggle for both land and religion. On the other hand, it inspired the Tsars to take interest in the fate of the Orthodox subjects under the Sultans and to assist in their deliverance. The academic Panslavism of Russia took a good deal of encouragement from the ideal of the unity of the Eastern Christian peoples. In recent years the religious division has lost much of its sharpness. The enduring political antagonism between Rumanians, Bulgarians, Serbs and Greeks, all members of the

Orthodox Faith, would indicate that national interests took precedence over religion.

The linguistic divisions are of no less significance for the understanding of Eastern Europe. Military conquerors as well as supposedly liberal governments attempted to impose external unity on the heterogeneous ethnic groups by linguistic assimilation, in the spirit of the dictum: "one King, one Faith, one language." Use of the language of the conqueror was pressed by forceful measures, and the native tongue was prohibited. Whenever this occurred language became the principal rallying point of national consciousness. It moulded the soul of nations, and perpetuated their tradition. It was of inestimable value in the course of modern national revival when the leaders of national movements sought the support of the masses. The familiar terms such as Russification, Polonization, Germanization, Magyarization, or Hellenization, suggested primarily the attempts of the ruling groups to eradicate, or at least to restrict, use of native tongue as the most common and the most natural medium of communication. In due course the preëminence of language as the criterion of nationality has been generally recognized.

If the linguistic frontiers could be ascertained with comparative ease, the racial divisions were blurred during the process of long mixing, until they disappeared almost completely. The fusion of the Nordic, Mediterranean, Lappish and Caucasian races has been going on ever since the quaternary period. This dilution in turn produced new composite types, of which the Baltic, Alpine, Dinaric, and Litoral have been most frequent in this area. Morphological and blood tests proved that each of the varied ethnic groups betrays a mixture of several types, and that no correlation exists between racial and linguistic marks. The German speaking people in particular are racially less homogeneous than their neighbors. No reliable conclusions can be drawn as to the correlation between physical characteristics of individual ethnic groups and their mental capacity. Similarly psychological tests do not lead to conclusive results. The racial idea has been introduced to Eastern Europe by the theoreticians of the doctrine of inequality of races. Scientifically it could contribute little to a better comprehension of the local problems except that knowledge of the true nature of race could have become a powerful weapon in the struggle against intolerance and oppression, and could have acted for more unity instead of more segregation.

From the point of view of economic structure, the area between the Baltic, Black and Adriatic Seas has been known as "agrarian Europe." One-third of the Czechs and Austrians, more than half of the Magyars and Greeks, two-thirds of the Estonians, Finns, Slovaks, and Letts, and more than three-quarters of the Poles, Ukrainians, Lithuanians, Rumanians, Bulgarians and Yugoslavs depend on agriculture. Within each group the unequal distribution of land under the feudal system produced a class differentiation of profound significance. Among the Czechs .02 per cent of the population exploited in an irrational manner 27.7 per cent of land at a time when 40,000 landless people had to emigrate annually to the United States to escape starvation. Similar conditions prevailed throughout the area with the exception of Serbia and Bulgaria where small holdings or collective holdings were familiar. In the nineteenth century serfdom was abolished, but the freed peasantry had no land to live on. The landlords were mostly foreigners, or belonged to the oppressing privileged class, to landed aristocracy, absentee proprietors and Church, and held the monopoly of government and of the socially, economically and politically dominant super-structure. Consequently, the rural history of Eastern Europe was largely the history of peasant revolutions, and the national movements assumed a mixed national and social character. However, in the decisive years of World War I and the Bolshevik revolution the struggle for national freedom took precedence over social emancipation. The people felt themselves Poles, Finns or Rumanians first, and workers, peasants or professional class afterwards. Above all they wanted to free themselves from foreign domination. After having achieved political independence they thought of attacking the problem of economic and social improvements.

The Peace Settlement of 1919

The Peace Treaties of 1919 and 1920 sanctioned a new Eastern Europe. According to Masaryk, one of the principal authors of this new order, it was to consist of national states erected on the ruins of the old monarchies from the Baltic Sea to the Mediterranean, where "all nations should be good neighbors." It was assumed that as soon as Eastern Europe was organized politically along more natural lines of liberated nationalities, and as soon as Germany was barred from control over Austria-Hungary, the Balkans and Turkey, that there would be no fear of German domination. A more natural organization of the zone of small nations would benefit the western powers for they would have a smaller burden to carry. It was to be a Europe based on the acceptance of the national principle as the most vital social reality. Masaryk warned against the pangermanists who raised nationalism to a mystical chauvinism and impressed upon their nation, intoxicated by frequent military victories, the idea of an elect race. He urged the subject nationalities not to foster nationalism to extremes. The struggle for liberation was essentially democratic and social. It was a spontaneous reaction to the militaristic spirit exemplified in the phrase of Treitschke that "there was something ridiculous in the idea of a small state," and that "morality was the endowment of small men undertaking small things, whereas the state must carry out big things." Masaryk conceived the new Eastern Europe as a part of a democratic and non-militaristic Europe, where the power-political concept of buffer states would have no meaning, for both large and small nations would exist in their own rights.

At the same time it could not be denied that there would be a material difference between strong and weak states. The strong nations could defend themselves more easily than the weak ones. It was therefore the policy of the Entente Powers to make the new states as strong as possible. Moreover, the weaker peoples believed that they were entitled to assistance on the ground both of international morality and practical policy. If the doctrine of the physically fittest was to be universally endorsed, they argued, it would inevitably lead to constant wars and consequently to the dehumanization of mankind. The makers of the new Eastern Europe clearly envisaged the need of an effective international organization and of a system of wide international agreements both political and economic, as a corollary to the practical application of the national principle. The Peace Settlement of 1919 did not make any serious attempt at reorganizing Eastern Europe on a federal basis. The opinion prevailed, however, that some such federation, if freely entered upon, would contribute to the consolidation of the sector. A real federation would be accomplished only when the nations were free to unite of their own accord; it would have to grow out of their needs and not out of dynastic or imperialistic motives.

The guiding principle behind the new order in Eastern Europe was that of nationality. The criterion of nationality was largely language. On general grounds the suitability of this principle was open to argument. But so was any other principle, whether historical, economic, cultural, geographic or strategic. Actually in no section of the area did the lines of division coincide to offer an ideal national boundary. The oldest geographic and at the same time historical boundaries were those of the Bohemian provinces, Bohemia and Moravia, and of Hungary. Yet it was just these two boundaries which ran counter to the line defined by ethnography. The ethnographic borders of Poland would have challenged history, economics and strategy. President Millerand's refusal to accept the Hungarian historical claim for the reason that "even though millennial, it is not bound to continue when it has been recognized as contrary to justice," caused repeated commotion in the Budapest parliament. Foreign Minister Teleki of Hungary considered it sounded "as if the thousand year possession of Hungary were illegal." At the Peace Conference Count Apponyi in stressing the cultural principle complained that the percentage of literacy among the Rumanians was only 33, whereas among the Magyars it was 80. He maintained that from the point of view of the broad interests of mankind it could not be a matter of indifference to include a Magyar minority within the hegemony of an inferior civilization, meaning Rumania. He was reminded, however, that from the point of view of the broad interests of mankind the Magyar majority which was responsible for the government of Hungary was also responsible for the illiteracy of the Rumanian and Slovak speaking population.

The reason why nationality was laid down as the basis of the new order in preference to any other principle was to be found in the existence of the national feeling which by its vitality pushed into the background all other considerations. Nationalities in 1918 represented living realities demanding political body. By the time the Armistice was signed in November, 1918, the liberation of each Eastern European people was in fact an already accomplished reality. Throughout the years of 1917 and 1918 the individual nations proclaimed their independence, and before the Peace Conference began its sessions, they had established their governments, occupied the territories they claimed, and in several instances passed provisional constitutions. Their delegations came to Paris not for the purpose of asking for independence, which they had already attained, but to demand the recognition of their specific territorial claims. They appeared at the Peace Conference not in the role of supplicants with cap in hand, but as delegates of states, some of which had been previously recognized as allies and cobelligerents. The Peace Conference had the task of examining and deciding upon these claims and upon the means of setting up independent states with some prospect of continued existence.

The primary object of the peacemaking of 1919 and 1920 as far as Eastern Europe was concerned was to establish national homes for the peoples whose liberation had been proclaimed as one of the peace aims. Ethnic considerations took a preëminent place in defining the new boundaries. Factors of geography, communications or defense were not ignored, however, when a strictly ethnic boundary would weaken the position of the new states and deprive them of the essential elements of security. The idealistic conceptions of the new-world-in-the-making as propounded during World War I under the stress of mass slaughter made room for sober pondering over the maps and in the course of personal contacts with individual peace delegations. The Europe of tomorrow as it was visualized by many practical optimists attending the Peace Conference was full of promises but also full of apprehensions lest the forces of reaction frustrate the fruits of the victory. The final settlement in Eastern Europe bore the imprint of this mixture of hopes and anxieties. It was a large scale compromise between the past and the future, an experiment which had equal chance of success and failure.

The fact that 4,000 miles of new frontiers were added to the already much compartmentalized Europe was among the most adversely criticized provisions of the Peace Treaties. However, this drawback could have been offset by the introduction of effective policies which would have reduced the restrictive or wholly negative functions of international boundaries. The superimposition of economic, geographic or strategic frontiers over strictly ethnic lines of division and the resulting creation of minorities on the "wrong" side of the borders was another feature commonly regarded as a weakness of the postwar system. Yet was it wholly impractical to expect that by a right kind of policy the sensitiveness of the imperfect boundaries could be reduced in due course, if not entirely obliterated? Was it not a fact that the codification of minority protection under international supervision constituted a novel method of redress which imperfect though it was could be developed into a potent agency of co-operation?

On the other hand, the postwar Eastern Europe was simpler than its predecessor. It was also more just. The number of people subjected to alien rule was decreased by more than one half. The liberation of whole nations from hostile domination eliminated certain sources of unrest and thus removed some of the causes of potential frictions and wars. The new frontiers were drawn with greater care and knowledge than at any previous Peace Congress. Controversial issues were scrutinized on the spot by investigators able to distinguish causes from effects. At least twenty-six investigations were undertaken before the final drafts were submitted to the respective Councils. It was generally conceded that if it were found to be impossible to do justice to both sides, the balance should be inclined towards the Allies rather than towards the former foe, but that the principle should not be carried too far, if the ultimate goal was to produce the bases of a durable peace.

The claims advanced by the spokesmen of the new states were often excessive, and as such were refused sympathetic hearing, or melted down to a compromise. Several opposing claims were settled outside the Conference directly by the parties concerned. An important part of the Settlement, namely the western borders of Russia, was effected against the better judgment of the Conference. Four nations, Poland, Hungary, Rumania and Turkey, challenged the Paris decisions, and were either permitted to retain the fruits of their unilateral acquisitions, or dissuaded from persisting in the arbitrary course of their policies. Most of the Baltic Settlement was only indirectly related to the main Conference agenda but was reserved to direct dealings with the Bolshevik Government. The absence of Russia from the Peace Conference made it easier for the Poles, Rumanians and Turks to obtain the maximum satisfaction of their claims. On the other hand, it introduced in the postwar relationships an element of insecurity which weighed heavily upon the subsequent attempts at stabilization. If Russia felt that she was barred from access to the Baltic and the Mediterranean Seas, Germany in turn resisted the Settlement which she regarded as aimed against her expansion to the east. Italy, too, failed to secure a firm foothold along the eastern Adriatic coast and in eastern Mediterranean. These three dissatisfied powers gave the lead to the postwar revisionist movements. They were assisted by Hungary and to a lesser extent by Bulgaria, the two minor powers aspiring to recover the lost provinces. The new Eastern Europe was thus born into a world of contesting forces which exercised an unrelenting pressure upon its future course. Eventually the same forces contributed to the outbreak of another war.

After the World War the problem of the reorganization of Eastern Europe on the basis of national states was in a measure taken out of the hands of the great powers and vested in the sovereign governments of the peoples immediately concerned. The interests of the great powers did by no means cease to exert influence upon the relationships between the smaller nations. Yet the local governments were given the opportunity, such as they had never enjoyed in the past, to shape their future more in accordance with their own desires than under the exclusive impact of political strategy of outside factors. Their sovereignty was slightly curtailed owing to minority obligations under the new international order, and in practice their freedom of action was also circumscribed by the material and moral ties which grew out of their specific relations with the individual Powers during the War. On the whole, however, they were free to embark on a road of their own choice, and correspondingly they assumed a large measure of responsibility for the future of that part of Europe which lay within the sphere of their combined influence. How they acquitted themselves in their new roles is discussed in the second part of this volume. As a preliminary a brief sketch is drawn of the evolution of each group inclusive of the way in which their histories were affected by the Peace Settlement after the first World War.

The Greeks

The history of modern Greece started in 1830, after the Wars of Liberation when the Great Powers recognized her independence under their joint protection. At that time Greece had only 700,000 inhabitants as compared with two millions in 1913 and six millions after the World War. With the progressive dissolution of the Ottoman Empire new provinces were added step by step to Pelopennesus, until modern Greece comprised Epirus, Thessaly, Macedonia, Thrace, Crete and islands in the Ionian and Aegean Seas. Thus numerous little states which had once contributed to the history of the classical age of Greece were forged into a fairly homogeneous body destined to play an important part in the Eastern Mediterranean. Modern Greece did not extend to the African and Asiatic territories formerly occupied by something like 150 little sovereign city states, but the dream of the supremacy of Hellenism in the Eastern Mediterranean has been kept alive and sometimes found its expression in the political formula of the Ionian Empire. It is generally believed that the modern Greeks represent a consolidated ethnic group which has grown out of several elements that during the Byzantine rule replaced the earlier Hellenes. The Greeks themselves entertain no doubts that they trace direct descent from the ancient race. This consciousness of a long, glorious and uninterrupted tradition proved a great asset in their nineteenth century national movement for independence. The fact that modern Greece is associated with the ancient Heroic Age helped to arouse popular sympathies for the Philhellenic movement in the western countries and for the Greek cause in general.

During the World War Greece remained neutral until the French deposed the pro-German King Constantine. In 1917 the new government, led by popular Veniselos, joined the Allies. By the Treaty of Sèvres of 1920, the Greeks doubled their territory and realized practically all their claims. Greater Greece appeared in the form of a state situated around the Eastern Mediterranean. It included Eastern Thrace and Smyrna with a large part of Western Asia Minor, inhabited partly by a Greek majority and partly by Turks. Cyprus was retained by Great Britain and the Dodecanese Islands went to Italy, in spite of their predominantly Greek population. Veniselos was well pleased with this outcome. "By combining the culture of her old civilization with the vitality and spirit of her younger generations Greece will become a factor of progress, of peace and of order in the Near East," he wrote to his friend Lloyd George.

However, Greater Greece was to last only to 1923, when a new Peace Treaty was signed with Turkey, that of Lausanne. The Lausanne treaty marked the ascendency of Turkey and a sub-stantial eclipse of Greece, whose Asiatic acquisitions had to be abandoned. This retreat of the Allies was due to several causes: the internal divisions in Greece, where the revival of the tradi-tional feud between Veniselos and Constantine weakened the army and brought about its debacle in Smyrna; the rise of Turkey which under the leadership of Mustapha Kemal refused to accept the humiliation imposed by the Treaty of Sèvres; and the differ-ences amongst the great powers. The French negotiated secretly with Kemal behind the backs of the British who themselves were divided as to the course to take. The Italians sided openly with Turkey helping her to weaken the Greek resistance. All through-out the Peace Conference Italian policy was more or less hostile to the Greeks who were regarded as a rival to the Italian designs in Eastern Mediterranean.

The Turks

As in the case of Greece the history of modern Turkey would take in a much smaller area than that of the late Ottoman Empire. At their height the Sultans controlled more or less efficiently the whole of northern Africa, a large part of Asia eastwards to Persia, and northwards to the Caucasus, and all the Balkans, subjecting to

their rule in the fourteenth and fifteenth centuries the early Slav,
Rumanian and Greek states and principalities. After the abortive
attempt to capture Vienna in 1683 they retired to the Balkans. The
Ottoman rule there has been described as despotic, and the cruelty
with which the repeated uprisings of the subject peoples were
suppressed caused the successive governments to be labelled as
corrupt, vicious and unfit to rule over alien races. The Ottoman
rule was regarded as synonymous with material and cultural de
struction, and the removal of that rule was welcome as the beginning of economic prosperity and rise in culture. On the other
hand, it should be admitted that few systematic attempts were
made to extinguish the customs and peculiarities of the subject
nations. Their resistance to the Turks, coupled with the ineffi-
ciency of the oppressors, enabled them to carry on through the
four to five centuries of what they described as the Dark Ages.

The World War brought the continued process of decomposi-
tion of the Empire to a fatal end. At the same time the defeat of
the Turks introduced a salutary element in their future evolution
as a nation. The Young Turks aimed at revitalizing the imperial
leadership. In 1908 they overthrew Abdul Hamid and took over
the government. Their revolt was not strictly national in character. Trained in German militarism, the Young Turk leaders
aspired to save the Empire, bankrupt financially, and losing one
province after another. Two often conflicting imperial ambitions
loomed in the background of their movement: Pan-Islamism,
uniting all Moslems of India and Asia Minor under the Sultans
and against the British Empire, and Panturanism, uniting all
Turkish speaking peoples of Asia and Europe, particularly Russia.
The occupation and the threatening partition of the Empire in
1918 aroused the Turkish national consciousness. The years between 1918 and 1923 saw the birth and the consummation of the
Turkish national idea. The shift of the center of the war of independence from the Allied controlled Istanbul to Ankara in
Anatolia symbolized the change in the orientation of policy.

Mustapha Kemal, "the Atatürk," since known as the founder of the modern Turkish state, defied the Peace Conference, and having gathered a fairly efficient army embarked on the struggle to clear Asia Minor of the Allied forces. He took full advantage of the dissensions amongst the victorious powers and succeeded in securing a revision of the Treaty of Sèvres. Most of his claims were eventually recognized. In particular Eastern Thrace and Western Anatolia were restored to Turkey, thus making her supreme in Asia Minor between the Black Sea and the Mediterranean. A compulsory resettlement of Greeks from Anatolia in exchange for Turks from Greece was designed to make Turkey ethnically homogeneous and to remove causes of possible friction in the future.

The Treaty of Lausanne was accepted in western Europe, and especially in England among the liberals and supporters of Lloyd George's policy in the Near East as "the most humiliating incident in the history of western civilization." For the Turks it marked the beginning of a new national life. The old capitulations were abolished and the new Government was placed in a position of full sovereignty, even though the territory of the former Empire was restricted to correspond better to the ethnic distribution of the population. Only one-thirtieth of the territory was still in Europe, with one-thirteenth of Turkey's fifteen million inhabitants. Under her capable leaders Turkey entered an era of regeneration. The Caliphate was abolished, the Islamic religion disestablished, and the whole political, economic, social and cultural structure of society was subjected to radical modernization. In international affairs Turkey approached the western Powers, her World War enemies, and was earmarked to play an important role in the Mediterranean and the Balkans.

After having gone through imperial adventures of several centuries the Turks finally retired to the lands where their Ural-Altaic ancestors had settled nine hundred years earlier.

The Bulgars

In 679 A.D. the Bulgars, a Turanian race akin to the Huns, Avars, and other Asiatics, crossed the Danube Delta on the way from the Lower Don region to the Balkans. There they mixed with the Slavs who in turn had from the third to seventh centuries absorbed or expelled the Thraco-Illyrian race originally found in the peninsula. The Bulgars conquered the Slavs and gave them their name, but accepted their language and were assimilated by the conquered. It took several centuries, however, before their Asiatic system of despotism merged with the Slavs, whose social institutions betrayed an innate democratic leaning. The Bulgars accepted the Greek Church and fell under the influence of Byzantine culture. Twice between the ninth and the fourteenth centuries they built up their own empire, which at one time extended to the Adriatic, and under Tsar Simeon and Ivan Asen reached a high level of power and culture. The history of the medieval independence of Bulgaria passed through continued struggle with Byzantium for Balkan supremacy. From 1018-1186 the country was subjected to Byzantine Emperors. The real subjection came, however, with the invasion of the Turks in the fourteenth century. Bulgaria became the vassal of the Sultans, and did not recover independence until 1878.

The delay in the rise of the national revival of the Bulgars was mainly due to their geographic isolation. They eventually gained freedom, largely thanks to Russia. In March of 1878 the dream of the united Great Bulgaria became a reality. At San Stefano Russia dictated the Peace Treaty to Turkey, creating an autonomous Bulgaria which comprised all Bulgarian provinces. However, the Congress of Berlin the same year frustrated the idea of Great Bulgaria. Disraeli was particularly bent on preventing the Tsar from using the Bulgarian state as an instrument of alleged expansion to the Straits. Bulgaria was divided into several parts, with Macedonia placed under direct authority of the Sultan. Thus while the British Prime Minister was being hailed for this "peace with honor," a violent irredentism was created in the Balkans which under the name of "the Macedonian Question" was to pre-occupy Europe for more than half of a century. It became one of the causes of the Balkan Wars, and it brought Bulgaria to the side of the Central Powers during the World War. In 1908 Prince Ferdinand, taking advantage of the situation brought about by the Young Turk revolution, proclaimed full independence and as-sumed the historical title of the Tsar. Before the spoils of the first Balkan War of 1912 were apportioned amongst the members of the anti-Turkish Balkan League, the second War broke out between the victors in 1913. Bulgaria found herself, largely because of her own fault, in the face of united enmity of Serbia, Montenegro, Greece, and finally Rumania.

By the Treaty of Bucharest she lost Southern Dobrudja, rich in soil, to Rumania, but obtained a strip of the Aegean coastline with the harbor of Dedeagach. During the World War Bulgaria shifted her traditional loyalty from Russia to the Central Powers in the hope of recovering Macedonia, then in Greek and Serbian hands. Realizing her miscalculation of the outcome of the War, she was the first Central Power to sue for armistice in September 1918. This step accelerated the approaching collapse of the Central Powers, but because of the strong position of Rumania, Yugo-slavia and Greece in Paris, Bulgaria failed to derive any benefit from her separate and belated withdrawal from the World War.

Ever since the Congress of Berlin the Great Bulgaria of San Stefano had been the symbol of the national aspirations of all patriotic Bulgars. However, the circumstances under which they came to Paris were hardly propitious. Their case was considered as of minor importance. With the exception of the American ex-perts they had few friends. Rumania and Yugoslavia on the other hand were supported by France, and Greece had a protector in Lloyd George.

The Bulgarian Delegation claimed Southern Dobrudja, a part

of Macedonia, and Eastern and Western Thrace, chiefly on ethnic grounds. Western Thrace would in addition offer her an un-hampered access to the Aegean Sea. Alternatively the Bulgars proposed the establishment of an independent Macedonian state under international protection or mandate, and the internationali-zation of Western Thrace. The Peace Treaties of Neuilly of 1919 and of Lausanne of 1923, and the Conference at San Remo, left Southern Dobrudja to Rumania, placed Thrace under Turkish and Greek sovereignty, and divided Macedonia between Yugo-slavia, Greece and Bulgaria. Although the claims of the rival Balkan Powers were slightly restricted, the changes introduced by the Peace Conference could hardly satisfy the Bulgarian aspira-tions. The country was cut off from the Aegean Sea by a strip of Greek territory about twelve miles long, so that Greece might have a contiguous overland route to Eastern Thrace. The demand of Southern Dobrudja, a sovereign access to the Sea, and a recti-fication of the Yugoslav frontiers constituted the basis for post-war Bulgarian revisionism. The principle and practice of the Conference of Paris that the possessions of the ex-enemies of the Entente should not be enlarged at the expense of the victors and their friends was attacked by the Bulgars as barbarous. It will re-quire a different kind of international society, however, before victors will be willing to surrender their territories to the van-quished.

The Albanians

The western coast of the Balkans is partly taken up by the Albanians, a mountain people given to pastoral and agricultural life. With tribal trends prevalent throughout most of their land, and with insufficient communications, the Albanians are very slowly emerging from their primitive self-sufficing home economy. Mostly of Moslem Faith, but with important Christian minorities, they have their own literary language of the Indo-European family of languages, and have developed their own national feeling. The two factors often overlap, particularly in the shifting border areas. Historically the Albanians lived first under the Roman Empire, and afterwards were ruled at one time or another by Bulgars, Serbs, Normans, native Chieftains, Venetians and Turks. The nineteenth century wave of nationalism did not find them indifferent. By helping the Turks in 1908 they hoped to be rewarded with autonomy. Instead, the Turks started upon a course of forcible Ottomanization. The Albanians revolted in 1912, and the following year an autonomous Principality of Albania was recognized by the Conference of the Great Powers in London under their protection. Albania comprised only a half of the ethnically Albanian population of the Balkans. The strategic raison d'être of the state was to bar the Serbs from the Adriatic Seacoast.

The new state led a precarious existence. Prince William of Wied, whom the Powers appointed to the Albanian throne, never reached his destination, but entirely unprepared for the task, was forced to leave Durazzo at the beginning of the World War. The Greeks occupied southern Albania, the Italians the central portion with the port of Valona, and in 1915 the Serbs took northern Albania. The latter were driven off by the Austrian troops, while Italy took over the Greek occupied territory. In 1917 General Ferrero proclaimed Albanian independence at Argyrokastron under the protection of Italy. Early in 1919 an Assembly gathered at Durazzo to acclaim "the noble principle of President Wilson" with regard to the right of small peoples to independence. It established a provisional government under Turkhan Pasha and sent a Delegation to the Peace Conference. It also appealed to Italy to drive out the Serbs from Northern Albania, and to send in technicians and capital to assist in the development of the country.

At the Peace Conference the Albanians claimed full ethnic frontiers, which went beyond both the limits set by the Congress of Berlin and the London Conference. The Italians first raised counter-claims to central Albania in accordance with the provisions of the secret Treaty of London of 1915. That treaty envisaged the partition of the country between Italy, Greece and Serbia. Later the Italians under pressure abandoned this claim and stated that they would be contented with sovereignty over Valona and a mandate over the country. Yugoslavia opposed Italy in favor of an independent Albania in the spirit of the motto, "the Balkans to the Balkan peoples." In 1920 a revolt broke out in southern Albania. Italy had to evacuate her troops from Valona, and in August of the same year she recognized Albanian integrity and sovereignty with the exception of the island Saseno at the entrance to the Valona Bay. Italy occupied the island in order to prevent Valona from being used as a base by an enemy power.

Having obtained de facto recognition by Italy, Greece and Yugoslavia, the Albanian Government asked for membership in the League of Nations. On British recommendation the country was admitted to the League even before it was recognized de jure by the Conference of Ambassadors. In 1921 the Great Powers acquiesced in Albanian sovereignty within the frontiers of 1913 with some rectifications. At the same time the Conference recognized Italy's special rights in the maintenance of the territorial order along the Albanian coast of the Adriatics. It stated that any interference in the integrity of the Albanian frontiers might endanger strategic security of Italy and that therefore should Albania be unable to uphold her integrity, she could appeal to the League of Nations, and the Great Powers would recommend to the League to entrust Italy with safeguarding the status quo. It became clear that Italian interest in Albania was to constitute an important issue in the Balkans.

The Yugoslavs

The history of the Yugoslavs falls into separate histories of the three ethnically related Slav peoples who in the sixth century penetrated into the Roman provinces in the Balkans: Serbs, Croats and Slovenes. Since the political boundaries in the Balkans did not coincide with the ethnic divisions, and the individual provinces developed under different rulers, a true picture of the past can only be obtained by tracing the history of each of the territorial units in which the Southern Slavs lived. Serbia, Bosnia, Herzegovina, Montenegro, Dalmatia, Istria, Croatia, Slavonia, and the Banat are the principal territorial divisions the political development of which conditioned the national and cultural evolution of the Yugoslavs.

The Serbs created their early state in 840 A.D. in the region of the river sources of Ibar, Drin and Vardar. Thanks to their diplomacy of cautious opportunism they maintained themselves between the rival pressures of the Western and the Eastern Empires, until in 1389 the Turks inflicted on them a mortal blow at Kosovo. Under Dushan the Great the Serbian state extended to the much desired coast of the Adriatic, but it failed to reach Salonica Bay of the Aegean Sea. After four centuries of vassalage under Turkey, Serbia was the first Slav country in the Balkans which gained autonomy in 1832 and full independence in 1878. She became the rallying point for the dream of the unification of Southern Slavs.

The Croats had an independent medieval state between the Drave and Save rivers and the Dalmatian coast. In 1102 they joined the Magyars as an autonomous unit of Hungary. Dalmatia passed to the commercial empire of Venice except for the port of Ragusa (Dubrovnik). In 1804 Dubrovnik was engulfed in the Illyrian Provinces established by Napoleon. Since then the concept of the union of Southern Slavs took the form of Illyrism, strongly supported by the Slovenes of the late Habsburg Empire. The Croats favored federalism in opposition to Great Serbianism propounded by some Serbs, partly on account of their two-thirds majority. Montenegro was able owing to her mountain location virtually to retain her independence throughout the Turkish occupation of the Balkans down to 1919, when she was absorbed in modern Yugoslavia. Bosnia and Herzegovina were administered by Austria-Hungary from 1878 and annexed in 1908. These differences in political systems together with geographic, religious and cultural divisions slowed down the process of unification, but were unable to stop it. Migration among the Southern Slavs produced a fusion of the different groups which tended to strengthen the feeling of community of fate. Outside hostility on the part of the Habsburgs, the Magyars, and the Italians added to the solidification of the idea of unity.

Although many Croats and Slovenes fought as Austro-Hungarian soldiers in the ranks of the Central Powers, a good many of them volunteered for the Entente and Serbia. In 1917 representatives of all three groups decided in a conference at Corfu to unite in the Tri-Union Kingdom the democratic constitution of which would be ratified by a common parliament after the World War. At the Peace Conference the major difficulties arose not in connection with the ex-enemy claims of Austria or Hungary, but with the claims of the Allies, Italy and Rumania. The frontiers with the ex-enemy states were settled rightly or wrongly with comparative ease. The final disposition of the Styrian district Klagenfurt was decided by a plebiscite in favor of Austria. The settlement of the Adriatic border with Italy and of the Banat region with Rumania was beset with difficulties and was eventually consummated outside the Conference by direct agreements between the two parties.

By the Treaty of Rapallo of 1920 Italy renounced Dalmatia which she had claimed on strategic ground in accordance with the secret Treaty of London, except the city of Zara and the islands of Cherso, Lussino, Lagosta and Pelagosa. She secured sovereignty over Fiume harbor, but the Sushak suburb was given to Yugoslavia. On the other hand, Italy kept Istria, Gorizia and Gradisca, of which only the last was Italian by population. The Yugoslavs failed to secure the internationalization of Trieste, the most important Adriatic port, and lost half a million Slavs to Italy. Thanks to American pressure, the national principle was applied with more justice than if the Treaty of London had been enforced. Similarly the secret Treaty with Rumania promised the latter the whole of the Banat of former Hungary. Both the Rumanian and Yugoslav delegations supported their respective claims on the ground of priority of settlement. Moreover, the Rumanians stressed the historical unity and economic indivisibility of the region, while the Yugoslavs asked for its division on ethnic grounds. Eventually the principle of division was accepted, which incidentally gave Yugoslavia a better strategic frontier by moving the boundary further from Belgrade.

The Rumanians

The Rumanians regard themselves as the descendants of the ancient Daco-Ruman stock, which had grown from the merger of the Dacian tribes and the Roman colonists, brought in by Emperor Trajan. It is not known to what extent the Roman Legions were withdrawn when Rome was not able to hold the exposed Dacian Province effectively. The role of the native Prince Decebalus of the pre-Roman era is remembered, but not much is reliably known of the formation of the early Rumanian Principalities. The Magyar push eastwards gave an impetus to the creation of Wallachia and Moldavia in the fourteenth century. Of all the Germanic, Magyar, Asiatic and Slav influences the last was the most enduring. Sometimes Rumanian historians described the Rumans as Daco-Romans transformed by Slavs. Christianity reached them chiefly from Bulgaria.

Historians usually divide the history of Rumania into the period of Turkish vassalage which lasted to 1714, the regime of the Greek Phanariotes who, while dispensing the Sultan's authority, hellenized the upper strata of Rumanian society, and the nineteenth century period of national struggle for independence. Transylvania was kept outside Turkish rule and did not fall to the Habsburgs with the rest of Hungary in 1526. She retained her native Princes until 1699. When the Habsburg Monarchy was converted into a dual state in 1867, Transylvania fell under the

Magyars. In 1599 boyar Michael the Brave united all the three Provinces for a brief period. His action had little in common with the modern unifying nationalism, but it created a historical precedent of unity. King Carol could be seen wearing the white cloak of Michael the Brave as the symbol of national continuity. After the Crimean Wars the Great Powers assumed the protection of Wallachia and Moldavia and in 1878 the Berlin Congress approved full independence of the two united Principalities. In order to bring in Transylvania, "the cradle of the Rumanian nation," the Bucharest Government abandoned the Central European allies and joined the Entente powers in the World War.

At the Peace Conference the Rumanian Delegation presented a list of claims the total of which amounted to the unification of all Rumanians in Great Rumania. The territories to be included in the new state comprised Transylvania, where according to Rumanian sources the Rumans had an absolute, and according to rival Magyar sources, a relative majority; Bessarabia, which since 1812 had belonged to Russia but had a Rumanian majority of 50-75 per cent; Bucovina which Austria detached from the Moldavian Principality in 1775; the whole of the Banat; and Southern Dobrudja which Rumania acquired after the Balkan Wars in 1913 but which was being reclaimed by Bulgaria on ethnic grounds. The Rumanian Government was in virtual possession of most of these territories. It was also in a position to produce two resolutions in which the Bessarabian National Council demanded union with Rumania. The temporary weakness of Russia and her absence from the Peace Conference left the claim to Bessarabia practically uncontested. With regard to Transylvania the Magyars opposed the inclusion within Rumania of Magyar cities which projected into Rumanian hinterland. The Conference decided that the ethnic character of the rural regions should take precedence over the ethnic character of the cities, upholding thus the Rumanian view that the cities were the centers of Magyarization. Bucovina was divided between Poland and Rumania, and the Banat between Rumania and Yugoslavia, both on ethnic grounds. Rumania thus obtained almost full satisfaction, but was to face three revisions in the future: Russian, Magyar, and Bulgarian.

The Magyars

The Magyar horsemen, a mixture of the Finno-Ugrian and Turkish races, invaded the Danubian Plain in 892 A.D. under the leadership of Arpad. After having raided a good part of Europe they settled down, accepted Christianity from Rome, and impressed themselves permanently on Eastern Europe. King Stephen who in 1001 received the Holy Crown from Pope Silvester became the founder and the Patron Saint of the Magyar state. In reality the ruling Magyars were outnumbered by Slavs and Rumans who lived in Hungary as the result of conquest or free accession. However, the perpetuation of the privileges of landed nobility and gentry served to maintain their superiority over the common people, and was also one of the chief forces for the preservation of the state and of its exterior Magyar character.

The Turkish advance to Central Europe induced the Magyars, Czechs and Austrians to form an informal union in 1526, but this union did not save Hungary from the occupation of her central part by the Sultan. It was not until the defeat of the invaders near Vienna that Hungary was cleared of the Turkish troops. The informal union was gradually converted into a real union, in which the independence of the Hungarian and Bohemian Kingdoms was submerged by the centralizing policies of the Habsburgs. Subsequently, the Hungarian Estates fought against the Habsburg dynasty for the retention of their ancient privileges. In 1867, after the defeat at Sadova, Vienna reached a compromise with Budapest which enabled the Germans of Austria and the Magyars of Hungary, both ethnically in minority, "to manage their respective barbarians."

The national movement of the nineteenth century had seized

Hungary more than many other Eastern European peoples. In 1840 it led to the substitution of Magyar for Latin as the official language, and it culminated in the Kossuth revolution of 1848, when for a brief duration a Hungarian republic was established. At the request of the eighteen-year-old Habsburg Emperor Francis Joseph the Russian army was brought in to put an end to the revolt. Kossuth escaped abroad where he was often hailed as a hero of the struggle for freedom. It was not always realized that in fighting for Magyar nationalism, he was reluctant to accord the right of national self-expression to Croats, Slovaks and Rumans. The denationalization of the non-Magyars turned the Habsburg Monarchy into a battleground of the struggle of nationalities. Eventually it brought the Magyars to the Peace Conference in Paris where they faced all their formerly subject peoples claiming complete separation.

The presentation of the Hungarian case at the Peace Conference met with little success for two reasons. First, the Slovaks, Rumans, Ruthenes, Croats and Serbs, who had already joined Czechoslovakia, Rumania or Yugoslavia, could point out the bad record of the Budapest Government in the treatment of non-Magyar nationalities. Second, by reason of a deep-seated conception of the millennial Hungarian possessions as the exclusive domain of the Magyar group, the Hungarian Peace Delegation did not confine its case to the disputed border areas with Magyar majority but aspired to retain regions which were predominantly of non-Magyar ethnic character. The Budapest Government had attempted to forestall the unrest by breaking away from Berlin and Vienna a short time before the end of hostilities, but this eleventh hour measure failed to produce the desired effect. During the Peace Conference the Hungarian officials discussed a scheme through the mediation of Ambassador Paleologue which in exchange for economic concessions to France would leave the towns of Bratislava, Kosice, Satu Mare, Oradea Mare and Subotica within Hungary, with plebiscites in Slovakia, Ruthenia, Banat and

Burgenland. The defiance by Bela Kun of the Peace Conference, the resignation of Paleologue from the Ministry of Foreign Affairs, and the opposition on the part of the Czechoslovak, Rumanian and Yugoslav delegates frustrated the scheme. Only in Sopron a plebiscite was held which returned the city to Hungary while Burgenland remained in Austria.

On the whole Hungary lost two-thirds of her territory and over ten million people. Of these 35 per cent were regarded as Magyar by Hungarian sources. According to the statistics of Hungary's neighbors the percentage was slightly less than one fourth. Hungary lost mountains, mineral deposits and forests, and retained most of her industrial equipment and good soil. She signed the Treaty of Trianon of 1920 under protest and the Magyars never reconciled themselves with its provisions. The efforts to revise the Treaty and to recover the lost territory became the basis of Budapest postwar foreign policy. It was also one of the most unsettling factors in the Danubian Basin.

The Czechs and Slovaks

These two Slav peoples are ethnically and linguistically closely related so that many Czechs and Slovaks consider themselves to be one people. The differences are largely psychological and are attributable to the fact that for nearly a thousand years an imposed political frontier divided them from one another. Both Czechs and Slovaks came to their present habitat in the sixth century A.D. In the ninth century they formed the Moravian Empire, which was broken up by the Magyars. For the Slovaks this was the only historical reminiscence of independent statehood, for under the Magyar rule they were not recognized as a distinct nationality, and were deprived of practically all political rights and cultural and social opportunities. Serfdom, illiteracy and poverty had been their unalterable fate.

The Czechs on the other hand were able to build up around Prague an important medieval state which continued an independent existence for centuries until it was joined to the Habsburg Monarchy. They accepted Latin civilization and were formally a part of the Holy Roman Empire. Ethnically the Bohemian Kingdom became a Czech-German state when in the thirteenth century German settlers began to infiltrate in large numbers and occupied the frontier mountain regions and towns. The Kings were sovereign sui generis. The inhabitants were direct subjects of the Crown, and the Imperial laws did not apply to them. The Golden Bull of 1356 issued under the reign of their King Charles IV, who was at the same time Roman Emperor, confirmed their rights, including the free election of Kings. The Hussite Revolution in the fifteenth century, originating as a revolt against the abuses of Christianity, quickly grew into a movement for religious freedom and national and social emancipation. In particular it aimed at curtailing the privileges of the growing German element. The struggle continued under the Habsburgs, until the defeat at the Battle of the White Mountain in 1620 sealed the fate of the Czechs for three hundred years. The Thirty Years War reduced their number from three million to 800,000, and wiped out their national nobility. Throughout the Habsburg rule the idea of independent statehood as a freely chosen partnership with Austria and Hungary had been kept alive and formed the Czech national program.

The nineteenth century national revival was almost purely the work of "commoners." The deep changes in the national philosophy and the democratic structure of their society, both traceable to their historical tradition, distinguished the Czechs from the aristocratic and feudal society which surrounded them in Central Europe. Originally the Czech nationalists worked for the reconstruction of the Habsburg Monarchy on the traditional and federal basis. Unable to make headway against the opposing German-Magyar combination, they gradually abandoned this idea and during the World War rallied around the flag of complete freedom. T. G. Masaryk led the struggle for the dismemberment of the Monarchy into its constitutional parts. The Slovaks who led their own national struggle within Hungary, and developed their own literary language in order to mobilize the common people for their cause, went through a similar experience. Failing to improve their position they finally threw in their lot with the Czechs and fought for a united state.

At the Peace Conference the Czechoslovak Delegation presented eleven memoranda summarizing the following claims: the re-establishment of the ancient Bohemian state within its historical boundaries, union with the Slovaks within their ethnic limits, and the incorporation of Ruthenia, which was demanded by the Ruthenes who had severed their relations with Budapest. The state constituted on this basis would contain slightly more than a two-thirds Slav majority, forming the founding element of the republic. In addition over three million Germans, living in the provinces of Bohemia, Moravia and Silesia since the Middle Ages, or brought in after the Thirty Years War, were to be accommodated within the historical boundaries, plus a Polish minority in the Teschen district. With regard to the latter a conflict arose between the Czechs and Poles which was arbitrated by the Conference of Ambassadors in 1920 on the basis of dividing the disputed region between the two claimants. As to the Germans they did not cherish then any serious idea of a union with Germany. They had never formed part of the Reich, except in connection with the loose partnership in the Roman Empire. Germany in turn put forward no claims to them, for, with the exception of the little district Hultschin, inhabited by 8000 Germans, none of her lands was to be added to the new state. The demand of the 160,000 Lusatian Serbs living in Saxony and Prussia to be granted the right of self-determination and of union with Czechoslovakia as an autonomous unit was not considered seriously in Paris and was to be settled eventually not as a territorial but as a minority issue of Germany.

The case of the Germans was taken up by the new Austrian

socialist government. They desired to unite the German districts of Bohemia and Moravia with Austria. While this might have been feasible with regard to the contiguous southern fringes of the two provinces, the bulk of the Germans was separated from Austria by a solid block of Czechs. After weighing the different arguments pro and contra the Conference decided unanimously in favor of maintaining the historical, economic and strategic unity of the Bohemian lands, not unaware of but rather fully realizing that it was overruling the ethnic principle. By laying claims to all Germanic enclaves scattered throughout the late Monarchy the Vienna Government unwittingly aroused the suspicions among the non-Germanic peoples of the continuance of the old policy of domination. The claim to a corridor connecting Czechoslovakia with friendly Yugoslavia and the Adriatic ports was dismissed as contrary to the ethnic principle and as impracticable.

In respect of Hungary where no historical or administrative frontier existed which would provide a dividing line between the Slovaks and the Magyars, the Czechoslovak claim to a direct access to the river Danube and to Slovak rural areas surrounding partly Magyarized towns, caused the final borderline to deviate from a strictly ethnic boundary. A Magyar minority of 700,000 was left in Czechoslovakia and became the source of tensions between the two neighbors. The time element which worked towards a rapprochement between Vienna and Prague soon after the Peace Settlement, failed to produce analogous change between Prague and Budapest. The wave of Hungarian revisionism continued to run high. In spite of the complexity of its ethnic structure Czechoslovakia emerged as an economically well balanced state.

The Poles

A Northern Slav people, the Poles, settled in the Vistula basin between the Sudeten and Carpathian Mountains in the south and the Baltic seacoast in the north. In 842 A.D. they united under the

Piast dynasty, and around 1000 the first Polish state under Boleslas extended as far east as Kijev. It continued to exist without interruption until the end of the eighteenth century. In 1410 the Poles defeated the Teutonic Order at Grünwald, halting thus for a time the German eastward advance. In 1386 Poland and the Duchy of Lithuania entered into a voluntary union which by the union of Lublin in 1569 was converted into one state, a royal republic with elective kings, an official Catholic religion, and a parliament composed largely of feudal lords.

In the sixteenth century Poland was the largest state in Europe, and in many respects the most liberal. The fact that the nobles enjoyed an exclusive privileged position towards both the titular ruler and the peasantry, a position which they did not always use for the advancement of national unity, weakened the state. The absence of a strong and prosperous middle class was equally fatal for the inner strength of the country, constantly threatened by the expansionist ambitions of Poland's neighbors. The Polish attempts to create a great federation of the peoples of the northern plain have been often called megalomania by critics. The Poles themselves grew convinced, however, that since they lived in an open plain so close to the expanding Germans and Russians, their nation could not maintain itself without an opening on the Sea, and the absorption of adjacent lands, even if inhabited by alien peoples. This exposed position coupled with the oligarchical anarchism of the Polish constitution contributed to the downfall of the long-lived state. Between 1772 and 1795 Poland was divided among the military autocracies of Prussia, Russia and Austria.

The nineteenth century of the history of the Polish people was marked by a series of sacrificial but abortive revolts, particularly in 1830 and 1863. Their result was a more intense Germanization and Russification of the dismembered nation. Prussia's policy aimed at a complete extermination of the Polish element. The Tsars attempted to assimilate it. Under Austria the Poles enjoyed more freedom. In Galicia the national tradition of the uprooted people had some chance of maintaining itself. Simultaneously the descendants of Polish exiles in liberal countries kept the plight of their nation before the eyes of the world as an open wound. Eventually, with the help of the Allies, the active sympathy of the United States, and the collapse of the Tsarist regime the Poles saw their country re-established.

At the Peace Conference the Polish Delegation labored for the reunion of all Polish lands within their pre-partition boundaries. The resurrected state was to comprise all of Galicia, formerly an Austrian Province, Upper Silesia, West Prussia and parts of East Prussia, recovered from Germany, and the Governments of Wilno, Grodno, Kowno, Minsk, Witebsk, Mohylev, Volhynia, and Podolia, formerly parts of Russia and inhabited predominantly by Lithuanians, White Russians, or Ukrainians. The Congress Poland, the territory which was reconstituted by Napoleon as the Grand Duchy of Warsaw but retained by Russia after the Congress of Vienna, was to form the undisputed center of modern Poland. In addition the Delegation claimed the Duchy of Teschen on ethnic grounds.

Not all Polish claims were accepted. Upper Silesia was subjected to a plebiscite which resulted in her partition between Poland and Germany. The City of Danzig was placed under the League of Nations even though it was left within the Polish customs union. The East Prussian districts of Marienwerder and Allenstein remained in Germany as the result of plebiscites. The arbitration award by the Conference of Ambassadors gave the coal mines and the railway of the Duchy of Teschen to Czechoslovakia and the City of Teschen to Poland. On the other hand Pomorze, or "the Corridor," was incorporated within Poland on account of its ethnic, commercial and strategic character, thus giving the new state sovereign access to the Baltic Sea. The Poles accepted some of these decisions with deep regret. The Germans protested vehemently against the terms as "contrary to justice and to principle." Their offer to transform the ports of Danzig, Memel and Königsberg into free harbors with special rights to the Poles was rejected as inadequate to grant Poland the promised free and secure access to the sea.

With regard to her eastern frontiers Poland capitalized on the general fear of the advance of Bolshevism to western Europe and the French desire to create a strong state on the German eastern flank. She refused to accept Lord Curzon's proposition of a border which would have given her a more or less ethnographic border with Russia and Ukraine, seized Wilno, causing thus the technical state of war with Lithuania which lasted down to 1938, and defied the Great Powers in Eastern Galicia. Having continued the military occupation of this ethnically mixed Ukrainian and Polish region, she succeeded in making the great powers modify their earlier provision for a plebiscite to take place in 1944 and give her full title to its continued possession. After the victory of Pilsudski over the Bolshevik army near Warsaw in 1920 Poland received from Lenin better terms than those suggested by Curzon, and shifted her eastern boundary deeper in the White Russian and Ukrainian lands. Moscow signed the Treaty of Riga as preferable to the continuance of war, but it did not reconcile itself to a permanent loss of these western regions. Germany regarded the settlement of her eastern borders as an outrageous dictate. She particularly resented the creation of the "Corridor," which separated East Prussia from the rest of the Reich.

Irrespective of how the Polish frontiers had been established in details, the very emergence of a large state between Germany and Russia was viewed by these two neighbors with anything but friendliness. Although less than one half of her pre-partition area the new Poland held the sixth place in Europe according to her population and size. The absorption of five million Ukrainians, one million and a half of White Russians, and about one million Germans represented a problem of considerable magnitude. It could not endanger the existence of the country, however, except in so far as it prompted Germany and Russia to intercede in behalf of their "unredeemed brethren."

The Baltic Peoples

This group of Eastern European peoples comprises two million Lithuanians, one million and a half of Letts, and one million Estonians. Their contiguous geographic situation across the Russian route to the Baltic harbors and many parallel features in their history make it convenient to treat the Baltic region under one title. In reality, however, each of these nations represents a distinct individuality.

Of peasant stock, given to cattle breeding and agriculture, the Lithuanians maintained intact their rich folklore and customs. Ethnically they are near to their northern neighbors, the Letts, but they speak their own Baltic branch of the Indo-European languages. The Letts, or Latvians, live mostly in rural communities around the Gulf of Riga. They claim to be one of the oldest nations of Europe, having inhabited their present territory as early as in the Iron Age. However, the heterogenity of their early social organization coupled with the exposed seacoast location made them an easy prey to foreign invaders. Owing to their long associations with Poland, one of the most Catholic peoples of Europe, the Lithuanians are predominantly Catholic. The Letts have a strong Catholic element, but the majority of them are Lutheran, thanks largely to the work of German pastors. The Esths, or Estonians, are preponderantly Protestants. Occupying the southern coast of the Gulf of Finland, with fifteen hundred lakes and eight hundred little islands, the Estonians form a transition between the Baltic and the Finnish element. Ethnically close to the Finns, they speak a similar Finno-Ugrian language, and like the rest of the eastern Europeans they earn their living largely from land.

When the Duchy of Lithuania joined Poland it brought to

her a territory three times as large as that controlled by the
Poles. It included the greater part of western Russia from Kijev
to Smolensk. The union strengthened the Duchy against the
Teutonic Knights and the Russians. On the other hand, exposed
to the higher cultural level of the Poles the Lithuanians were
Polonized and those among them who did not belong to the
gentry class lived in virtual serfdom. After the completion of the
Union Lithuania shared the vicissitudes of fate with Poland. Dur-
ing the three partitions she was split up between Prussia and
Russia. The former Russian Governments of Wilno, Kowno,
Grodno and Suwalki were largely Lithuanian in character. The
Letts lived since the Middle Ages in two states, Livonia and
Courland. Until the sixteenth century they were under the domination of the Teutonic Knights. Courland reached a considerable
degree of prosperity in the seventeenth century as an independent
Duchy. Livonia was conquered by the Swedes in 1621. Parts of
present Latvia were also under Polish rule. Peter the Great occupied Riga and Livonia in 1710 and in 1795 the whole Latvian
territory was united under Russian supremacy. Throughout these
changes the Letts lived as subject peoples, mostly as serfs. Their
land was taken by Germans or Russians and their industry was
controlled by the Hanseatic League. The opening of their harbors
to world trade benefited largely the alien element. The Estonians
were the object of a crusade which King Waldemar of Denmark undertook against them in 1219. Unable to master them the
King sold the country to the Teutonic Knights. In 1521 the
nobles and the cities placed themselves under Swedish protection,
but by the Treaty of Nystad in 1721 Charles XII ceded the province to Peter the Great.

In the nineteenth century all the three Baltic peoples were
aroused by the national movement that swept over Europe. The
repressive Russian rule stimulated their national revival. The
Lithuanians suffered probably even more than the Poles. In 1840
the Polish Code was replaced by the Russian one, and in 1863

Lithuanian was forbidden. In 1905, the year of the Russian Revolution, the Lithuanians worked for autonomy within the Tsarist Empire, but their attempts were frustrated. A great part in their national movement was played by Lithuanians in the United States where 34 periodicals were published. Similarly the national revival of the Letts passed through the usual forms of a literary renaissance, economic self-help, and revolts against the alien governments. The Estonians also labored for autonomy within Russia, but it was not until 1917 that the Provisional Government united Estonia with the Estonian populated northern part of Livonia as one autonomous Russian Province.

In 1917 and 1918 the national movements in the Baltic region reached the stage when they could express themselves in decisive action. Favored by the external circumstances, such as the general recognition of the right of small nations to independence and the Bolshevik Revolution, the Baltic peoples proclaimed their sovereignty and established provisional governments. It took more than two years of bitter struggle, however, before their independence was recognized and peace re-established. First, their peasant armies faced the Germans, who had occupied their territories during the negotiations of the Brest Litovsk peace, and intended to convert them into German dependencies. In this the Germans were assisted by the Baltic Germans, forming six per cent of the local population but owning sixty per cent of the land, and working for the union of the Baltic provinces with the Reich. Then, as the Germans retreated after the Armistice, the national revolutionary armies confronted the task of driving out the Bolsheviks who were pushing in as the Germans were getting out.

Of the western countries England was foremost in extending help to the battling nationalities. In 1920 the Bolsheviks came to terms with all three peoples and signed separate Peace Treaties with them recognizing their complete freedom. Thus, the Bolsheviks were the only Russian government which acceded to complete separation of the strategically and commercially important seacoast. It was too much to expect, however, that Moscow would foreswear interest in the fate of this region entirely or for good. The Baltic nations themselves fully realized that their future was dependent on the relative strength and the interplay of the German and Soviet power factors. Lithuania in addition was to face the pressure of Poland.

The Finns

The Finns, populating the large isthmus between Sweden and Russia and between the White and the Baltic Seas, are of the same Ural-Altaic ethnic origin as the Estonians, and speak a similar Finno-Ugrian tongue. Yet they feel themselves more Scandinavian and stress their cultural ties with Sweden with which country they had been connected politically for seven centuries. In 1157 they were conquered by the Swedish King Eric IX, and thus brought in closer contact with western Europe. Swedish and English missionaries converted them to Christianity and introduced to them elements of western civilization. In the sixteenth century Sweden converted them to Protestantism and elevated their country to an autonomous Duchy. This semi-independent status of Finland was maintained throughout the subsequent generations. It was tampered with only by the last Tsar Nicholas II at the turn of the last century.

Russia secured the Karelian and the Viborg provinces after a war with Sweden in 1721, by the Treaty of Nystad. The rest of the country inclusive of the strategic Aland Islands was lost to Russia by Gustavus IV in 1809. Tsar Alexander I granted Finland a free constitution and confirmed her status of an autonomous Grand Duchy. Beginning in 1899 a régime of rigid Russification and centralization was being substituted for the earlier milder course. During the World War some 2,000 Finns volunteered for the Russian army. An equal number volunteered for the German army to fight Russia.

In December 1917 the Finnish Diet proclaimed independence.

Then followed nearly three years of struggle which was characteristic of the unsettled conditions in Eastern Europe at a time
when foreign wars, competing rival nationalisms, and policies of
conquest merged with social upheavals. The Socialists leaning
upon a Red Guard, the Russian soldiers and the Bolsheviks endeavored to safeguard the fruits of the Russian revolution, and
to realize independence by means of a friendly agreement with
Russia. The extremists among them envisaged the establishment
of the Finnish dictatorship of the proletariat. The bourgeois
parties organized a white Guard, and determining to cut loose
from Russia and exterminate Bolshevism, appealed to Germany
for assistance. General Goltz with 12,000 men landed in Finland
and together with Finnish General Mannerheim defeated the
Socialists. Some 74,000 of them, men and women, were made
prisoners, 10,000 died in concentration camps and a good many
were slaughtered by the White Terrorists in reprisal for the earlier
Red Terror. The pro-Germans in Finland were well disposed
toward and actively engaged in establishing a German monarchical system, which found a wholehearted response in Germany.
The same circles conceived the Finnish Civil war as the war for
national independence in which the Whites, assisted by the Germans, fought against the Russians, who allegedly used the Finnish
proletariat and landless peasants as a tool of Bolshevik imperialism. There were also a few Finns who thought of marching on
Petrograd with the White Army of the Tsarist General Yudenich.
They would have liked to seize the Russian capital and use the
seizure for exacting better terms from the Bolsheviks during the
peace negotiations. Their objective was to create a Greater Finland which would include Eastern Karelia, inhabited by ethnically akin people, which was then under occupation by the Allied
Expeditionary Army. The defeat of Germany and the retirement
of the Allies from Murmansk changed the whole situation, and
incidentally secured for the Finns independence not at the hands
of Germany, but of the western powers and Russia. Economically

exhausted and feeling the aftermath of the civil war Finland then reoriented her policy toward the western powers from whom she was receiving help.

By the Treaty of Dorpat in 1920 she also came to terms with the Bolsheviks. She had to surrender the idea of a Greater Finland and abandon the claim of Eastern Karelia, but received an outlet to the Arctic Sea at Petsamo. The Treaty could not, however, heal the bitterness and resentment on either side. It remained a factor which was to play considerable importance in postwar Russo-Finnish relations.

Summary

As the result of the principal and subsidiary settlements and decisions Eastern Europe emerged from the chaos of the World War as a belt of small and medium size nations entitled to live in their own rights. This political rearrangement was not an accident, but a logical link in the chain of historical developments. It corresponded to the wishes of the majority of the peoples directly concerned. Each of the fourteen states had its historical antecedent. Eight of them existed before the outbreak of the World War, and the others functioned de facto and on their own strength before the Peace Conference began its work. The following table gives in round figures the size and population of the postwar countries situated in Eastern Europe:

	Area in 1,000 sq. miles	Population in 1,000,000	Minorities in %
Greece	50	7	8
Turkey	295	16	12
Bulgaria	40	6	18
Albania	10	1	8
Yugoslavia	95	15	10
Rumania	114	19	26
Austria	32	6	4
Hungary	40	9	10
Czechoslovakia	55	14	30
Poland	150	34	30
Lithuania	20	2	20
Latvia	25	2	22
Estonia	18	1	12
Finland	147	3	10

The total territory of these states equalled the combined area of the five largest American states, i.e., Texas, California, Montana, New Mexico and Arizona. Its population was as large as that of the United States. Territorially Eastern Europe was five times the size of the Versailles Germany with twice as many inhabitants. The new boundaries represented a compromise between ethnography, politics, economics, geography and strategy. Each nation had a larger or smaller fraction of its people outside its state frontiers. Nine million Eastern Europeans had lived permanently in the United States. About 2½ million Magyars and six million Germans remained in the surrounding countries or were scattered heterogeneously throughout the region outside the national boundaries of Germany, Austria and Hungary. It is true that Austria was not permitted to join Germany, but neither was she compelled to live under an alien rule. She was to stay independent, an ideal to which many of her people had probably not been responsive in 1918, but for which they would have gladly given their lives twenty years later. The rest of the Eastern European nations constituting the bulk of the population were set free with the exception of the Ukrainians. Their position was complicated among other things by the fact that the vast majority of them lived in Russia forming an integral part of that state. The Eastern European settlement was not perfect. Its imperfection lay partly in the impossibility of drawing clear divisions in a mixed area, and partly in diplomatic expediency. Compared with the general benefits the Peace Settlement produced by lifting oppression from more than a dozen nations and by putting them upon the path of hope, the deficiencies of the Versailles regime were much over-advertised in postwar years. The fact remains that never before in the history of Eastern Europe had so many people been liberated and placed on the right side of political boundaries.

Part Two

The Quest for Stabilization and Peace

Diplomacy of Blocs

One of the most immediate features of the international development in postwar Eastern Europe was the attempt to link up the smaller states in some kind of consolidated political system which would give the new order a broader base. The empire concept was dead, but the need to realize some community of sovereign nations was widely felt. There had to be a breathing spell first. The dimensions of the task to be undertaken can be measured by the fact that the revolutionary process had placed over a hundred million of various peoples in an entirely new situation amidst a material and psychological chaos without analogy in modern history. Unfortunately, the western powers which had taken a prominent part in shaping the territorial contours of nearly every Eastern European state, either turned away or failed to formulate a unifying policy. The new states were left largely to themselves to attend to the solution of the problem of reconstruction.

The most comprehensive plan for future Eastern Europe was elaborated by T. G. Masaryk during the World War. It envisaged a zone of good neighbors from Finland to Greece, each developing its own resources and adhering to the principle and practice of international cooperation in a democratic Europe. In such a system even the problem of Austria would have been less acute, for there could have been no serious objection to her union with Germany if the latter were imbued with the same spirit of live and let live.

The Rumanian statesman Ionesco labored for the plan of a defensive alliance of the five states which had emerged from the common victory. His bloc would have comprised 90 million Poles, Czechoslovaks, Rumanians, Yugoslavs and Greeks, bound together by a single multi-national treaty providing for a concerted military policy. The alliance would have guaranteed the borders of each state and counterbalanced the German-Hungarian revisionist bloc in the west and revisionist Russia in the east. It would have provided for a permanent contact between foreign ministers, claimed a permanent seat on the Council of the League of Nations, and acted in unison in dealing with international problems of common interest. Take Ionesco hoped that the projected union would diffuse the common danger and spread the risks more evenly among those members to whom the peril might seem remote and those whom it affected more immediately.

An entente as wide as this was undoubtedly sound from the Rumanian point of view. In 1920 Rumania found herself in an unenviable position. She faced three irredentist and revisionist demands at a moment of great internal disorganization. A broad alliance would have given her the respite she needed for unifying the five provinces she acquired by the peace settlement. The question of Bessarabia was of particular concern to her. Russia took the view that the vote taken by the Bessarabian National Council favoring the union had not been a genuine expression of the will of the population. When the Supreme Allied Council recognized in March 1920 the annexation of the province, the Soviet Government protested on the ground that the powers were disposing of Russian territory over which they had no jurisdiction.

The Bessarabian issue left Rumanian-Soviet relations strained. In fact they had never become normal.

Under such circumstances neither Czechoslovakia nor Yugoslavia was willing to guarantee the Dniester frontier. Not only were they disinclined to take the risk of fighting Russia but they regarded Russia's return to European politics as essential to the balance of Eastern Europe. The momentum for creating a large-scale bloc became somewhat less urgent, when it became apparent that no bloc of vanquished nations had been in formation. None of the defeated nations was in a position to overthrow the new state of things however much it might have disliked it. Germany was passing through internal chaos, Russia was engaged in hostilities with Poland, Austria was too confused and too weak to act, and Bulgaria had every reason to be disillusioned by her diplomacy which had caused her two defeats within five years.

It was Hungary's lot to be the most recalcitrant of all the vanquished nations of Eastern Europe. For a while it seemed that Hungarian communists might ally themselves with the Russian Bolsheviks and thus create in the heart of Europe a revisionist bloc with both imperialistic and class appeal. The specter of such a combination was used by the Magyar nationalists to frighten the Peace Conference into yielding to their demands for the preservation of prewar boundaries. Count Andrassy assured the Supreme Council that Magyar nationalism could not be suspect of Bolshevik sympathies. If it tolerated the Soviet dictatorship, it was only as the desperate means to impress upon the powers the necessity of non-interference with Hungarian integrity. If appeased, Magyar nationalism would part company from Bolshevism. In its proclamation the Soviet Government at Budapest appealed to the people to help to build up a powerful proletarian army which would support the dictatorship against the Magyar capitalists and landlords, the Rumanian boyars, and the Czech bourgeoisie. The workers of Czechoslovakia, Yugoslavia and Rumania were invited to conclude a military alliance against world capitalism. Bela Kun's Soviets had a short life, however. They lasted only from March to July of 1919. In contrast to Lenin's achievements in Russia they failed to win over the peasants and to unite the nation for the recovery of the lost provinces. As in Finland their Red Terror was replaced by the White Terror.

In the camp of the victors the situation was not altogether satisfactory. Unappeased rival claims constituted a strong bar to unity. Nowhere were the difficulties of readjustments greater than in the region dominated by resurrected Poland. Contrary to expectations Poland did not line up with her liberated neighbors in an open policy of solidarity but pursued several independent concepts of her own. Marshal Pilsudski hoped in 1919 that England and the United States would approve of a close alliance between Poland and the Baltic countries and that they would give Poland Libava and Riga as compensation for doubtful Danzig. The Marshal also played with the idea of a Polish-Hungarian-Rumanian military alliance at the expense of Czechoslovakia. He would have preferred a common frontier with Hungary. Prince Sapieha had his mind set upon a transversal bloc of Finland, the Baltic states, Poland, Hungary and Rumania. Paderewski thought of the combination of Poland, Czechoslovakia and Rumania. Piltz, the head of the political department in the Polish Foreign Office, was credited with proposing a bloc of these three victors plus Hungary, Bulgaria and Greece. The more ambitious plan sponsored and fought for by Pilsudski consisted of the revival of the ancient Polish-Lithuanian state which would have extended from the Baltic to the Black Sea and would have included the Ukraine as a federated member. Had this dream been realized Poland would have surpassed European Russia in strategic and economic importance. All throughout that period Poland already regarded herself as a great power and saw herself in the role of leadership. This policy of grandeur could not be dismissed simply as political romanticism. As realists, the Polish leaders appreciated the fact that the exposed position of their country made it imperative that they should never be absent from the Councils of Europe.

It was most unfortunate that Poland should have entered post-war Eastern Europe with a feeling of grievance. As it happened, each compromise was received by her leaders as a new wrong. When Upper Silesia was divided by a plebiscite in accordance with ethnographic principle, the decision was decried as a monstrous outrage. To Paderewski the subsequent division of Teschen between the Poles and Czechs by the Conference of Ambassadors meant an insurmountable abyss between the two peoples. The establishment of the international status of the City of Danzig was criticized as barring Poland from the Sea. The uncertainty Polish diplomacy spread around itself could hardly contribute to the feeling of general stability.

The conclusion of the Treaty of Riga which fixed the Polish-Soviet borders on the basis of the military status quo of the moment could not allay the uncertainty as to the future. Three years later, in 1923, the Conference of Ambassadors approved of the earlier annexation of Eastern Galicia. The Soviet Government raised protest against the decision and coupled it with the refusal to recognize the solution as final and binding. An issue was thus created which was to become the source of constant mutual mistrust behind the Soviet-Polish foreign policies. Had Pilsudski accepted the Curzon line in 1919, Poland's frontier with Russia would have been probably less objectionable to the Bolsheviks. This line, lying some sixty miles west of the frontier actually established at Riga, left Wilno to Lithuania, a fact which the Marshal, a native of that city, could not be reconciled to. The Curzon line would have made Czechoslovakia a neighbor of Russia. It would have also cut off Poland from her Rumanian ally. These were two additional reasons why Warsaw would not consider it. From the very beginning Soviet diplomacy disapproved and counteracted Polish aspiration to the leadership in the Baltic area for fear that such a bloc would bar the way to the Baltic ports and that Poland might want to lead her little neighbors against Moscow.

Since most of the Russian western borderline was settled in a manner which the Kremlin masters described as transitional, no Eastern European government was anxious to contract any long term engagement for fear that a future Russian move might involve them in undesirable conflicts. The Baltic states particularly shied from entering any fast alliance with Poland. Finland was especially cautious and her parliament disapproved of even such mild proposals as benevolent neutrality and consultation in case of unprovoked attack. Neither Estonia nor Latvia were enthusiastic about accepting Polish leadership. Thus the negotiations for a Baltic bloc which dragged onwards from 1921 for several years brought no tangible results. Estonia and Latvia would have preferred a Scandinavian combination but Sweden refused to be tied to the new states of the Eastern Baltics. Every country wished to practice a policy of moderation and hoped that the Soviets would not in the future interfere with independence. The net result of all these negotiations was very modest indeed: a ten year agreement of mutual assistance between Estonia and Latvia signed in 1923 together with an agreement for an eventual customs union.

Lithuania did not participate in these discussions. Ever since General Zeligovski's seizure of Wilno she regarded herself as being technically at war with Poland. Her people's government declined to renew the historical union with the Poles and claimed full political independence, which Russia recognized in 1920 by the Treaty of Suvalki. The attitude of Lithuania was a considerable loss to Poland's prestige and interests. Control of Lithuania would have provided her with an alternative route to the Baltic coast by means of the river Niemen and the port of Memel. In 1923 the Conference of Ambassadors bowed to the Polish fait accompli at Wilno. The lesson was not lost on the Lithuanians, already suspicious of the support given to Poland by the Allies. Early in 1923 the Lithuanian troops invaded Memel, temporarily under the military control of the Allies, and the following year the port was as much as theirs, even if it was to enjoy a degree of autonomy. Thus by a defiant stand Lithuania saved her only outlet to the sea from outside interferences.

The tense Polish-Russian relations troubled also the feelings between the Poles and Czechs. The Czechs did not feel enthusiastic over Pilsudski's march against Kijev which they feared would make cooperation between the Slavs difficult. Having made peace with the Bolsheviks Prague observed strict neutrality during the Polish-Russian war, an attitude which caused bitter resentment among the Poles. Masaryk nevertheless desired a close understanding with the Poles. He was convinced that "without a free Poland there would be no free Czechoslovakia, and that without a free Czechoslovakia there would be no free Poland." In November 1921, after the termination of Russo-Polish conflict, Beneš and Skirmunt signed a friendly treaty which might have become the starting point for closer collaboration in other fields, but the treaty failed to receive ratification.

Rumania was the only Eastern European country to enter into a military alliance with Poland. The alliance provided for mutual assistance against eventual attack from the Soviets. Both parties were interested in keeping the acquisitions gained at Russia's expense during the Bolshevik revolution, and they agreed to act in common should Moscow attempt to recover Bessarabia or the regions inhabited by White Russians and Ukrainians.

The Little Entente

The diplomacy of blocs, simple though it seemed, turned out to be difficult in practice. The anticipation of active Russian interest on behalf of the lost regions drove the smaller Baltic states into separate isolation for they were unwilling to risk hostilities with Russia. Had the Warsaw Government been successful in winning the smaller states to its side and in building up through a close union a neutral bridge between the east and west, the position of the Baltic area as a whole would have been greatly improved. On the other hand, any marked degree of such consolidation would have displeased both Russia and Germany. None of these two great powers was apparently ready for any Baltic move immediately after the World War. But the prospect of a Russo-German rapprochement over the heads and at the expense of the peoples lying in between was to hang like a dark cloud over the Polish and Baltic lands throughout the years to come.

In the Danubian region, formerly controlled by the Habsburg Monarchy, a regional group emerged from the postwar chaos in the form of the Little Entente. Two factors contributed to its establishment in 1920 and 1921. The more immediate one was the refusal of Hungary to reconcile herself to her new restricted position and the outward thrust of Magyar revisionism against Rumania, Czechoslovakia and Yugoslavia. The other factor was the lukewarm attitude toward the new order in Eastern Europe on the part of the western powers. The opinion began to spread, partly as the result of revisionist propaganda, that Central Europe had been "Balkanized," the implication being that like the Ottoman Empire, or the Habsburg Monarchy, the new states would be unable to assimilate their alien groups and that local rivalries would make them an easy prey of the mischief-makers among the great powers. It was in response to such tendencies that the Czechoslovak Foreign Minister Beneš announced in the Prague parliament in 1919 the necessity of creating in Central Europe "a new system of planned collaboration between the new sovereign states." "If we accomplish it, our initiative will be recognized on its merits in Europe and we will be able to do so in harmony with our wishes and interests. If we are compelled to do so by others, it will be done against us and against our interests."

In a sense the idea of close cooperation between the peoples of Czechoslovakia, Rumania and Yugoslavia had its historical antecedents in their common struggle for freedom while under the

Habsburg Monarchy. At the Slav Congress held in Prague in 1848 a resolution was passed demanding the liberation of all Austro-Hungarian nationalities. Similar manifestations of solidarity took place during the attacks on Transylvanian patriots in 1894, at the Congress of Nationalities in Hungary in 1895, as well as in 1896 when the Rumanians, Serbs and Slovaks protested in Paris against the conception of the Hungarian state as the exclusive preserve of the Magyars. In 1906 Hodža and Maniu, representing the Slovaks and the Rumanians, established in the Budapest parliament a club of the representatives of the oppressed nationalities. In October 1918 the Hungarian soldiers of Rumanian nationality surrendered to the Czech National Council at Prague and thus frustrated the attempts of the Habsburgs to crush the Czech revolt. Examples of this kind could be multiplied. They would show that foreign oppression produced a community of sentiments which was to influence the foreign policy of the three peoples in the years to come.

Technically the Little Entente consisted of three separate bilateral treaties of mutual military assistance signed in 1920 between Czechoslovakia and Yugoslavia, and in 1921 between Yugoslavia and Rumania and Czechoslovakia and Rumania. The treaties were renewable and their principal purpose was to protect the three countries against unprovoked attack by Hungary. The Rumanian-Yugoslav treaty also included the maintenance of the Treaty of Neuilly which established the postwar borders of Bulgaria.

The Little Entente was one of the first effective political formations to emerge in Eastern Europe. It was also exposed to the most vigorous criticism by the opponents of the postwar order, particularly Magyars and Germans, but also by Italians. Its very name was invented as a gibe in a Hungarian newspaper trying to belittle the bloc as an insignificant imitation of the Great Entente of the World War. In many respects the Little Entente represented a novel departure in the diplomacy of blocs and alliances. Its principal characteristic was its restricted scope. It aimed at no far-flung arrangement, and its purpose was not obscured by any ideological admixture. Giving a political interpretation to the phrase "in necessarium unitas, in dubiis libertas, in omnibus caritas," the Little Entente envisaged united action in matters of identical aims, benevolent neutrality in questions affecting special separate interests of each party, and consultation in general problems. By this limitation of its sphere of operation, it differed substantially from the more general and all-inclusive scheme of Take Ionesco.

The Rumanian statesman would have made his country the center of a military bloc of five nations, each of which would be guaranteed by all members against all potential enemies. Military assistance of all partners could be invoked in case of a Russian aggression against Rumania, German attack on Czechoslovakia or Poland, or Italian action against Yugoslavia or Greece. The objectives of the Little Entente were more restricted. The members undertook to assist one another only in case of an attack by Hungary. Should any one of the three members be attacked by a power not provided for in the treaties, the other two members would cover the victim's rear by keeping Hungary neutral. The multiplicity of threats to the new order would have made a larger agreement more desirable. Yet the prevailing tendency to restrict international obligations to the most immediate interests worked against a wider and a more comprehensive understanding.

The Little Entente was not and did not intend to be a federation of states. Each member retained full sovereignty. Coordinated action was not sought through the surrender of any part of legislative, executive or judiciary functions, but by means of an agreed limitation of the exercise of sovereignty in specific questions. With their combined population of 45 million, and located as they were, amidst the belt of small nations with an uncertain future, Czechoslovakia, Yugoslavia and Rumania hoped to create a functioning international system which would gradually become the rallying point for other small nations of the area. Austria and Hungary were constantly thought of as the most desirable additions.

Among opponents the tendency prevailed at first to regard the combination as a kind of a diplomatic joke, a blow into the air. As its international prestige grew, however, it began to be regarded more seriously. In Germany good care was taken that Austria be kept aloof from any combination that might compromise a future Anschluss. In Italy there was fear lest the Little Entente should become a political substitute for the late Austro-Hungarian Monarchy. The most vehement opposition came from Hungary. For it was against the Hungarian policy of restoration of the ancient regime that the Little Entente was called to life. Considering the high pitch of Magyar nationalism and taking into account the fact that the Little Entente actually forged a ring around Hungary, the temper of Budapest politics can easily be understood. Much effort was therefore made to make it clear to the Magyars that the Little Entente was concerned solely with the maintenance of the status quo, and that once they accepted it, Hungary's active collaboration in Eastern Europe would be welcome. In January 1921 Beneš declared that "history teaches us that we cannot live with the Magyars in a state of everlasting enmity." Earlier, in September 1920, he told the Prague parliament that "it was not enough to show opposition to the Magyars," but that it was necessary "to understand and study their difficulties and to find a way out of the situation. A way to help them and thus in the long run to help ourselves."

In 1921 Beneš tried three times to induce Hungary to modify her attitude toward the new situation. The first meeting with Teleki and Gratz took place at Brück on Leitha. It was negatived by the first putsch of Charles Habsburg who tried to recapture the throne with the assistance of Magyar legitimists. The second meeting with Foreign Minister Banffy at Marienbad made more progress, but it, too, was frustrated by the insurrection in Burgenland, staged by Magyar irredentists. The last negotiations at Brno arrived at an agreement in principle but were again torpedoed by the second Charles putsch. Czechoslovak and Yugoslav mobilization and the enforcement of the law barring the return of the Habsburg to the throne of Hungary, formally exacted by the great powers, but actually initiated and insisted upon by the Little Entente, made the chances of an early reconciliation with Budapest grow slimmer. The ruling Magyars would have had to revise much of their traditional conception of the Hungarian state, change their semi-feudal structure and abandon the complex of self-assumed superiority. They were in no mood to carry out such revolutionary changes.

Policies of the Great Powers

The creation of the Little Entente has often been accredited to France, as if it were a premeditated step in her policy of European hegemony. In reality French diplomacy had little to do with its beginnings. Preliminary conversations were led by Beneš, Veniselos, Take Ionesco and Pashitch in the autumn of 1918 for the purpose of appearing as a concerted body before the Peace Conference. After its establishment the Little Entente developed independently of the Great Entente and grew organically in its own Eastern European climate. A comparison of the relative positions of the two Ententes at the Genoa Conference in 1922 proved this dramatically. Czechoslovakia, Yugoslavia and Rumania appeared at Genoa with an agreed program of economic collaboration. The Great Entente on the contrary revealed the fissures which had for three years undermined its structure and inner cohesion. Poland cooperated with the Little Entente not as its member, but as an outside power with certain parallel interests. The inclusion of Poland in the Entente had never been seriously contemplated. Poland regarded herself as primarily a Baltic power carrying out an independent policy. The Little Entente states on the contrary considered themselves as medium sized nations seeking strength in cooperation among equals and refusing to make the Entente an instrument of policy by any single extra-Danubian great power. The formula ran: "the Little Entente and Poland."

The Genoa Conference was called for the ostensible purpose of finding a way toward the reconstruction of Eastern Europe, and of bringing Russia back to Europe. The Little Entente demanded a hearing at the preliminary meetings but Lloyd George refused the demand on the ground that the presence of new smaller states would complicate the already cumbersome machinery of the preparatory organs. In reality he was interpreting the views of that section of British opinion which from the very outset of post-war period declined any responsibility in Eastern Europe. Moreover, he made it plain that England resented what she considered to be a French policy of European domination and that she might eventually counteract it by a thorough rapprochement with Germany.

The French upheld the Peace Treaties as a part of the new international law which should stand no injury. The British, safe and strong behind their new acquisitions, and unchallenged by an unfriendly navy, tended to make no distinction between former allies and enemies. Specifically they were not particularly concerned with the maintenance of the Peace Treaties in Eastern Europe. Both the French and the British desired no doubt to establish durable peace on firm foundations. But their methods were different, for their positions with regard to the European continent were unequal and the general traditions of their diplomacy varied. The British thought of achieving peace in Europe by breaking with the World War past and by giving the continent a fresh start. The French believed that the re-establishment of confidence should result from a change in the German mentality, and that only insistence on a strict policy of fulfilment of the Peace Settlement could produce the evolution from the psychology of negation to that of collaboration. The French point of view was repugnant to the self-complacent British liberals and pacifists. They would ponder a good deal over disarmament and protection of other peoples' minorities, but they showed little understanding for the needs of the new states. The differences between the British

and the French took the most curious turn when those who upheld the Peace Treaties were accused of being reactionaries, mili-
tarists and trouble-makers whereas those who attacked them were
regarded as democratic, progressive and peace-loving.

The Germans and the Bolsheviks drew full benefit from the
weakening cordiality of the War Entente. While Barthou, representing intransigent Poincaré, negotiated with the Russians trying to trade the French loans for the reparations which Germany
owed to Russia, the German and the Russian delegates signed an
important treaty at nearby Rapallo by which they renounced all
reciprocal demands resulting from the war and postwar period.
The French came forward with terms which if met would have
established in Russia a régime of capitulation and placed that
country under virtual hegemony of capitalistic nations. The Germans granted Russia most of what France had refused to accede.
In particular Germany recognized the right of the Soviets to ex-
propriate the property of German citizens and she waived claims
for damages provided that citizens of other countries would not
be treated differently. Foundations were thus laid for trade relations which enabled the Reich to sell to Russia during the next
eleven years goods in value of three billion marks at a profit of
30 to 40 per cent. Russia on the other hand sold Germany agricultural products worth two and a half billion marks in exchange for
industrial plants she needed for her first Five Year Plan.

For the nations of Eastern Europe the Genoa Conference provided much food for careful thinking. It brought home to them
again that the coalition of the victors of 1918 was not so con-
genial, and that in many ways it was a strange and ill-assorted
structure. The Little Entente and Poland felt extremely uneasy at
witnessing the display of the Anglo-French crisis, and at seeing
Russia join officially the front with Germany. They favored a
middle road between the French and the British policies. Negotiations with Russia should continue so as not to drive her into
isolation again. There was no need for reinforcing the Peace

Treaties, which was the French suggestion, for the League of Nations was already functioning, and it would suffice to restate respect for international law and the signed contracts. The inevitable evolutionary process would then take its course and gradually evolve a workable basis for collaboration between former victors and enemies. Another lesson the representatives of the Eastern European nations learnt concerned the realization that the future German-Soviet attitude toward the smaller states of the zone would very much depend on the respective reactions of the two countries toward one another. Thus when in 1923 France occupied the Ruhr and voices were heard that Poland might seize Eastern Prussia, the Moscow Government hastened to make known its willingness to march against Poland. The Soviets also supported the German protests against "the mad policy of French imperialism." Czechoslovakia drew practical conclusions from Genoa by negotiating a trade treaty with Moscow which amounted to the first Central European de facto recognition of the Bolshevik régime.

The crisis of Anglo-French relations at Genoa marked the continuation of the unhealthy state of affairs as it developed soon after the opening of the Peace Conference. Unable to obtain an unequivocal pledge of adequate military assistance from England, France sought compensation in treaty relations with the smaller Eastern European states threatened by Germany. An alliance with Russia would have been more desirable to many Frenchmen but the Soviet Republic did not border directly on Germany and was governed by a régime objectionable to French bourgeois society. The next largest country which could serve as ersatz ally was Poland. A Franco-Polish treaty was signed as early as February 1921. This was the beginning of the postwar French continental system. The Franco-Polish alliance grew out of the cooperation between Pilsudski and General Weygand during the Polish-Russian war in 1920. Poland took the place of Tsarist Russia as France's eastern ally. This was the reason why Clemenceau wanted her to be strong, very strong. The background of the alliance was simple enough. France had acquired from Germany Alsace-Lorraine and Poland had gained the Baltic seacoast and a part of Upper Silesia. Should Germany try to reclaim either of the two or both after she had made herself strong again, the Polish armies were designed to play an important part in French strategy. They were to make up for the deficiency of France's man power. On account of First World War losses, there were coming up only 208,000 recruits in France in 1936 against 600,000 in Germany.

The decision on the composition of France's eastern allies was not made precipitately. Influential groups in France would have preferred it if the World War had ended sooner than it actually did. The Habsburg Monarchy might thus have been saved otherwise intact, and reorganized more in keeping with its racial structure. France might have been able to lean upon a de-Germanized Austria-Hungary which would check the revival of German expansionism. Tardieu, for instance, regretted that the Allies had not been stronger in 1914 so that they might have defeated Germany before the Danubian nationalities were able to consummate their national aspirations. Once the Habsburg Monarchy collapsed beyond the possibility of revival, the task of France was to look for allies among "the lesser Princes."

For some time Austria had been thought of as the possible nucleus of some kind of Danubian federation under French sponsorship. However, Austria herself knew not whether she wanted to live or die. Consequently, in 1919 and 1920 some attention was turned toward Hungary as a possible support of the eastern system, "in view of certain outstanding qualities of the Hungarian nation," as Secretary General Paléologue, the chief promoter of the scheme, had put it. Paléologue was not at all enthusiastic over the formation of the Little Entente which he erroneously regarded as anti-French. Rumania was being dissuaded from joining Czechoslovakia and Yugoslavia, for instance. The negotiations between Paléologue and the Hungarian delegates proceeded under the handicap of most unstable conditions prevailing in Eastern Europe. There was a link between these discussions and military assistance to Pilsudski against Russia. Hungary was trying to buy better peace terms than those she was expected to sign at Trianon. The *quid pro quo* would consist of economic concessions to French business and financial interests, such as Schneider-Creuzot, and possibly others. According to Paléologue the French Government was convinced that "peace and order could be established in Central Europe only if the nations could mutually agree in ways satisfactory to all interested parties." Hungary would have received some territory earmarked for the Little Entente states, and become the focal point for French eastern policy. French generals would be called upon to reorganize the Hungarian army, and French capital would flow more generously into Eastern European channels. The whole scheme was dropped when Paléologue was replaced by Berthelot, an indication that it had not been taken over-seriously. Had it been realized, the postwar story of Eastern Europe would have been written differently though not necessarily with a happier ending.

The choice fell eventually on Poland. The treaty of 1921 provided for concerted measures for the defense of French and Polish territory and the protection of their legitimate interests. It also foresaw common policy toward the rest of Eastern Europe. French efforts did not stop in Poland, however. By 1924 the Little Entente was well consolidated with Czechoslovakia in the lead. In January of that year a treaty of alliance added that country to the French system of security. The treaty was somewhat more specific than the Franco-Polish agreement in that it enumerated all the instances in which consultations would be initiated with the view of formulating a united policy. The inclusion among the contingencies of any infraction of Austrian independence and of any attempts to restore either the Hohenzollerns or the Habsburgs were of special portent. The treaty placed Czechoslovakia at the center of the French policy of security in so far as Central Europe was concerned. Czechoslovakia was elevated to a pivotal position which was to last until Munich. The Franco-Rumanian treaty of friendship of 1926, and the Franco-Yugoslav treaty of like nature concluded a year later, completed the circle. It should be observed, however, that neither of these documents developed into anything approximating the Franco-Czechoslovak treaty.

In a sense it might seem as if the treaties between the three Central European countries and France marked a departure from the original policy of the Little Entente. At its inception the Little Entente intended to keep aloof from the influence of any single great power and to develop as an independent factor of international politics. The deviation from the original program was only apparent, however, and not real. The Little Entente did not abandon its determination not to become a tool of any great power in Eastern Europe. At the same time each of the smaller states realized that it faced problems transcending the narrow limits of local interests. Czechoslovakia felt the unchanging enmity of Germany, Rumania did not feel safe alongside of the Soviets, and Yugoslavia saw in Italy an old rival in the Adriatic. It was in consideration of these outside contingencies that each smaller state made every effort to secure the friendship or active assistance from some great power which had identical or parallel interests and which was willing to assume reciprocal obligations. The Little Entente began to realize with growing concern that its fate was closely tied up with the fate of Europe as a whole, and that in the absence of an effective collective security power-political groups were bound to be formed along the lines of national interests.

Beneš made no secret that he would have liked to obtain a similar treaty from England. However, England did not then feel the need for allies on the continent. On the other hand, Czechoslovak-French sympathies had an old tradition. They dated back to 1871 when the Prague Diet protested against the annexation of Alsace-Lorraine. During the World War France was the first great power which understood and supported Czechoslovak strug-

gle for freedom. Between Paris and Prague a lively exchange of
ideas had been going on for many decades. In London the Franco-
Czechoslovak alliance was received coolly and with remonstrances.
England went through bitter disagreements with Poincaré over
the latter's policy toward Germany, and on general grounds she
was apprehensive lest by having helped to defeat Germany she
was unwittingly nursing France as the next successor to continental hegemony. This trend of thought was probably one of
the major blunders England committed in her continental policy
in the postwar period.

Italy viewed the French links with Eastern Europe with open
displeasure. Rome believed them to be signs of a policy of encirclement, and blamed France for allegedly fomenting anti-Italian
sentiment in the Balkans, particularly among the Yugoslavs.
There was a great deal of exaggeration in these assertions. Italian
plans of expansion in the Balkans were sufficient in themselves to
put the Yugoslavs and Greeks on guard. Italy hoped to acquire
what she regarded as a position of security in the Adriatic. In her
conception such a position implied the control, or direct annexation, of strategic points on the opposite side of the sea. Such a
policy was bound to bring her into conflicts with Yugoslavia,
Albania and Greece. There was also a strong undercurrent of anti-
Slav feeling in Italy inspired by the fear that Russia might revive
her Balkan patronage. The impatient way in which Mussolini
exacted satisfaction from Greece for the murder by a marauding
band of General Tellini's boundary commission in 1923 could
hardly work for appeasement. By the bombardment of unde-
fended Corfu he made it clear to the smaller peoples what Italy's
reaction might be in the face of what she chose to regard as provocation. Yet a sense of respect and solidarity could not be obtained by such procedures. Europe had just entered the period of
the League of Nations, and incidents like this could not fail to
arouse suspicions of Italy's good faith.

When Mussolini came to power on October 31, 1922, his pronouncements were devoid of the bellicose spirit which colored his later statements. He declared that Italy had no intentions to tear up treaties, and no intentions for many reasons, political, economic and moral, to abandon her World War Allies. In his first speech on foreign affairs in November 1922 he warned the Allies, however, that should the Great Entente not become a really homogeneous bloc of balanced and equal forces its deathknell would be sounded, and Italy, having recovered her full liberty of action, would embark on other lines of policy in accordance with her own special interests. Mussolini aspired to win for Italy an equal position within the circle of the Great Entente, at the hands of which he thought she had received humiliating treatment at the Peace Conference. His recognition of Russia in 1924 showed him as a realist and the perpetuator of the traditional Italian policy of sacred egoism regardless of differences in ideologies.

The rivalries of the great powers disturbed the pro-Entente smaller nations in Eastern Europe. They felt that they owed a debt of gratitude to all the Allies, and were eager to enlist Italy as a friend of the new order. The Little Entente states in particular desired to see France and Italy occupying a place of equality as guardians of the new Eastern Europe to the realization of which they had contributed in human lives and material losses. They also wanted to show that no great power would be able to boast of exercising exclusive domination over them. This policy found expression in the Pact of Rome signed between Mussolini and Pashitch in 1924, and a similar treaty of cordial friendship between Italy and Czechoslovakia the same year. The signatories promised to support one another in upholding the Peace Treaties, to stay neutral in the event of attack by a third party, and to consult on measures to be taken for safeguarding common interests in case of international complications. Thus for a time Italy represented herself as a guarantor of the Eastern European status quo.

The formulation of policies toward the Soviet Union placed the small states in a difficult situation. Rumania would have welcomed it if Czechoslovakia and Yugoslavia had promised to assist her in the event of a Russian coup in Bessarabia. Neither of the two was willing to accept such an obligation. The danger seemed to lie beyond their national interests, and they both reckoned with Russia's eventual re-entry into European policy. For almost analogous reasons Rumania refused to underwrite the security of Czechoslovakia with regard to the German threat, and she refrained from guaranteeing Yugoslavia against Italy. No direct assistance could therefore be expected by any of the Little Entente states in a conflict with any one of the three neighboring great powers. The most that could be hoped for would be to keep Hungary in check. As constituted the Little Entente offered therefore only a partial safety, and that was against the weakest potential enemy. It left its members exposed to inward thrusts by eventual foes possessing superiority of force and resources. In regard to relations with Germany, Italy and Russia liberty or action was left to each state in order to allow it to take account of its own special situation in given circumstances.

In Search of Security

Belief after World War I in the omnipotence of signed agreements was so strong that treaty drafting became the principal preoccupation of diplomacy. Each continental state, with the exception of former neutrals, aimed at surrounding itself with as many treaty neighbors as it could possibly secure. Few probably realized that the spreading cobweb of agreements was a symptom of insecurity rather than an effective guarantee of safety. In their final aspect these defensive treaties were linked up with the safety of France. Their connecting chain was pegged to the Covenant of the League of Nations, but in substance, if not in form, they continued the traditional balance-of-power policy. There were important gaps in the structure which it was found difficult to fill. The most ominous was that along the eastern frontiers of Germany, affecting the future of Austria, Czechoslovakia and Poland,

and that along the western borders of Russia, bearing upon the security of Finland, the Baltic states, Poland and Rumania.

Parallel with this skeleton structure of balance of power a system of general security began to be studied and attempted within the framework of which local problems of safety could find solution. It was believed that aggressions were less likely to occur if they involved the risk of local wars becoming general. This was exactly how the majority of the smaller peoples in Eastern Europe viewed the security problem. They were afraid that unless an effective collective security stopped aggression in general, they were earmarked to supply the victims of local aggressions in a region which to the great powers in the west seemed remote and risky. The British Governments in particular turned deaf ears to all calls for a general system. Lloyd George and others argued that such wide responsibility would not carry the wholehearted concurrence of the British people. The leaders made no serious efforts to guide their people toward a better understanding of the indivisibility of European peace. They discouraged rather than promoted taking a wider view of both general and specifically British interests.

The Baldwin parochial formula that British frontiers lay on the Rhine sounded so convenient and reassuring that the impression prevailed that England had no cause for worry, since the Rhine also happened to be the concern of France. The French on the other hand worried considerably. The Peace Settlement brought them neither the Rhine borders nor the promised Anglo-American guarantee. The Anglo-French negotiations for a military convention reached a deadlock. Consequently, in the autumn of 1922 the French delegation to the Mixed Committee in charge of the preparation of the security system brought in the thesis of the indivisibility of disarmament and security. Lord Robert Cecil and Colonel Requin elaborated a draft of the Treaty of General Guarantee which provided for reduction of armament, obligatory aid to the attacked state by members of the League of Nations, and the allocation of responsibilities by continents and through the conclusion of regional alliances of mutual assistance. By 1923 eighteen states accepted the Treaty, among them the new countries in Eastern Europe. The most emphatic refusal came from Premier MacDonald. He objected to the idea of regional blocs, fearing that they would lead to mutually opposing camps. England did not want to become the policeman of the world overlooking the fact that she could hardly avoid the obligation since she held a good part of that world.

In 1924 both Herriot, heading the liberal radical government in France, and MacDonald, presiding over the first Labor Government in England, came to Geneva. MacDonald, who killed the Treaty of General Guarantee, expounded now before the League his concept of security through obligatory arbitration of disputes. The party refusing to have the case arbitrated would be branded as the aggressor. Herriot was not satisfied. He wanted to know what would happen to the aggressor. Thus the Geneva Protocol was born. Politis and Beneš were active in drafting its contents. The Geneva Protocol was based on the triumvirate principle of arbitration, security and disarmament. It did not permit any member state to wage war on his own initiative, but solely as a mandate of the League and in self-defense. All conflicts had to be submitted unconditionally for a pacific settlement. Penal provisions, including economic and military sanctions, would be started against the party which refused to carry out the arbitration award.

It was hoped that the obligatory settlement of international disputes by arbitration would increase general security and make possible the limitation of armament. Fifty-four nations accepted the Protocol, and sixteen signed it immediately, France being the first great power. In England it met the most severe criticism. Austin Chamberlain in the name of the new conservative government which replaced MacDonald arranged for the burial of what had looked like a hopeful enterprise. The conservatives opposed the Protocol as involving far-reaching responsibilities. The Foreign Office now again favored a limited pact, which would be restricted to the most exposed regions, and underwritten by the nations immediately concerned. Thus His Majesty's Government went back to what its predecessors had refused to accept barely a year earlier. The Labor Premier preferred general pacts to regional blocs. The Conservative Premier preferred regional pacts to general schemes. They both were guided by the principle of avoiding liabilities in Eastern Europe. It did not dawn upon either of the two that in 1939 the situation would be reversed and that their successors in office would not be avoiding but soliciting entanglements in Eastern Europe. Under the Protocol most of the leaks would have been closed with the result that England's real obligations would have been practically eliminated. Europe would have been made almost war-proof.

The Eastern European nations were keenly concerned about the acceptance of the Protocol which they hoped would become the cornerstone of world peace. None of the revisionist countries protested or objected even if they knew that it amounted to the crystallization of the existing status. They either did not believe in its practical functioning or, if they had believed, they must have placed the advantages to be derived therefrom above the discomfitures which it entailed. Hungarian Count Apponyi maintained at the Fifth Assembly of the League that the Protocol contained guarantees for the rule of law against the rule of force. He admitted that the existing state of things would also derive benefit from those guarantees but he characterized it as an accident which could not be avoided. The remedy according to him lay in the change of the political situation itself, and the possibilities for such a change would certainly not be less if abusive power was being checked.

In the Locarno Pact of 1925, which represented the last stage in the struggle for European collective security, France, Germany and Belgium undertook the pledge to respect one another's boundaries and not to resort to war. England and Italy were the guarantors. With regard to Eastern Europe the British Government upheld its traditional policy of no commitments. France on the other hand signed identical treaties with Poland and Czechoslovakia and thus as far as she was concerned she linked security in the west with that in the east. Neither England, Germany, nor Italy was bound, however. Germany agreed to sign arbitration treaties with Poland and Czechoslovakia, and in a way these four documents were taken as marking the extension of Locarno spirit eastwards. Yet there were to be still two separated Europes, one on the Rhine, where Germany renounced any territorial claims, and one on the Vistula and the Danube, where Germany conceded to forego force but did not renounce her ambition to change frontiers peacefully. This was all Stresemann would concede and Briand agreed to accept. In writing to the ex-Crown Prince in September, 1925, Streseman stated that rectification of the eastern frontier of the Reich, recovery of the Polish Corridor and of Danzig, and an alteration of the boundary of Upper Silesia were to remain as outstanding items in the list of Germany's territorial demands. Immediately after Locarno the German Press resumed anti-Polish propaganda thus bearing out the contention that Locarno meant very little indeed in the way of an effective *détente* in Eastern Europe. By accepting certain existing facts in the west Germany made it clear that she was not giving up the principal objective of her policy, i.e., expansion in the east. Indeed, she felt that she made a considerable sacrifice in abandoning the west, a sacrifice for which she ought to be compensated in the east.

Czechoslovakia accepted Locarno as a not negligible step toward the ultimate ideal of general security, a step which in view of the general defectiveness of international society it would not be wise to belittle. From the juridical and military point of view the improvement consisted in the provision that should the Council of the League fail to reach unanimity and Germany assume liberty of action against Czechoslovakia, France was entitled to render the latter automatic military assistance. Chamberlain expressly endorsed this French interpretation of the Locarno system. Thus French action against Germany in fulfilling the treaty of guarantee with either Poland or Czechoslovakia would not be considered as a violation of the main Rhineland Pact. In spite of this the Poles were not pleased. They resented the inference that while some frontiers in Europe were accepted as definite, her own should be left open to question. Yet it was reserved for the Soviet Union to be most alarmed by the Locarno prospects.

In Moscow the rapprochement between Germany and the western powers, the suspected switch from the eastern to the western school of foreign policy, was taken to mean Germany's abandonment of the Rapallo collaboration. The Soviets were to be left to themselves to carry the label of political isolation. Russia feared that Germany might be drawn into a campaign against the Soviet State. To appreciate the Moscow point of view it had to be realized that ever since the Allied interventions and blockade of 1918 to 1920 the Bolsheviks lived in constant fear of a capitalistic crusade and charged the League powers with plotting an international crime against the Russian proletariat. In 1926 Stresemann mollified Russia's fears by writing a note to Ambassador Krestinski in Berlin to the effect that no action of the League could force Germany to be used against the Soviets without her approval. Sanctions could come up only in case of alleged Russian aggression. As a member of the Council Germany would have a voice in deciding who was the aggressor. Russo-German relations were based firmly on the Rapallo treaty and Russia had now a friend at Geneva. In order to bring her relations with Russia into accord with the new position Germany concluded the Treaty of Berlin in 1926. The Treaty provided for non-aggression and neutrality in a conflict with a third power, and for non-participation in any inimical alliance. The Treaty of Berlin recalled the Reinsurance Treaty which Bismarck signed with Russia in 1887.

One positive result of this search of security in Eastern Europe was the encouragement it gave to the conclusion of numerous conciliation and arbitration agreements. Poland entered into such arrangements with Finland, Estonia, Latvia and Czechoslovakia, Germany with Finland, Estonia, Poland and Czechoslovakia, and Italy with Austria and Germany. Another result was the good impression it created in the United States. While Washington would not commit itself to any political entanglement it could give Europe heartier moral support and financial credits. The signature in 1928 of the Briand-Kellogg Pact was also no mean contribution to strengthening the belief in the rule of law. The Pact of Peace outlawed war as an instrument of national policy. In that it went further than the abortive Geneva Protocol or the Covenant which admitted war under specific circumstances. It was also more universal than the League, for in addition to 54 members of the League it was signed by nine non-members. It appealed to the better spirit in nations, expressing an ethical postulate which peaceful peoples unhesitatingly endorsed. Yet it provided no mechanism to stop a policy of force by its violators. Thus the Briand-Kellogg Pact made no material change with regard to the problem of general or specific security. The ease with which so many nations renounced force on paper made many people suspicious of the adequacy of treaty making, particularly when such public pronouncements were compared with the daily evidences of recalcitrant spirit as reflected in the Press and in the activities of subversive groups working with full connivance if not with the moral and financial support of governments.

Franco-Italian Rivalry

Preëminent among the reasons which led France to her policy of Eastern European alliances was the conviction that unless she made common cause with other continental powers forty million Frenchmen might have to face eighty million Germans alone. The apparent reconciliation at Locarno and the entry of Germany in the League, noteworthy as it was, failed to produce the impression of a real understanding. In Eastern Europe, partic-

ularly as far as Italian and German comments indicated, Locarno
was construed as marking the decline of French influence. Mussolini at once began to fortify his position in the Balkans. Already
in October 1924 the Duce went out of his way to boast about his
foreign policy. Denying that it was original, he nevertheless
admitted that it was independent.

Mussolini's attention had from the very start been fixed on
Albania. Inasmuch as Albania was located at the narrow part of
the Adriatic opposite Italy and held a strategic position in the
Balkans, Italy was determined to secure a firm hold over her international position. The opportunity presented itself when in 1924
Zogu, an Albanian Bey, entered the country from Yugoslavia and
made himself ruler. Once in Albania Zogu forgot his Yugoslav
friends and oriented himself toward Italy. Anxious to preserve the
independence of the country as well as his personal rule he was
tempted into a compromise with Fascist Italy which placed the
future freedom of Albania in grave jeopardy. The arrangement
became known as the Treaty of Tirana of 1926. It was a treaty
of friendship and security providing that neither party would
conclude with other powers any political or military agreements
prejudicial to the interests of the two signatories. The mutual
recognition that any disturbance threatening the political, legal
and territorial status quo of Albania was contrary to the interests
of both parties aroused great indignation throughout the Balkans
and especially in Yugoslavia. It was felt that the principle,
"Balkans for the Balkan peoples," had suffered a great setback.
The maintenance of the existing political status quo meant in the
Yugoslav opinion only one thing, namely, the right of Italy to
interfere in Albanian internal affairs should a change in government be imminent. The Conference of Ambassadors in 1921 recognized that the violation of Albanian frontiers would constitute
a menace to the strategic security of Italy. Albania as an independent country should, theoretically, apply to the Council for
assistance, if attacked. If now Italy chose to shortcut the stipula-

tion and to arrogate to herself the right of protection, this meant
an important departure from her policy of maintaining the Peace
Treaties, and an aggravation of the situation in the Balkans.
Mussolini explained the thing away by saying it had been dictated
by the special geographic position of the country. "The ancient
ties of security, even if undefined, had dictated our attitude.
There are situations which cannot be shaped by abstract theories,
but are moulded by fate and the permanent laws of nature."

Albania became a virtual protectorate of Italy. A year later, in
November 1927, the Treaty of Friendship was amplified into a
defensive military alliance by which Italy sought "to protect her
own legitimate interests in the Adriatic." Yugoslavia regarded
herself as the country most threatened by Italian designs. From
Belgrade anxiety spread throughout the Eastern European zone,
and especially to Prague and Bucharest, the Little Entente capitals,
and to Paris. France had no territorial ambitions in Eastern
Europe whatsoever. She counted on the Little Entente as potential allies in case of emergency, but otherwise she cherished no
offensive plans either against Italy or Germany. She did, however,
exercise a check on Mussolini's ambitions. Inclined to expansion
nationalist Italy saw herself unduly restrained by the French attitude, and having failed to forge the Little Entente into an instrument of her own policy, she decided to counterbalance the French
Eastern European alliances by a policy of her own.

There were two faces to the Italo-French rivalries. One was
turned towards north Africa, and the other towards the Balkans.
They were inseparable parts of the same problem created by the
ascendancy of the Italian imperial idea. In Mussolini's view the
fate of Italian empire was not assured unless both the African
and the Balkan objectives were reached. Among these the elimination of the influence of third great powers was of primary importance. In 1925 Mussolini referred once again to his concept
of imperialism: "It may mean a system of government, but it
also means the possession of force and domination. Empire is

the sign of vitality and the will of power, the foundation of all living organisms. Every nation with a strong stamina for advancement is forced by its own character to expand its power and its prestige beyond its own boundary. If people talk of an Italian Empire it also means an attitude of mind, a combative conduct which the Italian people must learn to practice."

By this time Franco-Italian rivalry became acute. Both countries hastened to complement their respective treaty systems. On the French side a treaty of friendship with Turkey was signed in 1926, as well as with Rumania, and the following year with Yugoslavia. On the Italian side activity was even keener. In 1926 a treaty of friendship was concluded with Rumanian Premier General Averesco. The following year Italy signed an additional agreement recognizing the annexation of Bessarabia, a recognition necessary to bring the Allied decision of 1920 into force. Treaties of friendship and arbitration with Hungary in April 1927, Turkey in May 1928, Greece in September 1928, and Austria in February 1930 were the next successive moves by Italy to paralyze the effectiveness of French diplomacy.

In surveying in 1928 the events of the past decade Mussolini turned suddenly against France, though indirectly by way of the Little Entente. In his view the Entente had no great community of interest and its policy of status quo was negative rather than positive. Hungary on the other hand performed according to Mussolini a historical mission of importance in the Danubian region for a thousand years. It was in the interest of Italy that the Treaty of Trianon was revised. Similarly Bulgaria, the other revisionist country, had proofs of Italy's friendship and could rely on her in the future. By this historic speech at Milan Mussolini ranked himself openly on the side of the revisionist countries. "No treaty has ever been eternal because the world moves forward, nations rise, grow, decline, and some times pass away for good. The eternity of treaties would mean that humanity by a monstrous miracle had become sterilized at a given moment, that

it had died." With that the head of the Fascist Government
repeated his prophecy made the previous year in the Cham-
ber. There he had said that between 1935 and 1940 Europe would
find herself at a most significant moment in its history. As a result of the evolution of the Peace Treaties the nations should see
at that time the emergence of certain conditions which would
bring a new era in relations among the various countries of
Europe. Social problems would then arise, but they could be
solved by governments in a pacific manner But since a contrary
eventuality must also be admitted, nobody could be surprised if
Italy followed the example of all other states and wished to have
the necessary military force for the defense of her future. Paris,
Prague, Belgrade, Bucharest and Warsaw understood the implications. Mussolini had in mind certain definite treaties for the revision of which he had been working. They were exactly the treaties
which constituted the magna charta of the liberated peoples.
Mussolini thus started a policy of supporting Hungary which he
intended to use as a tool of his scheme for preventing Central
Europe from consolidating itself as an independent factor. It was
on this road that he was soon to meet his Berlin partner.

Revision or Restitution

Strange though it might seem, the intensified talk of revisionism
was related to the aftermath of Locarno and to the *détente* created
by the Briand-Kellogg Pact of the renunciation of war. Anxiety
made itself felt in the revisionist countries lest the temporary climate of general appeasement should solidify the status quo. The
Magyar revisionists for instance condemned "Marxist Germany"
and accused her of outright dishonesty. Premier Bethlen tried to
console the members of the Budapest parliament by telling them
that Locarno might even help Hungary for it removed the distinction between the victors and the vanquished, and it could lead
to the abolition of international military control. Yet to the extremists it appeared as a national calamity. They felt that Hungary

was isolated more than ever, and that something had to be done to break the ring around her. The opportunity presented itself in connection with Mussolini's efforts to build up his own Eastern European system of cooperative states. His Milan speech of 1928 indicated the change. This was the first significant *volte-face* of Italian foreign policy. More reversals were to come later. Leaning upon Mussolini's support the Magyars from now on became even more intransigent and opposed every attempt at economic or political rapprochement in Eastern Europe. Secret armament, the support of illegal military formations, open acquiescence in irredentism, and increased propaganda abroad became the daily routine of their diplomacy. Long before Goebbels coined the maxim that the chief purpose of propaganda was not to be truthful but to produce results, the Magyar revisionists had mastered the technique.

At the Peace Conference the problem of peaceful revision received considerable attention. In fact, the makers of Europe in 1919 were the first to suggest that their work should be subject to periodical scrutiny. This was the first great international conference at which the victors were willing to create the machinery of revision of their own work. Colonel House suggested to President Wilson that the territorial guarantee in the League Covenant should be subject to such modifications as might become necessary in the future in following out the principle of self-determination. A majority of three-quarters of the League members would decide whether such modifications were necessary and proper for the peoples concerned. All territorial changes would be compensated for in equitable manner, for the peace of the world should be placed above territorial frontiers. Wilson went even further in his original draft of the Covenant by adding social and political changes as sufficient reasons for the revision of treaties. The world Wilson had in mind was to be stable enough to permit normal international relations, and elastic enough to allow the forces of evolution to take their course without recourse to force. Just how this could be practically accomplished in a world of competitive national policies nobody clearly foresaw. Wilson was reminded that if the peace of the world was to be superior to every question of political jurisdiction or boundary, it would be enough for an unscrupulous government to create fresh boundary problems if it fitted in with its ambitions. International relations would thus become a sequence of appeasements in which stronger nations would be favored against the weaker ones.

One could well understand the anxiety of the drafters of the Covenant to avoid the danger of inelastic settlements. On the other hand, there was at least an equal danger that once the principle of bargaining with other peoples' territory had received international sanction, it would encourage irredentism and make instability permanent. Thus legalized revision would defeat its purpose. Moreover, it would work chiefly against the smaller nations, for it was highly improbable that great powers would have their boundaries tampered with. In its final form article 19 of the Covenant was sufficiently emasculated to be acceptable even to the most ardent practitioners of power politics. It said that the Assembly might from time to time advise the reconsideration by member states of treaties which had become inapplicable and the reconsideration of international conditions whose continuance might endanger the peace of the world. There was no procedure provided for dealing with such situations. The states were not given the right to request revision. The Assembly might recommend that the parties concerned reconsider the objectionable treaty but it was under no obligation to do so. The signatories of the Covenant were not obligated to accept such recommendation. The matter was essentially one of policy and not of law. Both sides understood that revision of treaties was a problem of power and not of jurisprudence.

The whole discussion of the problem of treaty revision proceeded with an eye on Eastern Europe. It was expected that that area might present the first opportunity to test the principle in practice. However, no Eastern European country discontented with the Peace Settlement thought seriously of availing itself of this opportunity. The reasons were several. It was not easy to prove that the territorial provisions of the Peace Treaties were inapplicable. As a matter of fact the Treaties were very well applied. In order to succeed, revision of a frontier would have to be agreed to by the country at whose expense it would be undertaken, and this against equitable compensation. Abstention from further revisionist agitation and loyal adherence to a security system would have to be among the prerequisites of any boundary deal. Moreover, the change should not be of the nature of crippling the victim of revision. It would have to be limited to such rectification as would promote better feeling and more stable relations.

Were the conditions in Eastern Europe conducive to local readjustments of imperfect boundaries? The perusal of the voluminous revisionist literature reveals that what was in fact demanded was not rectification but full restitution of the old régime, and in some instances a wholesale reversal of power political relations. Bulgaria for instance demonstrated a good deal of moderation. She did not ask for more living space, but restricted her demands to the regions in Rumania, Greece and Yugoslavia which were inhabited by Bulgarian majorities. The number of people involved was less than a million. Only access to the Aegean Sea was claimed on economic rather than ethnographic grounds. Hungary on the other hand introduced what Premier Teleki described as the element of functional historiography. The Magyars claimed the restitution of the ancient Kingdom within its historical boundaries. In fact, about a million Magyars could have been shifted to the "right" side of the Trianon border without creating more than a million strong non-Magyar minority on the "wrong" side of the boundary. The rest of the regions claimed contained mixed population with a non-Magyar majority. To restore the ancient Kingdom meant to throw millions of Slovaks, Rumanians and Croats back into subjection. As to the Germans their minority in Poland numbered less than a million. The grievance of Germany derived less from the existence of this minority on the Polish side, but rather from the fact that she saw the way eastwards barred by the revival of the Polish state. Again this was not a case of rectification, but of restoration of a situation generally recognized as unjust. The restitution would return several million Poles to Prussian rule. In Czechoslovakia no desire existed then among the Germans to be absorbed by the Reich. They had never belonged to it, and their economic life gravitated to the historical lands of Bohemia, Moravia and Silesia.

The revisionist countries were fully aware of the fact that no international agency could give them all this. On the other hand, the anti-revisionist countries realized that restricted local readjustments would scarcely transform discontented nations into contented ones. Boundary readjustments had been made in the past among friends and could be made even among opponents under proper international authority. Full restitutions of territories inhabited by alien peoples raised an entirely different problem, however. The realization by the claimants that neither the League nor any other body could give them complete satisfaction deterred them from resorting to its revisory provision. They were far from eager to have their propaganda methods exposed and threshed out before an international public. They hoped to help themselves to much more once the political and military situation changed in their favor, and concentrated their hopes and efforts on speeding up that change.

The Role of the Peasant Class

Travelling across Europe from west to east one cannot fail to observe how the ratio of population gradually rises until it reaches its climax on the borders of the Soviet Union, the Eurasian continent. In Eastern Europe the density of population is on the average close to 150 inhabitants per square mile as compared with

43 in the United States. If the annual increase in western European countries moves far below 10 per thousand, in Greece it stands at 11, in Lithuania 11.3, Rumania 13.3, Yugoslavia 14.3, Poland 14.8 and Bulgaria 15.7. In these last six countries the net reproduction rates, representing the dynamic element in man-land ratio, are much higher than in Scandinavia and western Europe. Among the Czechs and Austrians only 32 and 39 per cent of the population were occupied in agriculture, but a vast majority of all other peoples represent a farming population. The same area which supported 17 Americans or 21 Danes, had to provide for 59 Rumanians, 63 Yugoslavs, or 66 Bulgarians. The percentages of farming population were 53 in Hungary, 54 in Greece, 65 in Finland, 67 in Latvia and Estonia, 76 in Poland, 77 in Lithuania, 78 in Rumania, 79 in Yugoslavia and 81 in Bulgaria. Though it could not be asserted without exaggeration that the Eastern Europeans were unable to secure the minimum indispensable to physical survival, the absence of large unutilized areas combined with the growing population exercised a great pressure on the land as a means of livelihood.

One of the earliest postwar measures to remedy the situation was the inauguration of the long overdue reform of the system of land tenure. In the Soviet Union collectivized agriculture became the instrument of state socialism. In the smaller states of Eastern Europe land reform laws were passed as a social necessity by duly constituted democratic governments. The legislators aimed at removing the crying discrepancy between the few large landed proprietors, often absentees, and the masses of land hungry peasantry and the submerged class of unemployed farm laborers. As in western countries the principle on which the redistribution of land was carried out was that of private ownership. There was one difference, however, which made these land reforms appear more revolutionary than those in the west. In western Europe a steady evolution had been taking place from the system of large estates to smaller holdings by means of gradual land settlements.

In Eastern Europe the anti-social and anti-national attitude of the politically ruling landed classes, ethnically different from the masses, was primarily responsible for the delay of land reform. World War I eventually wiped out the empires and the feudal elements on which the empires rested. The land reforms assumed the character of a revolution within the laws.

The individual features of the reforms varied according to the social differences in each country. In the Baltic countries where before the World War 60 per cent of the land belonged to one per cent of population, and where the Germanic nobility, alien to the masses, owned 85 per cent of estates, large proprietorships were almost completely liquidated. In Poland, Czechoslovakia, Rumania and Yugoslavia large estates were not entirely abolished, and former owners were permitted to retain from 25 to 500 hectares. Agrarian reforms in Finland, Hungary and Bulgaria resembled more the settlement schemes. In Hungary the ruling land-owning gentry was treated particularly leniently. After 1921 big estates in Hungary still comprised more than one-half of the total land area and over two million peasants out of the total population of less than nine million represented the class of unemployed and casual laborers. In Bulgaria only 0.1 per cent of agricultural properties were worked by paid laborers. Nearly two-thirds of all holdings on the other hand were dwarf units below five hectares. Bulgaria had no feudal class comparable to Magyar magnates, Polish szlachta, Rumanian boyars, or absentee nobility among the Baltic peoples and Czechs and Slovaks. Consequently the Bulgarian reform was concerned chiefly with the fairer distribution of land between small properties. As land was divided among all heirs, plots tended to become very small which made the use of machinery and fertilizers difficult and costly. In Finland as the result of land settlement about one family out of three owned land. The problem of compensation was solved most radically in Latvia where no compensation was offered, and in Rumania where the depreciation of currency reduced the price to a fraction of the real value. In other countries compensation was calculated variously on the basis of the average prewar price, the cadastral yield, or the rent paid prior to the reform. The law applied equally to citizens and foreigners. The fact that most big estates were in alien hands gave the reform a nationality bias, although its original and real character was that of a social measure.

Altogether about fifty million acres passed from large owners to small holders, involving the living conditions and social status of at least three million families. Land was distributed among small peasants, landless farmers, ex-soldiers, municipalities and co-operative settlements. The land reforms were the most important element in the transformation of the traditional structure of Eastern Europe. The social effect of the measure was the creation of a new middle class destined to become the backbone of the nations. It would be erroneous, however, to assume that these reforms were in themselves sufficient to solve the economic problems of these countries. In many respects they created new tasks and problems. The large number of small farms could not prosper unless they could be given to intensive cultivation and receive ample equipment and inexpensive credits. In Poland six to nine million peasants could not make a living from the land prior to World War I. Partition of very large estates was therefore a logical measure. On the other hand 57 per cent of farming land was split up into more than two million small units. The consolidation of these units into larger self-sustaining holdings was suggested as the solution. Some nine million hectares were actually consolidated by the postwar Polish governments.

The peasant class bore the principal burden of World War I. It was expected that once it increased its ranks and found a solid ground in the enlarged ownership of means of production that it would become a powerful political factor in the life of the new nations. Yet for several reasons this objective was not generally attained. In Czechoslovakia the agrarian party became the leading political factor. Its policy of the protection of agriculture gave rise to conflicting interests with the exporting industries. The prosperity of the country was increasingly dependent on foreign markets. The traditional composition of the governments, based on the coalition of the principal factions and comprising all classes of the population, worked eventually towards the habit of compromise. In Rumania the National Peasant Party came to power in 1928. Previously the country was in the hands of the old Liberal Party which favored banking and industrial interests, and was not particularly concerned with the welfare of the rural population.

The outbreak of the agrarian crisis soon after the peasants came to power prevented them from playing the role to which they were entitled by their numbers. In Bulgaria the Stambolijski agrarian party held power from 1914 to 1923. It lost its hold over the country partly owing to the impetuous nature of its leader, and partly as the result of the peculiar circumstances through which Bulgaria passed during the War era. Few leaders had so many enemies as Stambolijski. The Bulgaro-Macedonians accused him of treachery on account of his amity for the Serbs. The high bureaucracy saw in him a republican enemy of the monarchy. The army caste hated his anti-militarism, and the town proletariat had a grudge against him for his suppression of the railway strike in 1919. His violent death at the hands of his political enemies ended the once high prospects of Bulgarian peasant rule.

In Yugoslavia the Serbian agrarian party founded in 1919 soon lost its peasant character. In Croatia on the other hand Stephen Radich's Peasant Party grew into the strongest element in Yugoslav politics though less because of its class program than for the support it gave to Croat nationalism as opposed to Serbian centralism. The national program of the Peasant Party made it the rallying point of most Croats irrespective of class allegiance. The extremists in the Party went as far as to favor complete separation from the Serbs. In Hungary the strength of the semi-feudal political machine and the lack of class consciousness made the formation of a truly representative peasant party particularly difficult. In Poland the peasants had been divided into three groups, unable to compose their differences. They wavered between the rightist and leftist tendencies incapable of striking a middle course. The influence of peasant leadership was cut short by the Pilsudski coup in 1926 which did away with party government. Witos, once the peasant Prime Minister, was put in jail together with several other deputies of liberal and socialist leanings. He managed to escape and lived in exile in Czechoslovakia until after Munich he was recalled home.

In Eastern Europe a land-philosophy guides the peasants' way of living and thinking. The soil is not regarded as an article of commerce nor even as a means to higher income. The peasants do not desert their farms when they fail to produce for them, for they are devoted to the land for the sake of the centuries of labor they and their forebears have put into it. They are as much masters as they are the slaves of the land. One form of revolt against oppressive governments is to grow just what they need for themselves and not more. On the whole, given a chance the Eastern European peasants would make almost the ideal stuff for building up strong democracies. They would be also a factor for peace and tolerance. In the field of international relations they could be relied upon to be supporters of general understanding. The thing they lack most is political experience, and this arises from inadequate tradition. They were thus unprepared to reap the full benefit of their changed status. The long economic depression immobilized their latent forces for a time. It is not too much to expect, however, that the weight of the Eastern European peasantry will tend to grow, and that in due course its influence will be exercised in favor of freedom.

Economic Nationalism and Internationalism

The origins of economic nationalism go far back to the nineteenth century when Germany, Russia, the United States, Canada,

Australia, France and other states began to use the economic weapon as an instrument of national policy. In Eastern Europe the struggle for social opportunities and economic freedom was inseparably connected with the fight for national liberation. While resisting political oppressors, the submerged nations were at the same time struggling against their economic exploiters, whether they were holders of land monopoly, or owners of the means of industrial production. "No political independence without economic liberty," was the motto of the Finns. "The Czech question is a social problem," was Masaryk's formula of the Czech national struggle. The victory of the ideal of freedom had a hollow sound unless the means whereby the higher social structure was to be built ceased to be the preserve of the political masters of yesterday. Having secured recognition of their national aspirations, the new nations embarked on a policy of consolidating their domains economically. The national state was conceived as the application of the principle of self-government, as an organized defense against the return of the kind of social discrimination the liberated people had previously received at the hands of their socially privileged political masters.

The intensity of economic nationalism appears in more realistic light when related to the general stage of economic development in which the individual peoples found themselves at the time of their political liberation. The agricultural yield in Eastern Europe was from one-third to one-half of that in the west. With a much higher density of population the purchasing power of the peasants stood below one-sixth or one-fourth of what it was in western Europe. Throughout the zone hundreds of millions of working days could be provided if the available unemployed labor could be utilized. In the Balkans one-third of the productive potential was idle. The picture of grave social maladjustment was general. The degradation of millions of people was so deep that in some parts it drove them into danger of losing the will power to struggle against these conditions. The World War brought on new hardships and the impoverishment of those classes whose position had been less unfavorable. The enormous cost of the four years of struggle both in direct losses and forfeited gains absorbed about four-fifths of the national wealth of the Habsburg Monarchy and five times its annual national income. In the Polish inhabited regions eleven million acres of land were put out of use during the German-Austrian-Russian military campaigns. The economic life of the whole zone was almost completely immobilized. Frequently economic values were deliberately destroyed by the shifting armies, as happened in Latvia, Poland, Rumania and Serbia. The civil wars in Finland and Hungary added to this dismal picture of destruction. It was in these war and postwar losses and not in the Peace Treaties that the economic distress of Eastern Europe should be sought. It was also in the light of these factors that what had been called the economic nationalism of the small states should be studied.

The Peace Settlement did not provide for a general and organized plan of the transformation of Eastern Europe from prewar to postwar conditions. There was no precedent and no formula as to how the new and enlarged states could best fit in the world economy. They were left to themselves to work out their future as best they could. The task of establishing economic units out of regions which had been cut loose from their traditional connections was not a small one. The major feature of the change in the Danubian region was the dismemberment of the prewar economic system of 52 million people, and its replacement by the national economies of Austria, Czechoslovakia and Hungary. Thus a great part of what used to be internal trade became now foreign trade and was subject to the influences of governmental commercial policies. In the Baltic area a large new economic unit of over 32 million Poles arose plus four smaller national economies of Finland, Estonia, Latvia and Lithuania. In the Balkans the change was of less importance, and was marked by the enlargement of Serbian and Rumanian economy.

The problems the new states were facing were those of readjustment and of inner economic expansion. The fulfilment of national aspirations opened up fresh creative energies and new opportunities which accelerated the process.

Already before the World War the tendency of agrarian regions towards industrialization and that of industrial regions towards agrarianization made itself strongly felt. The establishment of separate economic areas encouraged these parallel movements. The reasons were political, economic and social. The nations wished to strengthen their defensive potential by increasing domestic output of the land, and by creating more industry. They were also influenced by the consideration of fiscal incomes to pay for growing public expenditures, and by social motives of providing employment for the surplus rural population. The process of industrialization was much criticized by liberal economists. Yet it was in many ways an inevitable phenomenon. The view that agricultural countries with growing population and untapped natural resources and idle labor were to remain forever in that state of economy was basically wrong and untenable. The older manufacturing countries will have to reconcile themselves to the knowledge that backward countries will sooner or later strive to better utilize their resources. Although Eastern Europe is not over-rich in natural resources, its arable land, forests, water power, ores, oil and the availability of labor constitute a wide enough basis for the establishment of a measure of industry supported by domestic forces and raw materials.

The way in which individual nations of Eastern Europe adapted their economies to the new conditions proved their vitality beyond doubt. Finland made a marked recovery by concentrating on finished and semi-finished products. The Baltic states overcame the difficulties which arose from the separation of their economy from the vast Russian rear. Poland put her finances on a sound basis. Czechoslovakia which was most hit by the dislocation of the Danubian trade gradually recuperated by reorganizing her industry along specialized lines and became the principal German competitor in Southeastern Europe and to some extent overseas. Hungary increased her national income from industry within fifteen years from 16 to 26 per cent. Austria and Czechoslovakia made particularly strenuous efforts to place their industrial products in western Europe. The first postwar decade was in many ways harder for these two manufacturing nations than for the agrarian countries.

In the years preceding the world economic crisis the manufacturing nations of western Europe initiated a policy of autarchy in foodstuffs. Prices began to rise, and since domestic production did not suffice to cover the demand, imports from Eastern Europe increased. Consequently, the international trade of the agrarian countries gained more rapidly than that of the industrial states. The period preceding the years 1928 and 1929 marked comparative prosperity. The index of agricultural production stood at 89.8 in 1925, that of industrial output at 81.6, as compared with 100 in the peak year of 1929.

The way in which the six Danubian countries, Austria, Bulgaria, Czechoslovakia, Hungary, Rumania and Yugoslavia managed to adjust themselves during that period to one another and to world trade has not always been appreciated with accuracy. Taking 1913 as the base year of 100, the index of world exports rose to 177.3 in 1929. European exports rose in that period to 150.3. The exports of the Danubian countries as a whole rose to 200.4. The economic relations within the Danubian basin changed considerably as the result of the new political map, but the volume of trade between the area as a unit and the outside world maintained itself fairly well. At the same time the inter-Danubian trade went through a process of shrinkage which reflected the growing degree of the adaptation of the national economies to the new political status. National economies began to correspond more to the specific domestic conditions. The tariffs which were imposed as a means of protecting either domestic farmers or infant industries played a secondary role in the reversal which followed the world economic slump. The real reasons for the Eastern European economic crisis lay elsewhere, namely, in the general drop of agrarian prices. A reduction in tariffs would have eased the position of Austria, for instance, but by itself it would have been insufficient to bring about recovery. It may be of interest to recall that the indices of tariffs against the outside world was 24 in 1925, i.e., six points higher than in prewar years, but much below the United States level of 37.

Up to 1929 the economic conditions in Eastern Europe tended to develop normally. Considerable credit for this should be given to the new factor, economic internationalism, which contributed directly to this work of normalization. The most outstanding example was the 1922 reconstruction of Austrian finances by international action of the League of Nations. It consisted of 26 million pounds sterling of non-political international loan, guaranteed by eight countries, inclusive of Czechoslovakia. In 1924 similar assistance was given to Hungary whose government was able to raise a loan of 10 million pounds without guarantee. Greece obtained a 9,700,000 pound Refugee Settlement loan to help her to place 1,400,000 refugees on land and in new industries, as a part of the compulsory exchange of population with Turkey. The fact that only four per cent of the advances were left unpaid at the date fixed for their redemption proved the success of this scheme. In 1926 Bulgaria received a similar loan of 2,225,000 pounds to establish 220,000 refugees from Greece. In 1927 the loan through the League of Nations placed Estonia on sound financial feet. Altogether nine financial schemes were undertaken by the League, all in Eastern Europe, where private capital was unlikely to take initiative.

The first postwar decade closed on a hopeful tune also with regard to the so-called eastern reparations. These reparations consisted of several items. First, the Peace Treaty obligations of the defeated states, Austria, Hungary and Bulgaria; second, of the obligations of Poland, Czechoslovakia, Rumania and Yugoslavia as the succession states to make compensation for the state property and to take over a share of the national debt of the empires to which they succeeded; and third, of paying the so-called liberation debt incurred in connection with the assistance rendered them by the Allies in their liberation. At the conferences held at the Hague in 1929 and in Paris in 1930 the reparations due from the small states were reduced to 30-33 per cent of the original sums. Austria was freed entirely. The obligations of the smaller Allies were also cut down, in case of Czechoslovakia the total reduction being 25 billion crowns. The settlement of the eastern reparations brought to a close the question of compensation arising out of the land reforms. For twelve years the countries which had carried out the land reform had to fight for the recognition of that measure as a matter of their national policy within their constitutional rights and not subject to international bargaining. The Hungarian landlords having properties in Rumania claimed that the land reform restricted their right to private ownership which they alleged was contrary to the Trianon Treaty. The Rumanians refused to make restitution on the ground that the reform was not a liquidation of a World War measure, but a legislative act applied by a sovereign state to its own citizens as well as to foreigners. The legal dispute lasted seven years. It was responsible for much bad feeling in Eastern Europe, especially owing to the fact that prominent international lawyers engaged in publicity on behalf of both disputants. Eventually the issue was settled in 1930 by the establishment of two funds out of which compensations were to be made in accordance with the decision of the mixed tribunals. The funds derived their assets from the compensations agreed upon by national legislatures of the land reform countries, and out of the Hungarian reparations, plus contributions by the principal Allies. As the result of this settlement the land reform issue lost much of its distributing aspect.

The work of the Hague and Paris was received in Eastern

Europe as one of the most significant steps toward the liquidation of the financial problems of the Peace Settlement. It was hailed as an augury of better days. Unfortunately this optimism was not shared by all. A number of developments manifested themselves at the turn of the decade which revealed a state of deep tension throughout Europe. In September 1930 the National Socialists in Germany obtained a great election victory in securing 6,401,210 votes and 107 seats in the Reichstag. The Naval Conference in London opening in the spring of 1930 showed the persistence of Franco-Italian differences. Germany and Hungary demonstrated no willingness to change their basically negative attitude toward the existing order. Above all, however, the foretaste of the economic depression with its profound effect on the position of the Eastern European countries was already strongly felt throughout the area. The optimists still believed in the ultimate supremacy of the factors working for understanding and compromise over the factors leading to intransigency. The more realistic observers realized, however, that the years of idyllic interlude were coming to a close.

Summary

The first postwar decade ending with the year of 1929 witnessed a progressive internal consolidation of the states of Eastern Europe. It was the first time in several centuries that the small peoples living between western Europe and Eurasia were to a degree their own masters in their homes. Each of them made great strides toward making up for the losses they had suffered in the past when they had been treated as mere geographical extensions of other powers' interests. In the field of national economy, culture, social conditions and the fullness of life generally the new nations gave a good account of themselves. Illiteracy was one of the bequests left by Russia and the Habsburgs. In Poland in 1921 one-third of the population could not read and write. Among the Slovaks, Ukrainians, Rumanians and other formerly submerged nationalities the proportion was sometimes even higher. A decade of political independence reduced illiteracy to a small fraction of what it had been before, while schools of every kind were provided for the young generation.

In the field of international relations the chief preoccupation of the liberated nations was to ensure that the territorial conditions established after the World War become safe and enduring. In this direction the results were not altogether satisfactory. The quest for general collective security fell wide of the mark. Neither the League, nor Locarno, nor the Pact of Paris offered effective guarantee of the new order. England's refusal to underwrite any risk east of the Rhine made it impossible for that country and France to evolve a united Eastern European policy which would have either firmly protected the established conditions, or paved the way for a reasonable and loyal rectification of the Peace Settlement which would not undo its positive achievements. The early dissolution of the Franco-Anglo-American cooperative front increased the vulnerability of Eastern Europe in the face of the forces which under the title of revision actually worked for the restitution of former domination. These forces were joined by Fascist Italy which accomplished a *volte-face* from a status quo power to a revisionist power, trying to secure a foothold in the Balkans.

Thus none of the three great powers surrounding the zone of the small states could be regarded as favoring the new order. Germany, the Soviet Union and Italy all hoped to draw benefit from its dislocation. No concerted policy of revisionism was yet formulated by these three powers, mutually suspicious of one another, but the cooperation between Germany and the Soviets nourished the uneasiness of the peoples located on the converging routes of the traditional west-to-east and east-to-west expansion. Consequently, the security of Eastern Europe was put under the strain of a heavy burden which could not be borne without the assistance of outside powers. This became the more evident after it had been found that no all-inclusive regional system among the smaller states of the zone was practicable. No nation was willing to accept more than the most immediate risk close at home. The Little Entente was the only regional system which during the first postwar decade developed a degree of solidarity. But it was limited and the Little Entente did not succeed in becoming the nucleus of a wider system.

Under such circumstances Eastern Europe developed as an area of small sovereign states, obligated to help one another in certain restricted contingencies, but representing no pooled potential of defense. So long as Germany was not prepared to march there was little to fear. The real danger lay in the possibility of the restitutionist powers resorting to force. In 1930 that probability had to be admitted. The common belief that another war was unthinkable lacked its former ring of conviction. Peoples who had enjoyed ten short years of freedom after centuries of subjection had no illusion as to the seriousness of events to come.

Part Three

The Years of Crises

The World Slump

For agricultural countries of Eastern Europe with little free capital and limited credit balances abroad it was of great importance that they should reach an active foreign trade. The balance of exports over imports would permit them to make essential payments to foreign creditors. With the exception of Czechoslovakia which had, as a rule, an active trade balance, the conditions in other countries varied. After 1930 they all reached a favorable balance with the exception of Austria. In spite of the progress made during the preceding decade the exports of the new states did not meet fully their requirements. Converted to per capita basis their foreign trade amounted to 10.4 dollars in 1913, 21.7 dollars in 1929, and only 7.1 dollars in 1934, the year when the crisis reached particularly low ebb. The agricultural countries had a favorable balance in foodstuffs and agrarian raw materials. The two manufacturing nations, Austria and Czechoslovakia, were active in finished goods. Both groups had a passive trade in industrial raw materials and semi-finished products, an indication of limited resources of minerals and non-agrarian raw materials generally.

After having reached the climax of upward development in

102

1929, with the deterioration of the world economic crisis Eastern Europe entered an era of grave depression. To understand the special nature of the local economic difficulties it is necessary to examine the credit position of the countries concerned. Compared to the year of 1929 the total exports of Poland, Czechoslovakia, Austria, Hungary, Rumania, Yugoslavia, Bulgaria and Greece fell to almost one-half in 1934. In the critical years 1930-1932 their imports from outside sources dropped from 7.4 to 2.7 and exports from 6.1 to 2.3 million Swiss francs. Because of lack of funds with which to buy raw materials and goods in western Europe and overseas the imports fell more substantially than exports. The adverseness of the trade balance fell from 1,378 million Swiss francs in 1929 to only 136 million in 1931. One of the negative features of postwar economy in Eastern Europe was the fact that the creditor nations ceased to be buyers of goods. Before World War I Bulgaria, Rumania, Serbia and Hungary were also borrowers in foreign money markets but they were able to pay their debts to Switzerland, Austria and Germany by their exports. After World War I the lending countries bought less and became often competitors of the borrowing countries in world agricultural markets. Great Britain, France, Holland and other nations reduced their purchases, and Germany and Italy, the nearest large importers, found themselves in the borrowing camp with no capital to spare. Before the World War Germany had 25 billion marks placed abroad, but in 1931 she owed 23 billion marks instead.

In 1932 the external debt of the eight countries combined amounted to 24.3 billion Swiss francs, of which 6.1 billion were private. The external debt service totalled 1.3 billion per annum. The yield from exports necessary to service foreign debts indicated the importance of foreign trade as a means toward meeting the liabilities abroad and keeping the channels of credits open. In 1931-1932, Greece had to spend 49 per cent of her exports for her debt service, Hungary 48, Yugoslavia 29, Rumania 28, Poland 24, Austria 22, Bulgaria 16 and Czechoslovakia 5. Of the total foreign indebtedness 2.77 billion Swiss francs were short term debts, largely private. For the service of their debts abroad the majority of these countries had at their disposal only the surplus of their trade balances. The drop in agricultural prices and the restrictions imposed on international trade added sensibly to the debt burden, some of which had been imprudently increased. The withdrawal of the short term loans by foreign lenders, followed by an increasing flight of capital beginning 1931, was the immediate reason which led to the financial crisis of Eastern Europe, and made the countries restrict free dealings in foreign exchange. It started in Austria with the collapse of the Creditanstalt on May 12, 1931, and it soon spread to the neighboring countries, particularly Germany and Hungary, where the Creditanstalt had been heavily engaged. It was not so much the volume of exports that had undergone the change as the fall in prices, and hence the growing scarcity of foreign exchange. The problem was one of markets and of prices. There was a correlation between the means of payment available and the export capacity, and between the export capacity and the price level of exportable goods. The great difficulty lay in the fact that an unduly high proportion of loans was in the form of short term obligations. A sudden movement to effect withdrawal on a large scale made transfer impossible and, in certain cases, upset the precarious balance of payment.

The acute crisis caused by the fall of agricultural prices was intensified because of the protective policies by the industrial nations which normally imported agrarian produce. Under such circumstances the problem of balancing the payments owed to foreign countries against foreign assets was rendered very difficult. The same could be said in regard to national budgets and to the flow of foreign capital. Of the nine states located between Germany and the Soviet Union, namely, Estonia, Latvia, Lithuania, Poland, Czechoslovakia, Hungary, Rumania, Yugoslavia and Bulgaria, only Czechoslovakia was able to reach a stable equilibrium of the balance of payments, a steadily balanced budget, and an equilibrium between the capital needed for her development and the capital actually available. With the exception of Czechoslovakia national income in Eastern Europe was low; less than twelve pounds sterling per head of population in Yugoslavia, ten pounds in rural and thirty pounds in urban districts of Bulgaria. The capitalization of national income did not suffice for any large scale development of national resources. All the Eastern European nations were therefore borrowers of foreign capital, and agrarian products occupied the dominating position in their economy. Frequent fluctuations in agricultural prices tended therefore to unbalance chronically their financial structure.

The foreign trade items in the balances of payments were of greater importance than in the richer industrial countries. Foreign trade represented often the only active item, unless some countries, such as Austria, could also benefit from transit trade and tourist traffic. The item of foreign debt was in each case unfavorable. As the economic situation improved the increase in imports of capital goods and raw materials lowered the credit side of the balance, while with a new depression the reverse process set in.

In prosperous years emigrants' remittances and the inflow of new capital resources from abroad were sufficient to cover the debt service. There were, however, only a very few prosperous years, in fact only 1928 and 1929. In 1929 the combined exports of the nine countries to outside markets reached the figure of six billion gold francs, and imports little less than seven billion. The deficiency of the balance of trade and the foreign debt service, amounting together to roughly two billion, were met to the extent of one-half of a billion francs out of the proceeds of emigrants' remittances, while the remaining one and one half billion francs were paid from newly contracted foreign loans. With the intervening depression the value of the agricultural exports, two-thirds of the total, fell by fifty per cent, while the drop in the price of non-agrarian imports fell by one-fifth only. The result was that instead of six billion, the nine countries received only

3.6 billion. The value of essential non-agrarian imports fell only from seven to 5.6 billion, so that the deficit in the trade balance rose from one to two billion. The debt service remained the same, but remittances fell off, and there was no more inflow of new foreign loans. To meet this situation the governments had to draw on the gold and foreign exchange balances. In a short time as much as half of these reserves were exhausted. A strict exchange control was introduced as an emergency measure, but as frequently happens, the emergency measure became permanent.

All throughout Eastern Europe the period from 1929 to 1936 witnessed a profound transformation of economy, Foreign trade sank deeply below the normal level and the flow of international capital was extremely restrained. Parallel with the stagnation in international trade, national efforts were spurred on to mobilize domestic resources. The whole region closed itself in, embarking more intensely upon economic autarchy.

From the budgetary point of view the decrease in the farm income led to the reduction in national revenues. At the same time the growing German and Italian rearmament and the approaching collapse of the effort toward a general security system compelled the smaller states to further increase their expenditures on armament. In Poland 55 per cent of the budget went on armament. Had more liberal trade policies been maintained in the outside world, had emigration been permitted to take its natural course, and had moderate external loans been made available, the price structure would have probably not reached such a critical state. A measure of liberalism on the part of the powerful democracies would have made it more difficult for Germany to increase her economic and political hold over Southeastern European area.

Political Rapprochement by Economic Methods

A summary should be given of the various attempts to reach a better political atmosphere in Eastern Europe by means of economic cooperation. If peoples engaged in peaceful trade, it was assumed, they were likely to understand better their mutual problems and needs. They might become business friends and among friends political issues might lose their sharpness and be adjusted in a friendly manner. Most of these attempts occurred in the years of the agricultural depression of 1929-1932. The only provision of the Peace Treaties which envisaged some sort of closer collaboration between the Central European countries were articles 222 of the Treaty of St. Germain, and 205 of the Treaty of Trianon. Under the influence of the British delegation Austria, Czechoslovakia and Hungary were encouraged to establish between themselves a special régime of customs preferences for five years in order to remedy the adverse consequences of the break-up of their former economic unity. The practical value of this régime would not have been very important. Hungary was not able to absorb much of the combined industrial output of Austria and Czechoslovakia, for her purchasing power was low and she had her heart set on her own industrialization. Hungary did not favor any economic rapprochement with Czechoslovakia for political reasons. She regarded it as a trap set to mollify her opposition to the consolidation of the postwar political system. Among the Czechs the idea produced some suspicion lest it mean the first step toward the resurrection of the Monarchy that had just been buried.

Among the great powers the opinion gained currency that the new states were unduly jealous of their newly won liberty. In point of fact the great powers could hardly have imposed upon their smaller allies limitations of sovereignty to which they themselves would refuse to submit. The lack of foodstuffs and monetary chaos immediately after the World War pushed the new states almost automatically on the road of protection. The policy of protective tariffs had been of good service to them particularly in times of the sudden fluctuations of exchanges such as occurred with the collapse of the German mark. There seemed to be no reason to abandon it. Measures which some people regarded as temporary remained to stay.

In 1922 at American initiative a conference of the succession states met at Porto Rose with the participation of the great powers. Common accord was sought there on measures for the expansion of commercial relations and communications between the heirs to the Habsburg Monarchy. The abolition of import and export prohibitions was agreed to under certain conditions, and a return to freer trade was recommended. The resolutions of the conference were accepted but never ratified.

The Little Entente was built originally for the purpose of political collaboration. From 1927 onwards it began to interest itself in economic problems of Eastern Europe. Under the guidance of the central organ of direction a united economic plan of commercial, financial and transport policy was to be set up each year with a view to cement political friendship by wider economic ties. The object was to intensify mutual trade by the rationalization of industrial and agrarian production and markets. Since Czechoslovakia could not absorb Rumanian and Yugoslav agrarian surpluses, and the two latter countries, both engaged in the process of their own industrialization, could not buy all Czechoslovak manufactured goods, the Entente did not aim at a closed or self-sufficient economy. None of its three members had such raw materials as rubber or cotton for instance. Due to the protectionist tendencies of Czechoslovak farmers and Yugoslav and Rumanian manufacturers a customs union was not feasible. A plan for a narrower Rumanian-Yugoslav customs union had been prepared for some time, but it did not materialize. Less radical forms of cooperation, had therefore been devised, such as preferential tariffs on the basis of bilateral quota arrangements.

It was felt throughout Eastern Europe that the doctrine of the old economic liberalism demanding complete freedom of trade was often exacted in a very abstract way and that it was deduced from conditions prevailing in the older and economically more

developed western industrial countries. It was also felt that freedom of trade could be of advantage to the stronger but that it
would act as a handicap to the weaker, just as war could. The
economic subjection might even be worse and more demoralizing.
It was remembered that Austria-Hungary had threatened Rumania and Serbia with a tariff-war before 1914. Rightly or
wrongly the feeling prevailed that the existing conditions made
free trade undesirable. In theory the advantages of international
division of labor and specialization of trade were freely admitted
but in practical politics half developed or insufficiently consolidated nations feared that their poverty would in the throes of
competition with stronger nations be made permanent. A more
sympathetic view was taken towards more general international
economic agreements in which the specific needs of local economy
would receive proper recognition.

In 1930 Hungary, Rumania and Yugoslavia in a joint reply to
the Tariff Truce Conference of the League of Nations recommended a system of preferential tariffs for agrarian products of
European origin as the best means toward stimulating the exports
from the depressed areas. The same year the Warsaw government took the lead in organizing what became known as the
agrarian bloc of Poland, Czechoslovakia, Rumania, Yugoslavia,
Bulgaria, Hungary, Estonia and Latvia. Lithuania was not invited
for she was still technically at war with Poland. The agricultural
preferences which this bloc demanded and which were incorporated in the Final Act of the second conference on Concerted Economic Action in November 1930 were subject to so many reservations by the non-agrarian nations that the practical value of the
plan became insignificant.

The year 1931 saw the continuation of the battle for preferences.
In February 1931, at the invitation of Briand, seventeen govern-
ments of grain producing and grain consuming countries met in
Paris under the auspices of the Commission of Enquiry for
European Union set up by the League of Nations. Both groups

of countries adopted a resolution favoring a preferential system for European wheat, maize and barley. A few months later Germany actually accorded such preferences on imports from Rumania and Hungary. A French memorandum was sent in May 1931 to the Commission recommending preferences for Eastern European agricultural states, together with a special preferential system which would also include lower exclusive tariffs on certain industrial products of Austria. This recommendation was apparently destined to counteract the Berlin-Vienna scheme for a German-Austrian customs union announced at the same time. Another proposal made by England envisaged a Danubian customs union to include the three Little Entente states and Austria, Hungary and Bulgaria. The German and Italian governments refused to agree to the proposal and the plan, never publicly announced, was frustrated.

On March 19, 1931, at the initiative of the Bruning government, Berlin and Vienna surprised Europe by publishing unexpectedly the text of an agreement to bring about an economic Anschluss by establishing an Austro-German customs union. The correspondence exchanged to that effect between the German Foreign Minister Curtius and the Austrian Vice-Chancellor Schober aroused sharp reaction, particularly in Czechoslovakia and France, but also in Italy, and in the other smaller states. The two governments agreed to maintain their political independence, but the wording of the text of the agreement, and the press which it received in Germany, left no doubt that it meant the extension of the policy of the Zollverein, and that the real purpose of this economic move was political, namely to create the Greater German Reich. The agreement stated that Germany and Austria would be willing to enter into similar negotiations with any other state, but no country was apparently willing to allow itself voluntarily to be gradually wound up. The Czechoslovak Foreign Minister pointed out that a regional plan involving control by one single great power would inevitably jeopardize the freedom of the smaller states. Moreover, the economic Anschluss was not conceived in the spirit of liberal European collaboration. It was a means toward creating a larger autarchic economy under German hegemony. Just like the Zollverein a century earlier, the new bloc would embark on a policy of restriction of trade with outside countries. The fact that German tariffs on agricultural products were higher than in Austria and four times as high as in Czechoslovakia indicated the true nature of the scheme. It was one thing to organize a larger economic area by agreement among countries of comparable size and equal strength, and it was quite another thing to extend the economic and political power of a large country aiming at domination. The Anschluss was particularly directed against Czechoslovakia whose competition in Southeastern Europe Germany was determined to eliminate. Ever since the middle of the nineteenth century the policy of Prussia was directed toward forestalling the rise in Central Europe of an economic system which would consolidate itself outside German control and leadership.

The Council of the League requested the Permanent Court of International Justice to express its opinion as to whether the contemplated union would be contrary to the Geneva Protocol of 1922. Eight judges expressed the view that it would be contrary to both the Protocol and the Treaty of St. Germain, for it would jeopardize Austrian economic freedom and thus threaten also her political independence. Seven judges representing the United States, Great Britain, Germany, Holland, China, Belgium and Japan were of contrary opinion. In the meantime both governments abandoned the project. The German Foreign Minister stated that his country would actively cooperate in the preparatory work for the establishment of an all-European federal union, initiated under Briand. Some of the criticism addressed to Germany in connection with the attempted economic Anschluss was to be accounted for by the way in which Berlin handled its scheme. It looked as if Europe were to be placed before an accomplished fact.

On September 8, 1930, delegates from the twenty-seven members of the League met unofficially at Geneva to decide what action should be taken regarding the Briand plan as announced to 26 European governments in May. It was at this meeting that Schober suggested that regional economic agreements might lead to European union, without, however, hinting as to whether negotiations for Austro-German union had already been in progress. After discussing the answers sent in by the governments the delegates constituted themselves into the Commission of Inquiry for European Union with the Secretary General of the League as their Secretary.

Among the answers the German reaction was of particular interest as it referred to Eastern Europe as the future living space of the German people. Another point of the Memorandum was concerned with the interdependence of political and economic conditions. Most governments agreed that there was a close interdependence between the two without the one being definitely subordinated to the other. The Hungarian government used the occasion for pressing its revisionist demands adding that it would not join any organization that would preclude any possible future revision of the Peace Treaties and make the existing order unalterable. The Polish and Rumanian governments opined that economic cooperation could be organized without preliminary political cooperation. The political cooperation should rest upon the principle of respect for treaties and territorial integrity of states. Czechoslovakia answered that cooperation among European states manifested itself more predominantly sometimes in the political and sometimes in the economic sphere since the two groups of problems stood in a continual relation of interdependence one to another. The Scandinavian countries recommended the reduction and gradual abolition of more than twelve thousand miles of Europe's economic barriers. The Scandinavian countries pointed out that they could not associate themselves with any general scheme of guarantees or security that would involve military obligations. Poland on the other hand favored general military guarantees and pointed out that the principles of the Geneva Protocol should be constantly kept in mind. Germany, Italy and some other states recommended that Russia, Turkey and other non-members should also be invited. England stressed economic cooperation rather than political, and, with an eye fixed on her Dominions, declared that she would have to satisfy herself that the measure taken for closer European cooperation would not cause anxiety or resentment in any other continent.

The Briand plan was based on the principle of freedom of sovereign states to join the federation, and on the rationalization of European political and economic problems. Matters on which agreement would be easy to reach, and where the need of an all-European settlement would be particularly desirable should be examined first. Considering that not a single state refused adherence, it could be assumed that the idea answered a general and vital European need. Had the cooperative elements in Europe and particularly among the great powers kept in check the elements of non-cooperation, the federal idea might have entered on the evolutionary road of gradual realization. Unfortunately Briand's idealistic realism coincided with the rising wave of exclusive ultra-nationalism as represented by the growing power of national socialism. Barely a week after the publication of the Inquiry Hitler's followers grew to nearly six and a half million. In 1920 there were only seven.

By way of reaction to the project of Austro-German customs union the French Premier Tardieu proposed to the British government in 1932 an alternative plan for the organization of Austria, Czechoslovakia, Hungary, Rumania and Yugoslavia into a special economic system without the interference of the great powers. The five smaller states were asked to agree on common

policies, and the four great powers, France, Italy, Germany and
Great Britain would extend to them financial assistance. The assistance would take the form of releasing the small states from the
obligations of the most favored nation treatment in inter-regional
trade, and of an international reconstruction loan to which France
would subscribe, as the initial installment, 40 million dollars. The
preferential tariffs were to extend to 10 per cent to start with, and
would cover agrarian exports from Hungary, Rumania and
Yugoslavia to Austria and to Czechoslovakia, and industrial exports from these two latter states to the agrarian group. The Little
Entente states favored the plan as a serious attempt toward the
economic betterment of Danubian relations. They asked that the
great powers decide first upon a concerted action so that the creation of the system would not be regarded as directed either against
Germany nor Italy. The reaction in Germany and Italy was negative. It was pointed out there that the plan would benefit mostly
Czechoslovakia which Germany was particularly determined to
prevent from happening. The British liberal economists echoed
the German objections calling the plan another French trick devised to protect the interests of French investors. However, the
British government invited the three great powers to discuss the
scheme in London on the occasion of the World Economic Conference in June 1933. The German and Italian delegates did not
vote openly against it, but by demanding representation on the
preliminary conference of the five small nations they made it
plain that they would permit no organization in Central Europe
that would not be of their own making and under their control.
The plan broke down on this question of procedure but in reality
it was deliberately wrecked on political grounds. Germany repaid
the French and Czechoslovaks in full for having obstructed the
Austro-German union the previous year. From the economic
point of view the plan would not have made the Danubian region
self-supporting but it would have increased its internal trade especially if it were accompanied with better rationalization of the

economies of the five countries. Yugoslavia was tied to the region to the extent of 32 per cent of her total foreign trade, Austria 30, Hungary 29, Rumania 25 and Czechoslovakia 22. The rest of their trade was dependent on extra-Danubian markets.

In September 1932 the problem of assistance to the Eastern European countries was discussed at the conference at Stresa. In addition to the five states mentioned under the Tardieu plan, ten more countries participated in its sessions: Bulgaria, Poland, Greece, Italy, Germany, France, England, Belgium, Switzerland and the Netherlands. The Agrarian Bloc came to the conference with the agreement that preferences on agrarian products should be included in the recovery plan. England opposed this on the ground of the incompatibility of the preferences with the Imperial preferences, and Italy took a similar line in consideration of her South American trade. Both insisted on the maintenance of the most favored nation treatment. The conference thus proceeded amidst two rival conceptions of commercial diplomacy. The French delegation suggested a general convention which would lead to a multilateral type of Central European economy whereas the Italians favored bilateral agreements. It was recommended that cereals coming from the Eastern European countries were to enjoy preferential treatment in the importing industrial nations in western Europe. In addition a special revalorization fund was to be set up to which the importing countries would make contributions. This would raise the prices of products of the hard hit agricultural states. The Italians suggested that subsidies be paid to each agrarian exporting nation in proportion to its average exports in the last three years. The importing countries would grant these subsidies out of special funds collected by means of a tax levied on each country according to the amount of its total foreign trade. Overseas grain exporting countries would enjoy a lower tariff. It was pointed out that each group would benefit: the Eastern European countries through higher prices, the industrial importers through the increased purchasing power of the agrarian nations, and the overseas exporters of agricultural products through the lowered European customs tariffs. The Germans did not oppose the plan. Doubtful of its reception, however, they had their own scheme prepared. It consisted of a convention between Germany, France, Italy, Austria and Czechoslovakia for the purchase of cereals from Hungary, Rumania, Bulgaria and Yugoslavia on the basis of bilateral agreements involving preferential treatment and lower tariff rates. This plan would have benefited Germany against Czechoslovakia, for Germany had not been self-sufficient in agrarian products and was able to absorb a great share of the surpluses whereas Czechoslovak agrarian production reached almost the point of self-sufficiency.

The decision was left to the London Conference where the criticisms of the Stresa plan were again inquired into. The difference of opinion on the point of Eastern European preferences versus most favored nation principle were not bridged, but several delegations aware of the severity of the agricultural depression in Eastern Europe seemed to be sympathetic to the idea of making an exception. There were 67 countries represented at the London Economic Conference. Cordell Hull stressed the significance of the occasion by stating that the success or failure of the conference would mean the success or failure of statesmanship throughout the world. The conference in fact was a failure and the United States contributed substantially to making it so. The Stresa resolutions were dropped. The year 1933 brought to a virtual end the postwar era of diplomacy by conferences. With the National Socialists in Germany a new factor came to Europe which gradually assumed more weight and developed its own techniques.

The Revolution in Germany

Of the four post-World War I revolutions, the Communist one in Russia in 1917, the Fascist in Italy in 1922, the militarist in Japan in 1931, and the National Socialist in Germany in 1933, the last one produced the most far-reaching consequences for Eastern Europe. Russia and Japan were regarded in western countries as lying outside the borders of western civilization with which they entertained only superficial connections. Italy was an inseparable part of the western society, but her power-political inferiority made her unlikely to reach a position of preëminence. Germany on the other hand occupied the central place in Europe. She was the strongest and the most dissatisfied great power, and had on two recent occasions proved, in 1870 and again in 1914, that she could throw Europe, and a good part of the outside world, into a maelstrom with the most portentous repercussions. At first the western liberal opinion was chiefly embittered by the ruthless application of the National Socialist doctrine of race, suppression of freedom and of civil liberties, the spirit of tribalism, and of the glorification of intolerance and violence. Gradually this moral indignation grew into a more coherent attitude of fear lest the translation of the revived spirit of militant Prussianism into the totalitarian national state meant the inauguration of one more attempt to establish German hegemony over Europe.

As in almost everything that went on in Europe after 1918 the reaction to the ascendency of Hitler to power was anything but uniform. Probably the Czechs, Poles and French were the least surprised people in the world, while the British were perturbed as never before throughout the past fifteen years. France had built her postwar policy on the hypothesis that the Weimar republic was a sham and that sooner or later the German people would again place the temporarily silenced militarism upon its old pedestal. The rise of Hitler to power, and particularly the smooth way in which the transformation of the Weimar republic to the Third Reich occurred, was received as the justification of the supposed French intransigence. England on the other hand had been trying to restore Germany to the position of equal partnership. In a debate on foreign affairs in the House of Commons in April 1933, three months after the German coup, Sir Austin Chamberlain went out of his way to denounce "the savagery, a racial pride, which cannot allow to any fellow-subject not of pure Nordic birth equality of right and citizenship within the nation to which he belongs." He doubted the wisdom of discussing "with such a government" the Polish Corridor and of putting another Pole under its heel. He openly charged the Germans with ingratitude for British good offices in fighting their battle against the French. The same moral denunciation was sweeping throughout the United States, but as in England it was largely restricted to verbal protests and private boycott activities without producing much change in the policies of the two democracies. Winston Churchill took the oppositional view that now was the time to stop discouraging France from building up her armament, for a strong France would free Great Britain from the obligation to come to her rescue in another Franco-German conflict. Great Britain was not yet in the mood, however, to intervene effectively in continental affairs. Deeply sunk in sterile, shortsighted and deliberately inactive Baldwinism, shared by many conservative, liberal and labor leaders and politically naïve intellectuals, she saw no reason to prepare to take a share in averting what a handful of her individuals clearly recognized as a new danger to the Empire and to western civilization. Her governing class continued half-heartedly to try to save Europe by keeping out of the so-called continental entanglements for fear of commitments and by persisting in its selfish attitude of self-complacency which was undermining the will of the people to build up the energy necessary for steering effectively an alternative course. As regards the United States its indignation was equally "academic," and each successive failure in Europe was construed by the moulders of public opinion as one more argument to justify the postwar policy of isolation without international responsibilities.

In Eastern Europe the reaction to the revolution in Germany was on the surface less ostentatious but inwardly more realistic. "Mein Kampf" had been read there ever since its appearance in print, and was accepted not as a mere propaganda tract but as a truthful reflection of ideas and programs which had filled the minds and hearts of generations of Germans for several past decades. The raw phraseology of the book expressed poignantly the metaphysical German pride of race and of the yearnings and will for more power. It reiterated Fichte's faith that Germanism would prevail because of its own intrinsic superiority over all other forms of civilization. There were specific passages in the book which read ominously in their possible bearing on the security and the very existence of the Eastern European nations. "In less than a century two hundred fifty million Germans will live upon this continent, not crammed together as factory coolies but as peasants and workers whose labor will reciprocally vouchsafe life to one another." "We the National Socialists must unwaveringly hold to the aim of our foreign policy: to secure the soil due to the German people on this earth. We start anew where we halted six centuries ago. We reverse the eternal Germanic migration to the south and west of Europe and look eastwards. If we speak today in Europe of new soil we can but think first of Russia and her subject border states." "Since one needs strength for this and France, the mortal enemy of our people, strangles us pitilessly and robs us of power we must take upon ourselves every sacrifice to destroy French endeavors to hold mastery over Europe. Any and every power is to-day our natural ally who like us feels the French lust for domination on the continent to be intolerable." The evangel of the German foreign policy was determined not to permit the existence of two great continental powers. "Every attempt to create along our borders a military state, or even a state which might be capable of maintaining an army must be regarded as an attack against Germany. It is our duty and right to prevent the rise of such a state, and if it exists to destroy it."

At no other time had the will to domination been defined so openly and with such naked clarity. In the face of such a program the feeling of precariousness of one's own existence on the part of the smaller German neighbors could have hardly been underestimated. The final settlement with France was conceived "not an end, but merely a means whereby the German people will be able at last to expand in another quarter." The presence within the Eastern European states of German minorities "all of which must be embraced within the German Reich," was to be used as a powerful weapon of German policy in the approaching hour of manifest destiny. Most of them had already been enrolled in various cultural, gymnastic and benevolent societies linked together by the master minds in Berlin, Munich and Stuttgart, and were waiting for "the day." Rarely in history had Europe witnessed the massing of such a powerful army ready to attack from within or from without at the command of a single man. The small neighbors of Germany knew that a great majority of Germans supported the program as expounded. "Mein Kampf" denounced a peace which the average German was brought up to regard as oppressive and humiliating, and capitalized on the economic and social discontent of the masses who were made to believe that the roots of all their troubles lay at Versailles. There was much less confusion among Germany's small neighbors concerning the true aims of National Socialism than there was in England, the United States and in some so-called neutral countries. It was clear to Germany's eastern neighbors that the first major step of the Nazi policy would be to wipe out the memory of Versailles as the symbol of defeat, but that this was to be only the first episode, a preliminary incident, after which Germany would resume the march toward her self-assumed predestination.

As with Mussolini in 1922, so with Hitler, the first public pronouncements on foreign affairs were pacific and reassuring. The militant and intolerant attitude was reserved for "the internal enemy" first. Consequently, "after the Saar territory had been restored, there was to be no rational or moral ground left for a war with France." In the words of the Interior Minister Frick the Hitler government sought to live in peace and friendship with all the world. In insisting upon her own national claims the new Germany recognized, according to Hitler's word, the equal sacrosanctity of equally valid national claims on the part of other peoples. The enlargement of the Reich was limited strictly to the redemption of German population at that time subject to alien rule, and even that limited policy of national unification was to be pursued through peaceful methods with express repudiation of force. Paris seemed unalarmed and convinced that the deeds of the new régime would be even more moderate than the speeches. Indeed, as the change of the régime in Germany was taking some time to work itself out within the Versailles frontiers, Europe seemed or pretended to be not unduly concerned. Even the consensus of Polish official opinion, not shared by all Poles, appeared to be that the Germans would have so much internal trouble with the advent of Hitler government that the question of territorial changes in Eastern Europe would be relegated to the background. The people outside Germany were generally slow in grasping the depth and the dimensions of the change, and found it more convenient not to look it straight in the face.

Nevertheless, certain international transactions did take place on the part of the peoples who felt that in the long run they would hardly escape being affected. Of these the promotion of the Little Entente to a more homogeneous diplomatic body under its new Pact of Organization was the first reaction to the changing international situation. The failure of the League to stop Japanese aggression in China and the abortive proceedings of the Disarmament Conference were as much responsible for this move as the accession of National Socialism to power. The Pact of Organization was signed at Geneva on February 16, 1933, by Beneš for Czechoslovakia, Jevtich for Yugoslavia and Titulesco for Rumania. The Pact aimed at a complete unification of the foreign policies of the three countries, and for that purpose it provided for the establishment of the Permanent Council of Foreign Ministers with a permanent secretariat as the organs of common policy. The three states retained their sovereignty but agreed to renounce the right to conclude separate treaties with third parties or take unilateral action of international import without the Council's unanimous approval. Their existing bilateral treaties of alliance as well as the tripartite arbitration treaty of 1929 were welded into one diplomatic instrument to last for perpetuity. The Little Entente thus appeared as a novel international factor, a kind of a composite diplomatic great power, representing 45 million peoples, willing to place their commonweal above separate interests. Subsequent political developments in Europe were to show to what extent the composite character of the Little Entente proved to be its weak point. The Pact was open for the adhesion of other small states in Eastern Europe, such as Hungary, Austria and Bulgaria. Its purpose was to impress upon the great powers the determination of the small states not to become pawns of rival policies, and to be given the same serious consideration as had long been enjoyed by the equally small but older nations of northwestern Europe.

By Hungary, Italy and Germany the Pact of Organization was received with resentment. Hungary accepted it simply as one more curb to the recovery of the terra irredenta, and hastened to make it known that rather than trade her revisionist claims for membership in the Entente she preferred to close her ranks and play Italy's, Germany's or anybody's game if that would sooner or later help her to the former territories. Italy had no particular cause to resent the combination for none of her real interests were endangered. Yet she attacked the move out of opposition to any system of collaboration in Eastern Europe which, she feared, might develop into a factor limiting her freedom of action in the future. Germany resented and belittled the transaction. Her future policy was to ensure the non-participation of Austria in the Entente. With regard to Hungary the Wilhelmstrasse was continually adding fuel to Magyar revisionism, pointing out the advantages to be reaped from the associations with the Reich when the time came to remake the map.

The Pact of Organization gave Mussolini a fresh impulse to put in shape his cherished idea of Europe governed by the consensus of the four great powers, Italy, Germany, England and France. Italy was not the only great power which ever since the Corfu incident deprecated the role of small nations at Geneva. England was no less irritated by what she considered the intransigency of "the states of lesser calibre" during the League's discussions of the Manchurian affair. Some of these states made it unpleasant for Sir John Simon when he was trying hard to accommodate Japan and to make the League swallow the bitter pill. In a way it was therefore comprehensible that Mussolini chose Premier MacDonald as the first statesman whom he acquainted with the principles on which the Four Power Pact was to rest. The first draft was transmitted to MacDonald by Mussolini in Rome in March 1933. The Disarmament Conference reached a deadlock from which the British Premier was eager to extricate it. Mussolini believed that in the event of a complete breakdown of the Conference it would be easier to overrule the objections of France to German rearmament if the small states were eliminated from the deal, and particularly if France could be isolated among the great powers. A directorate of four powers would also be in a position to enforce the revision of the territorial clauses of the Peace Treaties and thus satisfy one of the foremost demands of Fascist Italy. In addition to the restatement of the principle of the revision of the Peace Treaties through the League machinery, German equality in armament, and a common line of action in all political and non-political European as well as colonial questions, the Four Power Pact provided for its renewal after the expiry of ten years. Mussolini aspired to revive the Concert of Europe without Russia. The original draft of the Pact went through a process of at least four modifications, however, with the result that the final text, initialled by the four powers in June 1933, was so innocuous that it became virtually meaningless. Moreover, since the Pact failed to be ratified, it became a dead letter.

The purge of Mussolini's draft was largely the work of the Little Entente, Poland, France and of the small countries which raised vehement protests against what they termed the attempt of the four powers to impose their will on other states and to dispose of the rights of third parties. Beneš summarized the plan as granting exceptional position to the great powers against the small Eastern European states whose frontiers were to be revised in favor of creating a new balance of power in which France, the Little Entente and Poland would be weakened and the defeated powers strengthened. In his speech to the Czechoslovak Parliament in April, 1933, Beneš also indicated the following conditions on which rectifications of frontiers might eventually be made: no external pressure, direct negotiations between the interested parties, peaceful cooperation sufficiently long to produce an atmosphere of calm conducive to an agreement, no terror, pressure or blackmail by rival powers, equivalent compensation, and free consent of national parliaments and public opinion. Mussolini's efforts to eliminate small powers from European diplomacy did not stop there, however. In December 1933 the Fascist Grand Council made Italy's continued collaboration with the League conditional upon the radical reform of the League, reducing the role of small nations. By then, however, a clarification was reached between France as a great power and the Little Entente as representing small nations to the effect that, to quote Paul-Boncour, "the League combined happily the principle of equality for all nations with the fact that the great powers, as permanent members of the Council, were able to play a predominant part in directing the work of the League without exercising a decisive hegemony."

While the re-affirmation of the principle of territorial integrity and the bringing of the Four Power Pact in line with the Covenant made it acceptable to the Little Entente, Poland raised strong protests for not having been given the opportunity to participate in the negotiations. Her anger turned against France, her ally, whom the Warsaw government accused of having neglected to stand up for Polish rights. The indignation reached its climax when France was being openly attacked as having compromised her right to count on Polish assistance in the event of squaring the account with Germany. Thus in itself the still-born diplomatic document produced a significant change in Eastern Europe. It led to the gradual detachment of Poland from the traditional policy of friendship with France and to the *détente* in her relations with Germany. A series of conversations between Ambassador Lipski and the German government, held in 1933, culminated in the conclusion in January of 1934 of the German-Polish Declaration, in many ways a landmark in postwar Eastern European diplomacy. The Declaration could not be ascribed to that one cause alone, however. It sprang from the rapidly deteriorating international situation in general. Germany's withdrawal from the Disarmament Conference and the League on October 14, 1933, was one of the decisive contributory elements to this reversal of Polish policy.

The Declaration was historically important because it terminated, at least for a time, a wholly unhappy epoch of German-Polish relations. "The moment has come," so ran the ten year non-aggression agreement, "to start a new phase in the diplomatic relations of the two countries, which would under no circumstances resort to arms but would strengthen the relations that should prevail among neighbors." There was no reference to territorial issues in the Declaration but the phrase eliminating from the scope of the agreement such questions as according to international law were to be regarded as belonging exclusively within the domain of domestic affairs, could and actually was taken by the Poles as covering the territorial matters. Many Poles among the governing circles thought indeed that the document indicated a definite reversal of the traditional Prussian policy which up to then had been pro-Russian and anti-Polish. The National Socialist régime, so it was thought, would strike a new course and become anti-Russian, and if not pro-Polish, at least not anti-Polish. Hitler was accepted as an improvement upon Streseman for he had the courage and authority to break the tradition. Instead of aiming at the elimination of Poland with the help of the Russians he chose a contrary course of friendship to Poland and reserve toward the Bolsheviks. Such was at least the impression carried away by the Poles from Berlin and Berchtesgaden at the heyday of the German-Polish rapprochement.

As regards Pilsudski himself the available evidence seems to confirm his disillusionment about cooperation with Germany. As far as he was concerned, the problem of Polish independence and security would be solved if Russia could be beaten by Germany and Germany in turn could be beaten by France. He was not impressed by Hitler's announcements of peaceful intentions. He was convinced that Germany was quite capable of plunging Europe into another war within twenty years. The pact with Germany would give Poland more time to prepare her defenses, but it would not guarantee her peace. Hitler simply wanted to postpone the evil day. Like other statesmen of Eastern Europe Pilsudski warned the western powers in time but unfortunately Europe was not heeding their warnings.

In Germany the Declaration received a far less extensive interpretation. It was taken as a useful instrument to serve several purposes at the same time: the breaking-up of the isolation of the Reich, insurance of the eastern frontiers while the relations with France were tense, prevention of Poland from taking part in any schemes of Eastern European security, and at best the creation of a political climate which might provide a better background for a peaceful settlement of German territorial demands. Following closely the brusque departure of the National Socialists from Geneva the agreement with Poland was the first expression of the new activity of Hitler's diplomacy. At home Germany speedily increased building up a powerful military machine. Abroad she advertised willingness to conclude bilateral non-aggression arrangements with "cooperative" countries. If Hitler reckoned with a possible last minute hostile intervention, or even with a preventive war, he had neglected nothing to prevent the necessary psychological conditions from developing which might make such a move appear justified or easy of accomplishment. By winning Poland over to sign temporary appeasement he pulled out an important stone from the postwar structure and unbalanced the whole conception of Eastern European solidarity. One of the immediate results of his rapprochement with Pilsudski was the inauguration of an intensive campaign in the Polish Press against Czechoslovakia, the pretext being alleged oppression of the Polish minority in the Teschen district. The campaign did not lack an aspect of curiosity, for the same Colonel Beck who let it loose took the opportunity to denounce, at Geneva on April 10, 1934, the principle of international protection of minorities on the ground that it had been imposed discriminately upon certain nations while the great powers were under no such obligation.

The Balkan Pact

The establishment of the National Socialist régime in Germany and the growing agitation for treaty revision in Eastern Europe which Hitler raised to the foremost aim of his diplomacy was also partly responsible for the realization of the regional security agreement in the Balkans. The initiative came from the Foreign Minister of Rumania, Titulesco, who saw in the creating of a Balkan understanding a guarantee of the Rumanian-Bulgarian frontier. The Little Entente insured the western Transylvanian border of Rumania, the Treaty of Alliance with Poland and the 1933 non-aggression pact with the Soviets took care of her eastern province of Bessarabia, and a Balkan Locarno would complete this safety circle by guaranteeing the Dobrudja region against Bulgaria. On

top of these regional arrangements Rumania was a member of the
League and signed the Kellogg Pact, so that from the point of
law her future seemed to be pretty well established.

The idea of a Balkan union was much older than the National
Socialist régime, and the connection between the two was in
fact only incidental. As early as 1809 when Napoleon carved
out the Illyrian Provinces the ideal of a Slav federation in the
Balkans received some attention. Prince Kara George thought
of a greater Serbia as the nucleus of the union. Carasinin's project
of a Serbian-Bulgarian Entente in 1867 envisaged a united Yugoslavia with close cooperation with Rumania, Greece and Montenegro. In 1887 Stambulov proposed to Carol of Rumania a Bul-
garo-Rumanian personal union which the latter declined for fear
of antagonizing Russia. In 1905 a customs union between Serbia
and Bulgaria was actually ratified at Sophia but Austria induced
Serbia to abandon the project. A working Balkan League was
formed in 1911 and 1912 against the Turks. With the liquidation
of the Ottoman Empire in the Balkans and the removal of antagonism between Turkey and Greece after the World War a
way was paved for a rapprochement between the liberated small
nations on the model of the Little Entente. Between 1930 and 1933
four conferences were held by unofficial representatives of Albania,
Bulgaria, Greece, Yugoslavia, Rumania and Turkey with a view
to establishing cooperation in the economic, transport, postal and
technical fields. Some progress had been made on this non-
political plane.

Collaboration in the domain of politics encountered difficulties
chiefly on the part of Bulgaria. A Balkan pact of non-aggression
would involve that country's renunciation of the revisionist
claims against Greece, Rumania and Yugoslavia, and perpetuate
the status quo as established by the Treaty of Bucharest in 1913,
and reinforced by the Treaty of Neuilly in 1919. By 1933 the relations between Bulgaria and Yugoslavia improved considerably,
thanks to the firm hand adopted by the Sophia government in

dealing with the Macedonian komitaji, and the personal interest King Alexander and King Boris took in establishing better relations. The rapprochement was not limited to the crowned heads but corresponded to the popular wishes on both sides. Nevertheless it did not go far enough to bring Bulgaria within the Balkan Pact signed in February of 1934. The Pact included only Yugoslavia, Rumania, Greece and Turkey. Even in that limited sphere, however, it marked an important step on the road of converting the proverbial powder barrel of Europe into a quiet and at that time probably the most peaceful spot in Europe. The final liquidation of the terroristic International Macedonian Revolutionary Organization by the Bulgarian government indicated that even if staying outside the Pact, Bulgaria had no intention of being an obstacle in organizing the Balkans for the Balkan peoples.

The Balkan Pact was thus the first union of the Balkan nations to be formed not against the Turks, but having the new Turkish republic as one of its partners. The Pact provided for the mutual guarantee of the Balkan frontiers, consultation on general problems affecting their Balkan interests, assumption of no political obligations towards non-signatory states without the consent of the member states, periodical conferences of Foreign Ministers, a permanent secretariat, an economic council, and it left the way open to any Balkan state whose accession would be regarded as desirable. Bulgaria and Albania stood outside, the former on account of her revisionist policy, and the latter because of her dependence on Italy. Greece and Turkey made their reservations which somewhat weakened it but did not render it ineffective. In secret protocols, soon made public, Greece postulated by implication that no military assistance to Yugoslavia should be required of her in the event of Italian aggression. Turkey stated her case similarly in regard to the Soviet attitude toward Rumania. Italian action in the Balkans through Albania or Yugoslavia and of Russian action through Rumania or Bulgaria were regarded as possible. Neither Greece nor Turkey wished to be involved. In common with all nations they were willing to assume risks unlikely to occur and shied from wider responsibilities which really mattered. A united front against Bulgaria was far less important than a united front against Italy.

The economic significance of the Balkan Pact had also its limitations. A bloc of 60 million people occupying 600,000 square miles, i.e., a territory nearly three times as large as that of prewar Germany, and controlling a long seacoast of two continents, had no doubt wide possibilities. Mutual trade between the four countries was small, however, for their economies were parallel rather than complementary, and their purchasing power very modest. They had been engaged in parallel processes of industrialization destined to raise them above the low stage of one-sided agricultural economy. Most of this work was initiated by governments, although private initiative was not excluded whenever sufficient capital was available. Turkey had conceived the most comprehensive plan of industrialization modelled after foreign examples. Expressed in figures the mutual trade of the four countries amounted to roughly one-tenth of their total foreign commerce. The role of the economic advisory council was to unify transportation rules, postal services, collective marketing possibilities, etc. If given peace the Balkan nations would no doubt be able to give fuller effect to their cooperative efforts, provided that outside nations would buy their agricultural surpluses, and that they were granted sufficient credits to develop their natural resources, build roads and harbors, and buy industrial equipment.

The threat of German hegemony over Eastern Europe led to the Franco-Italian attempt in 1933 and in 1934 at the consolidation of the Danubian area on the basis of an economic rapprochement between the Little Entente states on the one hand and the Italian sponsored group of Austria and Hungary. The attempt began with the Four Power Pact, the final text of which was watered down to leave the question of territorial revision where it had stood. The consolidation of the Little Entente and the growing solidarity among the Balkan nations exercised also a decisive influence upon Mussolini in hastening the Italo-Austrian-Hungarian scheme of economic and political solidification. The main incentive to the new move was, however, the importance which Italy attached to the desirability of stopping the growing German interference in Austrian affairs. Austria was placed in the center of Mussolini's foreign policy. There was only one way to bar German penetration southeast, one way to prevent Germany's absorption of Austria. It consisted of an alternative plan to the Anschluss, a Central European system which would include Austria, strengthen her economic position and guarantee her independence politically. The Tardieu plan of organizing a loose economic Danubian cooperative bloc independently of the interference of the great powers was rejected by Mussolini as a French supported scheme. In 1933 the Italian government sent a memorandum to Geneva which marked a certain compromise between the Italian and the French view in that Rome abandoned its opposition to the preferential system. Rome retained a negative attitude to the French idea of a collective bloc, and favored as before bilateral agreements. The result of the new Italian activity in Central Europe was the signature in March 1934 of three Rome Protocols, extending to Italy, Austria and Hungary. The question of closer cooperation with the Little Entente was left open.

The Protocols provided for political consultation and increase of trade by a triangular method. Italy agreed to grant preferential tariffs on Austrian iron and timber and Hungarian agricultural produce, mainly wheat, and she was also willing to pay higher than the world price. Through these economic concessions foreign policies of Austria and Hungary were aligned with Italy. Mussolini succeeded for a time in his dual objective of preventing a Central European consolidation outside his lead, and of detaching Austria from the influence of Germany. France and Italy were drawn a little closer for a short period owing to their parallel concern over the developments in Germany. At the same time the

rapprochement between Italy, Austria and Hungary, following
one year after the Pact of Organization of the Little Entente, led
to the division of the Danubian countries into two sharply defined blocs. Both blocs pursued the policy of erecting barriers to
southeastern expansion of Germany, but they found themselves
at cross-purposes on the problem of territorial revision. Moreover,
Hungary seemed to have a foot in each camp, i.e., in Italy and
in Germany, although the Italian orientation seemed to prevail.

Whether the Italo-French agreement on the Danubian issue
was only a gesture or a well conceived policy, the consolidation
of the two blocs under Italian leadership encountered great local
difficulties. The revival of monarchist propaganda in Austria, the
persistence of Hungary on revision, and the sharpening of Italo-
Yugoslav and Hungarian-Yugoslav relations in connection with
the murder of King Alexander stood in the way of supplying the
proper background for appeasement. Moreover, the German danger was less acutely felt in Yugoslavia than in Czechoslovakia.
The Franco-Italian attempts were not ended, and more was heard
of them in the following year. In the meantime the Rome Protocol
system received its first major test in July of 1934 when the Austrian National Socialists made their abortive putsch. Mussolini
dispatched Italian troops to the Brenner Pass as a warning to
Hitler that the Anschluss would be resented and if need be prevented by Italian forces. Mussolini did not save the life of Chancellor Dollfuss, the initiator of the new Austrian policy, but he
did give Austria a new lease of independence, short though it
was to be.

The regional idea found an echo also in the Baltic region. If
the lead in the Little Entente was for the greater part in the hands
of Czechoslovakia, and if in the Balkan Pact the initiative passed
alternatively from Rumanians to Turks or Yugoslavs, in the Baltic
area it was Latvia which gained considerable reputation as an
international factor working for peace and consolidation. As early
as 1922 her socialist leader Cielens urged the organization of the

Little Baltic Entente which, however, was repeatedly deferred on account of rival politics of Germany, Russia and Poland. Eventually it reached the stage of signature in November 1934. It was preceded by the defensive alliance between Estonia and Latvia, concluded in February 1934, and by fourteen years of strenuous efforts in search of a formula that would bring peace to the fragile Baltic structure. The Estonian-Latvian alliance was modelled on the Organization Pact of the Little Entente. Its provisions included regular conferences of foreign ministers, a permanent joint council for the coordination of legislatures and economic and political action, and joint representation in all international conferences. The Memel dispute with Germany and the Wilno conflict with Poland delayed the accession of Lithuania to the Baltic Union. Poland's opposition was eventually overcome and Germany's objection was met by the inclusion in the statutes of the union of a clause excluding specific Lithuanian problems from the common concern of the Union. The selection of Latvia to the seat on the Council of the League in 1936 was viewed as the international recognition of the new diplomatic group. The non-complementary character of the economies of the three Baltic states did not make them particularly suitable for an extensive collaboration in the economic field.

Experiments in Democracy

It was the hope and the vision of the leaders of the liberation movements during the World War to replace the autocratic monarchies in Eastern Europe by a system of free nations devoted to the practice of democratic principles of government. From Finland to Greece and from the Alps to the Black Sea a belt of liberal governments was to bring western conceptions of life to the peoples who for centuries had been the object of political and social exploitation and bias. At the manifestations organized by the representatives of the struggling nations during the World War in the Allied countries, and in the United States in particular,

pledges were made on behalf of the oppressed peoples that democratic principles would be incorporated in the organic laws of
whatever governments the peoples may establish in their proper
lands. At one of these conventions, held in Philadelphia on October 26, 1918, delegates of thirteen nationalities took part and
unanimously hailed the declaration of democratic faith. There
were Czechs, Poles, Slovaks, Serbs, Croats, Slovenes, Ukrainians,
Lithuanians, Rumanians, Italians, Albanians, Zionists and Greeks.
The imparting of this belief in democracy was one of the outstanding contributions which the United States made to the
cause of Eastern Europe.

Most of the constitutions introduced after World War I by the
Eastern European parliaments were imbued with what was believed to be true American or western spirit. Not infrequently the
revolutionary legislators had the ambition to outdo the older and
traditional democracies. Recruited mainly from liberal and socialist groups they wanted to disarm the executive and to give all the
power to the legislative branch. They remembered that it had
been through the executive decrees of the fallen monarchies that
most harm had been inflicted upon them arbitrarily. The postwar
tendency to reduce the executive to the mere holder of a title and
to subordinate him to the legislative body was general. In Estonia
the parliament received the power to form the cabinet. In Austria
the federal government was to be elected by a simple majority by
the National Council on the basis of lists of candidates set up by
the central legislative committee. The Polish constitution of 1921
reserved to the Seym alone the right to dissolve itself, and it also
provided for its own revision every twenty-five years. In Yugoslavia the Vidovdan constitution of 1921 gave the parliament the
right to decide on the constitutionality of its legislation. The concentration of all power in the elective assemblies was generally
taken as the best safeguard of popular rights. The influence of the
Russian revolution was indicated by the prominence given to
social legislation. Yet the Soviet example did not exercise as im-

portant influence as did the democratic conceptions of the west.

In most Eastern European constitutions provisions were included for the election of the parliaments on the widest possible basis of universal and secret franchise often with proportional representation. This led to the multiplication of political parties which in turn made the organization of a majority government an arduous process of bargaining and compromises. The stability of governments was intimately connected with the stability of political parties. There was a constant danger that the rigid party system forming the basis of the coalitionist governments might lead to the conversion of political factions into oligarchies, especially in view of the fact that the electors often voted on the basis of party tickets and not of individual candidates. To avoid sudden crises of cabinets on flimsy pretexts of procedure the Greek constitution made the too liberal use of the vote of confidence more difficult. To make the legislative machinery more adaptable to the changing needs of economy and to provide for more safety in emergencies the Czechoslovak constitution introduced a standing parliamentary committee to adopt emergency measures while the parliament was not in session. The government had the right to use the power of decrees provided that such decrees were approved by the parliament within two months. In Czechoslovakia the party system had demonstrated considerable endurance and stability. Although the constitution made no provision for vesting the power in the hands of the parties, these and their leaders, five to eight in accordance with the number of the factions forming the government, played the leading role in the management of the country. This expedient which developed in the course of political practice was often criticized as unconstitutional but it proved its usefulness. The country stayed democratic down to the day of its destruction from outside.

The presence of national minorities within nearly every Eastern European state turned attention to the problem of how to deal constitutionally with the minority issue. The new states were parties to the minority provisions of the Peace Treaties, or to special minority conventions with their neighbors. Protection of minorities and their right to send petitions to the League of Nations over the heads of their governments was a part of the new postwar international law. Respective provisions were also incorporated in national constitutions of the signatory countries. However, in spite of these provisions the minority issues continued to be one of the most burning problems weighing heavily upon the process of internal consolidation. The reason lay in the fact that some of the minority groups were the ruling groups before the World War, that they were contiguous to kindred peoples living in the neighboring countries, and that foreign governments, instead of regarding the minorities as a bridge, began to use them as instruments of aggressive policies to undermine the structure of the states which stood in the path of their expansion.

Under such circumstances there was little impetus to solve the minority issue on the basis of federal organization. Austria with a very small percentage of alien people was in fact the only country which adopted a federal framework. All the other states favored unitary constitutions. Yet in Austria the federal system had nothing to do with the minority question. It was based on the historical administrative provinces. The only arrangements for autonomy were those imposed upon the new countries by the Peace Treaties. The City of Danzig, Memel and the Carpathian province of Czechoslovakia were constituted along autonomous lines as provided for by international treaties. On the whole the tendency prevailed away from the federal idea and towards centralization. Fascist Italy and National Socialist Germany repudiated it as tending to weaken the state authority in matters of national economy, social problems and military as well as foreign policies. Everywhere among the surrounding great powers the tendency prevailed toward the concentration of authority in the hands of highly centralized government and unitary party organization. For Italy and Germany the concentration of authority was a corollary to aggressive policies. The problem of centralization versus autonomization of the small nations with minority groups was consequently viewed as primarily an issue of national security and safety in the face of the growing authoritarian aggressiveness.

A distinction should be drawn between individual countries and also between the former victors and the vanquished. In Germany and Austria democratic régimes were adopted under the strain of collapse. The innate anti-democratic feeling was temporarily shelved behind the screen of ultra-liberal constitutions. Yet it continued to live. The German example showed that it needed little effort to call it back. Among the liberated peoples the adoption of democratic forms of government was the outcome of victory. In many respects it reflected foreign influences, or outright derivations. The prewar dynastic régimes gave the masses none of the opportunities of self-government enjoyed in western nations with long democratic tradition. The wide democratic régimes established immediately after the World War failed in many instances to satisfy either the needs or the capabilities of the peoples. Thus within the two decades systems of government had to be changed frequently, in fact over forty different constitutional charters replaced one another. Some régimes were put aside by sudden coups, others through rapid evolutionary process. These changes were sometimes so sudden that there was little time to embody them in proper institutional framework. Pilsudski in 1925 used the parliamentary machinery to establish an anti-constitutional government. Where a strong and experienced middle class existed the appeals from either extreme right or extreme left were successfully resisted. Czechoslovakia belonged to this category. In Hungary, with the exception of the short-lived republic of Karolyi, a semi-feudal society continued to rule by its own kind of constitutional dictatorship which showed a high degree of resistance to change.

Most changes in political régimes were brought about largely as the result of the demand for a stronger executive. The positions were now reversed. It was the turn of the legislative to be subordinated to the executive authority. One of the first countries to abandon liberal government was Lithuania. An authoritarian system of government of national concentration was adopted there allegedly as a measure of strengthening the country in the face of Polish ambitions. The Pilsudski coup in Warsaw was referred to as providing a cause for the change. Pilsudski's principle of a strong presidential authority found its expression in the Polish constitution. Pilsudski felt that his chief responsibility was only to God and history. The most radical changes came about in Eastern Europe in connection with the economic crisis and the rise of totalitarianism in Germany.

After 1931 people began to blame the representative democratic institutions for the inability to solve economic issues and bring back prosperity. The movement away from the traditional institutions was general and only a few and firmly grounded régimes survived, often at the price of far-reaching compromise. France, Great Britain and the United States made no exception. Small wonder that the inexperienced democracies failed.

Latvia became authoritarian in 1934. The same year saw the constitutional life of Austria pushed back to the absolutism of the Holy Alliance era. Again it was the resurgence of outside menace rather than internal conditions which produced the reversal. Under the new constitution the equality before law could be dispensed with if objective reasons warranted it. The executive enjoyed the monopoly of initiating legislation and the members of the five corporations carrying on the administration of the country had to offer guarantees of Austrian, and not Reich, patriotism.

In Yugoslavia King Alexander overthrew the parliamentary system by a royal proclamation as early as 1929. He declared that parliamentary government had always been his own ideal, but that it was abused by blind party passion. The desire to preserve the unity of the state against external danger dictated his move.

King Boris of Bulgaria followed Alexander's example in 1934, and King George II of Greece in 1936. Carol of Rumania joined the ranks of the royal dictators in 1938. The one party system as developed in Russia, Italy and Germany had served the royal revolutionaries as a model, although they never brought it to a comprehensive system such as existed in Germany. Both in Yugoslavia and Bulgaria some latitude had been allowed to oppositional voices. A measure of credit can not be denied to the royal dictators for their good but ill-directed intentions. In several instances they made genuine attempts to check the abuses and to represent the cross-section of their population. But on the whole the results were negative. They killed the emerging sense of popular responsibilities of the masses, and by vesting their countries' fate in the hands of the few, strengthened the centrifugal forces of disunity.

In general, however, it would not be accurate to represent the existing régimes in the small Eastern European states as genuine totalitarian dictatorships. They should rather be regarded as truly emergency expedients, in no way characteristic of the basic predilections of the people. Democracies in Eastern Europe went by the board for several reasons working in combination: economic crisis, threat of foreign aggression from without and within, inexperience in self-government, and deficiency of democratic institutions. It may safely be assumed that constitutionalism as understood in the west will again be given its chance.

The Return of the Soviets

The prelude to the new Soviet policy of cooperation with France and the League of Nations dates back to the year 1932. In that year the Soviet Union concluded non-aggression treaties with Poland, Finland, Estonia and Latvia. In 1934 the treaties were extended for ten years. They gave the signatories the right to withdraw in the event that the other party violated the principle of non-aggression by attacking a third country. The next step proposed by Moscow was the proposal that the western neighbors of the Soviet Union accept the Geneva draft convention defining the aggressor. The move was announced by communist editor Radek in "Izvestia," in which a strong stand was taken against "imperialism which under the smokescreen of treaty revision prepares the most terrible and ruthless war that human brains could conceive." The convention was signed in London by the representatives of the Soviet Union, the Little Entente, Turkey, Poland, Latvia and Estonia. Lithuania signed it separately on account of her feud with Poland and Finland soon joined the other countries.

The definition of aggressor as given in these treaties was one of the most complete ever formulated. It took into account the various methods of aggression from within committed on the pretext of alleged political, social or economic disorders in neighboring countries. It also defined as aggressive the support of organized or armed units hostile to the interest and institutions of the contracting parties. In 1935 the Soviets consolidated further their relations with Turkey. Thus Moscow had surrounded itself with a contiguous chain of non-aggression pacts covering all the 1,800 miles of the Soviet western borders. Behind the belt of the small buffer states loomed the specter of Germany which in 1918, at the time of the Brest-Litovsk peace, held one-third of Russia's population under her military sway.

Nothing could probably better describe the complete change of political scenery in Europe than the reversal of German and Russian attitude toward the League of Nations. During the first phase of disarmament discussions the Soviet government supported Germany against France. However, soon it deviated from its germanophile stand, and when in 1933 the Disarmament Conference failed and Germany had taken leave of Geneva the Soviet Union was already in the opposite camp. It supported the League and on occasions its delegate, Maxime Litvinov, dominated the Assembly. The Soviet Union stood strongly for non-aggression, the indivisibility of European peace and collective security. In all this Soviet diplomacy was in a sharp contrast with all that the

National Socialists stood for. German National Socialism also produced reaction on the internal Russian front in that it led to the accentuation of Stalin's policy of building up socialism in one country alone instead of spending energy on a world revolution. The thirteen years of German-Soviet cooperation were to be followed by Soviet collaboration with the so-called anti-aggression group of powers.

The Soviet entry into the League of Nations was preceded by several events which had direct bearing on the modification of the Moscow policy. The German-Polish declaration of January 1934 was in the Soviet eyes fraught with incalculable eventualities. The men of Warsaw were not liked and trusted at the Kremlin, and the distrust was mutual. In March and April of 1934 it became known that the Anglo-Italian formula aimed at reaching a compromise between the German and the French views of disarmament would come to nothing. France made it known that she was not prepared to accept any proposal which would virtually reduce her armed status and legalize Germany's secret rearmament. The July National Socialist putsch in Vienna was suppressed, but it showed the menacing advance made along the road of nazification of Germans living outside the Reich borders. All such events indicated that Europe was entering upon a period of great uncertainty. The Soviet Union felt especially uneasy both in the Far East where it was facing Japan along the newly created long borderline of Manchukuo, and in Europe where anti-Bolshevik propaganda in Germany was steadily gaining in strength.

The gap created by Germany's absence from Geneva had to be filled if collective security was to survive. The Little Entente was interested in seeing the Soviets filling the vacated seat on the Council. It was generally felt that it would be better to have the Soviet Union in the League instead of outside it. The Czechoslovak Foreign Minister was particularly active in helping to smooth the road for Moscow's return within the orbit of western powers. At their meeting at Zagreb the three Little Entente states decided to recognize the Soviet government de jure, leaving it to each member to choose the appropriate time for giving effect to the decision. Rumanian Foreign Minister Titulesco and Beneš of Czechoslovakia acted at once, whereas Yugoslavia, which had been under the strong influence of anti-Bolshevik elements, refrained from following the example. On September 15, 1934, the invitation was sent to Moscow and in three days the Assembly admitted the Soviet Union by 39 out of 49 votes.

The presence of the Soviets at Geneva brought the problem of Eastern European security once more on the agenda of diplomacy. Ever since 1925, the year of the Locarno Pact, responsible statesmen were waiting for the moment when a similar system could be introduced in vulnerable regions east of the Rhine. Rustu Aras of Turkey, Politis of Greece, Titulesco and Beneš studied with others the ways in which the Locarno model could be adapted in the Mediterranean, in the Danubian basin and in Eastern Europe. The problems of revisionism and security reached a vicious circle. The revisionist powers insisted on no collective security without revision first. The status quo nations answered that without an effective system of mutual guarantees the peace of Eastern Europe would be continually disturbed. With the Soviet Union at Geneva the path seemed cleared for organizing an Eastern European Locarno on broader foundations. With the passing of Stresemann and Briand French foreign policy returned to the conception of a balance of power as outlined in the pre-Locarno era of Poincaré. The Quai d'Orsay sought an Eastern European security pact. Foreign Minister Barthou took upon himself to sound out the attitude of the Eastern European countries to such a pact. He was strongly supported by Litvinov and Beneš, and neither Italy nor England opposed the plan provided it did not increase their responsibilities. The scheme involved the conclusion of a series of bilateral treaties of guarantee and mutual assistance between the Soviet Union, Germany, Poland, the Baltic states and Czechoslovakia. France would act as a guarantor of the system, and the

Soviet Union would co-sign the western Locarno in order to bring both halves of Europe closer together in the spirit of the doctrine of the indivisibility of peace. How keenly the Kremlin government was interested in the plan could be judged by the note of February 20, 1935, in which it pointed out that 365 million peoples representing 70 per cent of the population of Europe, including France, England, Italy, the Soviets, the Little Entente and the Balkan Pact, favored a policy which had for its purpose the prevention of military aggression by means of mutual assistance pacts.

The two governments opposing the plan were those of Germany and Poland. The German attitude as formulated in April of 1935 after a series of conferences and exchanges of notes could be summarized as follows: Germany could not adhere to a pact containing military obligations, but at the same time she could not be prevented by such pacts from concluding simple treaties of non-aggression. The German government further stated that the amplification of non-aggression pacts through agreements for military assistance, as solicited by France and Russia, rested upon inherent contradictions. Either one believed in obligations which had been freely undertaken or one did not believe in them. If one did believe in them, then the necessity of military agreements did not arise. On the other hand, if one doubted the sincere fulfilment of non-aggression obligations, the same doubt was equally justified in regard to the fulfilment of the military obligations. If pacts of non-aggression were to cause wars, offensive action could in the opinion of the German government also originate from defensive agreements for mutual assistance. The road leading from the non-aggression pacts to the violation of peace seemed even longer and less easy than the road leading from military obligations of defensive character to offensive action. On the whole Germany was against any general or collective system of mutual assistance, but would not oppose a general pact providing for non-aggression, arbitration and non-assistance to aggressors, "even if precise identification of aggressors was fraught with difficulties." On March

16, 1935, Germany announced the introduction of conscription, repudiating thereby one of the military clauses of the Versailles Treaty. This unilateral action, coupled with the refusal to negotiate a pact of mutual assistance, deepened Soviet and French suspicions of Germany's intention to keep the way open for eventual expansion.

The Polish attitude to the Eastern European security system was described by Colonel Beck before the Seym Foreign Relations Committee on February 1, 1935. "The proposed pact was neither Locarno nor Eastern European," said Beck. "The Locarno pact was based on the British and Italian guarantee. The proposed plan has no such basis. Besides, the very name is not attractive to us. Experience with the western Locarno proved poor results because of its connection with a certain style of western European policies which paid absolutely no regard to our vital interests." This was a reproach addressed to France of the Briand era. In France and Russia the opinion prevailed that Poland was already deeply involved in the German orbit, and that for that reason she was checkmating all attempts to create in Eastern Europe a coalition of anti-aggression powers in which the Soviet Union would represent the strongest factor. Marshall Göring was reported to have hinted to Pilsudski on February 10, 1935, that a joint German-Polish action against Russia would benefit Germany in the northwestern part of the Soviet Union while Poland might gain her respective sphere of influence in the Ukraine. Pilsudski was said to have turned down the suggestion on the grounds that it was impossible to stand continually at the ready on such a long line as the Polish-Soviet frontier.

Poland's real anxiety was to keep aloof from participation in a collective system that might turn her into a battlefield. She felt that should Russia or Germany come in to fulfil the mandate, neither of the two could be dislodged, for both had designs on her territory. Poland also felt that the pact would relieve France of the direct obligations she had already assumed towards her, for her role as a Polish ally would be reduced to that of a mere guarantor. Had Great Britain associated herself directly with the plan Poland would have been probably more sympathetic. The Warsaw diplomats believed that under the leadership of the Austrian born Chancellor Germany would march to the south rather than to the east. The leading Nazis had been assuring them that Danzig and the Corridor did not really mean much to the new Germany, and that the old pro-Russian orientation of the Wilhelmstrasse had been definitely replaced by the new National Socialist conception. It seemed, therefore, as if Austria and then Czechoslovakia were to bear the brunt of the revitalized German might. Consequently Warsaw did not wish to guarantee Czechoslovak integrity within the proposed general pact. Poland did not approve of the Trianon Treaty which in her interpretation placed the Slovak and Carpatho-Russian "corridor" between her and Hungary. Then the settlement of the Teschen district did not meet Polish expectations, and supplied one more reason why Warsaw would not tie herself too closely with a country which the governing régime regarded as a seasonal creation. In short, Poland preferred to pursue an independent course of keeping Germany and the Soviet Union apart, a task which rendered her position particularly exposed.

The negotiations for the Danubian pact, conceived as a part of the ambitious scheme of replacing the Versailles system by a series of freely negotiated arrangements between Germany and the other powers, did not fare better than the Eastern European security plan, even if they opened under the hopeful signs of preliminary agreements between Italy, France and Great Britain. The initiative in this sector rested with Mussolini, and the discussions and declarations went down under the name of the Stresa front. Up to 1933 Mussolini had many diplomatic struggles with the French, and the leftist groups in France hated his régime on ideological grounds. In Central Europe the Duce's position was considerable until the rise of power of Hitler's Germany. Mussolini and Hitler knew exactly one another's ambitions and weaknesses and both watched anxiously their respective moves. At his first meeting with Hitler at Venice in 1934 Mussolini learnt that his supremacy east of the Rhine was to be circumscribed and reduced, since Germany also cherished concrete ambitions in the sector. For that reason Italy considered it opportune to champion a policy of status quo in Central Europe, or at least a purely theoretical form of revisionism, wrapped in general formulas of the Genevan vocabulary. The economic steps had already been mentioned in connection with the Rome Protocols. The political efforts to meet the menace of German expansionism were chiefly concerned with the increased Italian interest in the fate of Austria. The consideration of the Austrian problem, as the central issue in the vortex of the approaching struggle, gave Italian foreign policy once more a new orientation. It was not an entirely anti-German orientation, but an attempt to organize that part of Europe on the basis of a compromise between the policy of insistence on the fulfilment of the Peace Treaties and that of revisionism, without offending German susceptibilities but also without letting Germany have everything her own way.

Leaving aside the African concessions by France to Italy, covered in the historical conversations between Laval and Mussolini, a new system of security in Central Europe was one of the important items discussed in the course of conferences held in January 1935 at Rome, in February in London, in April at Stresa, and in May at Venice. The Little Entente, Austria and Hungary were counted upon as potential partners in the scheme. Direct and active cooperation of Germany was essential for the success of the plan. The Franco-Italian agreement of Rome provided for noninterference and respect for territorial integrity and independence of the participating states. An undertaking to that effect was to be negotiated between Austria, Hungary, Czechoslovakia and Yugoslavia as countries immediately interested in the preservation of Austrian independence, and Italy and Germany as the two neighboring great powers. The undertaking would be open to France, Poland and Rumania. England gave her blessing but faithful to her declared policy of aloofness from Eastern Europe indicated she would stay at a distance.

Germany wanted a precise definition of the term of non-interference before deciding on participation. Considering her designs on Austria, this was one of the most serious obstacles. Another stumbling block was the proposal that Austria's neighbors would accept a general undertaking of mutual assistance and of military help to Austria against unprovoked attack. Assistance was not conceived to be given automatically but after due consultations between the interested governments. Since international consultation usually meant in practice the last resort of indecision in the face of reality, the effectiveness of the scheme became problematical. To Mussolini it was clear that unless the general pact was supported by a military force—he spoke of 600,000 men perpetually under arms—it would not contribute much to guaranteeing the peace of the Danubian area. Germany was unlikely to guarantee the borders which she was seeking to abolish. Poland, another absentee at Stresa, was equally unwilling to guarantee any Central European territory, pointing out that her immediate interests were confined to the Baltic coast. Hungary, whose revisionist efforts were neutralized somewhat at Venice where they had been referred to the revisory stipulation of article 19 of the Covenant, would perhaps have guaranteed the borders of Italy and Austria on the basis of reciprocity, but she could hardly have been expected to behave similarly in regard to the frontiers of the Little Entente states for the revision of which she had been agitating ever since she had to sign the Peace Settlement. In regard to disarmament Laval and Mussolini suggested that the Little Entente states grant the ex-enemy states of Austria, Hungary and Bulgaria the right to re-arm after the negotiations of the Danubian security pact should have made such a course safe. The agreement was to be discussed at a special Danubian conference to be held at Rome in June 1935. The conference never met.

The Eastern European security pact was frustrated because of the opposition of Germany and Poland. Despite this failure France, the Soviet Union and Czechoslovakia felt that some kind of mutual assistance should be provided for. Litvinov, Laval and Beneš labored to save whatever they could from the original plan, even without Germany and Poland. The big scheme of mutual assistance between France, Germany and the Soviets with the inclusion of the surrounding lesser states eventually took the reduced form of a skeleton system of two treaties of mutual assistance between France and the Soviet Union and between Czechoslovakia and the Soviet Union. The treaties were signed in May of 1935 in Paris and at Prague respectively. If France or Russia should be subjected to unprovoked aggression by a European power the other state was to come immediately to her assistance. In view of the special geographical situation of Czechoslovakia her obligation to come to the assistance of Russia and vice versa was conditioned by the engagement of France.

French opinion was divided as to the efficaciousness and wisdom of the Soviet pact. Laval himself explained that the purpose of France in signing the pact was not so much to ensure Russian military help for herself but rather to forestall the ever present possibility that Moscow and Berlin might come to closer terms with one another. The way in which Laval managed to delay the ratification until February 1936 threw some light on his vain endeavors to effect the alternative policy of an understanding with Berlin. In Moscow the conclusion of the treaty was accepted with satisfaction even though it limited France's assistance to Europe only and did not provide for any help in the event of aggression in the Far East. It was also doubted how quickly French assistance would come considering the fact that the pact was subjected to the procedure of the League and that France would

have to consult the other Locarno powers before taking action. Berlin protested against the treaties as contrary to the Locarno Pact. France and England declared on the other hand in June 1935 that there was nothing in the Franco-Russian treaty which either conflicted with the Locarno Pact or modified it. As regards Poland Laval assured the Warsaw government that the Franco-Polish alliance of 1921 was unaffected, for it was dictated by nature and history. This explanation did not, however, change the cool attitude of Colonel Beck to Czechoslovakia. In order that Russian help could come to that country, permission from Poland or from Rumania to cross their territories would have to be obtained first. Under the League Covenant this was permissible. Yet Poland was in no way disposed to permit the Russian army to enter her territory. On the contrary, the apprehension, whether reasonable or not, that Russia might drive her way through Galicia added to Warsaw's irritation.

In Rumania the rapprochement between Prague and Moscow was accompanied by the efforts to settle the Bessarabian issue and obtain an analogous mutual assistance pact with the Russian neighbor. Titulesco considered friendship with the Soviet Union a cardinal point in the Rumanian foreign policy and worked indefatigably toward that end. One of the staunchest supporters of collective security, his labors were constantly interfered with by the opposition at home and also from outside. The Rumanian bourgoisie was frightened by the prospect of a closer cooperation with a régime which was its class enemy. At the moment when everything seemed to have been prepared to bring about the pact and when Moscow agreed to discuss the Bessarabian question, Titulesco was deposed from his office. Like the murder of his predecessor Duca in 1933, the assassinations of Chancellor Dollfuss of Austria and of Alexander of Yugoslavia in 1934, the removal of Titulesco from the Foreign Ministry in 1936 marked a setback to the elements working for the consolidation of Eastern Europe. Whether these acts were unrelated events or part of a conspiracy, they had far-reaching consequences for the course of Eastern European policies.

The pact-making fever of 1935 brought with it one more event which affected the Baltic sector. In June of that year the British government accepted Hitler's proposal that the ratio between the British and German fleets should be established definitely and for all the future in the proportion of 100 : 35. Germany had already been constructing a fleet which exceeded the limits laid down in the Versailles Treaty. By the Naval Agreement the British government hoped to limit Germany's unilateral action. In France the Naval Agreement aroused deep resentment for it placed the country before an accomplished fact only four months after the solemn British undertaking to maintain a common diplomatic front. Mussolini, too, regarded it as an offence against the Stresa solidarity, although his reaction was somewhat milder. In Eastern Europe it was less the Naval Agreement by itself that caused a good deal of worry as the political tendency of which it was the symptom. It was felt that Germany was having one more success in establishing friendly relations in the west in order to avoid enemies on two fronts and thus securing a free hand in the east.

The Anglo-German agreement tacitly conceded German domination over the Baltic sea routes. In Moscow the agreement was viewed as directed against her interests. It was not forgotten that during the World War when Russia controlled all the Baltic ports of Finland, Estonia and Latvia, she was unable to prevent the Baltic sea from becoming an exclusive German domain of operation, and this despite the fact that she had the cooperation of the British and French fleets. A conflict between Germany and Russia would be waged partly in the Baltic sea. The Naval Agreement represented a threat to the small Baltic states, especially to Finland, for they were put into the prospective precarious position of seeing their markets cut off from the rest of the world should war come.

Forging the Axis

Two grave events of 1935 and 1936 changed the political relationships in Europe and profoundly affected the situation and security of Eastern Europe. One was the Ethiopian campaign, and the other the remilitarization of the Rhineland. On October 3, 1935, Mussolini's African army of well equipped mechanized troops invaded Ethiopia, and on July 6, 1936, the sanctions committee of the League of Nations wound up. The recommendation to cancel sanctions was carried by 44 states against one, that of the Negus. Ethiopian independence ended on May 9, 1936, when Mussolini proclaimed the annexation of the Kingdom and the creation of the Italian East African Empire. The application of sanctions confronted the League with its major test. It failed in the end because it had been rendered ineffective by French and British preoccupation in permitting Mussolini to carry out his project rather than risk a Mediterranean war; they hoped to save the League by keeping up appearances. Non-participation of Germany, Austria and Hungary in the sanctions left too many loopholes, while the refusal to stop shipment of oil and other essential materials to Italy made it possible for Rome to prosecute the war to a successful end. Moreover, the League's pressure on Italy served Mussolini's purpose of rallying his people more solidly behind his Ethiopian venture, and of driving Italy into more economic autarchy.

Taking advantage of the League crisis, and convinced that the democratic nations were so deeply devoted to the policy of peace that they would maintain it at any price, Hitler ordered his troops to march into the demilitarized Rhineland on March 7, 1936, and to repudiate the Locarno Pact. As a pretext he took the ratification by the French parliament of the Franco-Russian mutual assistance pact of the previous year. He argued that the pact was not compatible with Locarno, a charge which had been refuted by the British and the French after the signature of the Soviet treaty.

For France this was "the gravest injury since the World War." Her safety on the Rhine and her ability to cooperate militarily with her Eastern European allies was gravely weakened. She was now separated from them by strong Rhine fortifications which Germany was erecting opposite the Maginot line. Sarraut declared over the radio that "France could not tolerate that Strasbourg should be within the firing distance of German guns." The German coup meant one more unilateral repudiation of the Peace Treaties, and the abrogation of an agreement freely negotiated and signed.

How did the western powers react to this violation of international contracts? There suddenly rose a brief undercurrent of public opinion in both France and England demanding "the creation of a bloc of peaceable but resolute nations determined to make a stand against aggression of all sorts." Yet there was also another and powerful undercurrent accepting the accomplished fact, for after all "the Rhineland was German territory." The French were obviously unwilling to take up arms, for much of their postwar trend of mind moved toward fighting no other war except the defense of French territory. The Maginot Line was the expression of fatal lack of coordination between French diplomacy and military strategy. The alliances with Eastern Europe called for an offensive warfare in front of and beyond the Maginot Line, whereas military strategists planned to defend the country in and behind the Line. The Germans were permitted to arm while they still could have been prevented. The fact that earlier the French had refused to treat with Germany while she was likely to be more accommodating was one of the peculiar features of France's diplomacy. Whether the reliance on collective security undermined her will to vigorous independent action, or whether dependence on Great Britain circumscribed her freedom of decision, at this particular juncture her inability to act proved to be most detrimental to her future position in Europe and to her security.

The only united action the signatories of the Locarno Pact took was the consultations between the French, English and Belgian army staffs at Brussells. Italy refused to take part for the sanctions had not yet been lifted. Eden on behalf of England in a rather meek speech promised France military assistance in case of actual attack. England did not want to hurt French susceptibilities, but she also was anxious not to anger Germany. She proposed that Germany consider the occupation of the Rhineland as symbolical, at least for the time being, until the Locarno Pact could be modified to suit the changed situation. Germany saw that her march into the Rhineland was unopposed and that surprisingly enough no action was going to be taken against her. The plebiscite approving the march by 98.95 per cent of votes prompted Hitler to ignore the verbal protests entirely, to state that he would under no circumstances withdraw from the Rhineland, and to repeat his willingness to conclude twenty-five year non-aggression treaties with Germany's neighbors. Hitler would also discuss the problem of the "humanization" of war, without however surrendering the right to the remilitarization and fortification of the Rhine.

The Locarno powers replied separately. France raised again the plan of an international army within a collective security system as opposed to the German conception of separate bilateral non-aggression treaties. England sent to Berlin on May 6 the ill-fated Fragebogen, in which she tried to elicit Germany's real intentions in western, central and eastern Europe. She wanted to know whether Germany was interested in concluding "real" agreements, i.e., agreements that she would not claim the liberty of repudiating on the pretext that at the time of their conclusion she had not been in a position to assume binding obligations. The Fragebogen further included questions of this type: what was Germany's attitude to the remaining Peace Treaties, did she accept the existing territorial order in Europe, and would the offered non-aggression pacts extend to the Soviet Union, Estonia and Latvia. There was no answer to the inquiry until in his speech of January 30, 1937,

Chancellor Hitler referred to it in passing. In his opinion the document owed its origin to the British desire to disentangle the situation as it existed at the moment when the Fragebogen had been written. In the meantime Germany settled several of its points "in the most natural manner through practical steps." "Today, when we have re-established complete sovereignty and equality of rights Germany will never again sign a treaty which would in any way be incompatible with her honor, or which would be inconsistent with vital German interests, and could not therefore endure in the long run."

The repudiation of the Locarno Pact, the liquidation of the Stresa front of Franco-Anglo-Italian diplomatic solidarity, the humiliating failure of the League over the sanctions, and the separation of France from Eastern Europe by means of the remilitarization of the Rhineland forecast the imminence of the end of Europe as conceived in Paris after the World War. The Polish Foreign Minister, perplexed, declared that he was adopting an attitude of waiting and seeing. The international scene was indeed teeming with spectacular moves. After having lulled the Poles into the state of a precarious truce in the east, the German government made sure to fortify the western front by frightening France and England into inactivity. Now the way lay open to revert to the east for further advance. The Spanish diversion served the purpose of impressing upon France her hopeless location between three potential enemies and of warning the British of the risk involved in any French entanglement.

In August 1936 obligatory military service in Germany was extended to two years, and through the years 1934 to 1937 the military budget increased from 32 to 67 per cent of the budget. The 1933 army of unemployed was by 1936 largely absorbed by the semi-military formations and the Labor Front, and the four year rearmament plan was put on foot with typical Russian thoroughness. The extension of the military service was explained by the growing armament expenditures in the Soviet Union. The

Russian military budget was in fact inflated from 1500 million roubles in 1933 to 14,900 million roubles in 1936. In England the increase was only from 13 to 20 per cent in the years 1922 and 1936 respectively, while in France it took 26.5 per cent in the critical year of 1936. Military unpreparedness of Great Britain dictated a cautious course in foreign policy. On November 20, 1936, Eden stated at Leamington that England would fulfil her obligation toward France and Belgium, but it was evident that official Downing Street retained its freedom of interpreting international developments and obligations entirely in terms of expediency.

The break-up of the Stresa front and Germany's entry into the Rhineland had the most serious consequences for Eastern Europe. In 1932 National Socialist military writer Professor Banse published a book dealing with the relationship between geographical space and the position of nations in wartime. He said that the Anschluss would bring about the collapse of Czechoslovakia, give Germany a common border with Yugoslavia, and strengthen Italy against France. Banse's work was minimized in Germany as extremist and fantastic, but it explained exactly the course which National Socialist leaders adopted as soon as they came to power. The union with Austria was for Hitler a matter of both patriotic emotion and a hard fact of strategy. It would create a pincer of steel around Czechoslovakia and make France aware of her weakness in Eastern Europe.

Much depended then on the attitude of Italy, the protector of Austrian independence. From the time of the Roman Empire down to 1919, that is for fifteen hundred years, the Middle Danube had been lost to Italy. It formed the center of Germanic expansion. From 1919, when Italy established herself on the Brenner frontier, she became the leading Central European great power. Through her hold over Vienna and Budapest she exercised predominant influence in the Danube basin. In 1935 the Third Reich resumed the traditional Germanic pressure along the river. Italy was also brought for the first time in her modern history into a conflict of interests with her traditional friend Great Britain. As recently as June 1928 the Duce said that Italian friendship with Great Britain was one of the cardinal points of the Fascist foreign policy. But within a few years English prestige sank deep in Italy and Italian self-confidence rose so high that Roman diplomacy openly challenged the British Empire at the roots of its African power and along its sea-route to India.

In "Mein Kampf" Hitler wrote that if Germany had to shed blood it would be criminal to do so in order to liberate 250,000 Germans in South Tyrol, when much nearer home millions of them lived under foreign domination. Italy had to be won over to preclude the repetition of the Napoleonic march to Central Europe through northern Italy. The resentment against the sanction powers paved the way for a co-ordinated Italo-German policy. The Axis was born the moment Germany refused to join the sanctions in 1935. It grew through the Spanish war into more precise shape. Several reasons combined to produce a favorable climate for the rapprochement. All throughout the postwar years Italy showed a varying degree of understanding for Germany's grievances in contrast to the habitual attitude of France. Both Fascist Italy and Germany considered themselves encircled and checked everywhere by France or Great Britain. Germany saw herself hemmed within the limited confines of the continental area. Italy called herself the prisoner of the Mediterranean. Both nations were controlled by political régimes repudiating democracy. Both had wide ambitions in Eastern Europe which could not be satisfied without resort to arms. Both had good reasons to limit the areas of mutual rivalries and to act in concert on plans for future action.

In regard to Austria Berlin dropped her tactics of 1934, and sought Italian agreement. The absorption of the little republic was to be performed bit by bit under Mussolini's nose. First in July 1936 he was approached with the proposal to accept con-

ciliation and compromise which would respect all his vital interests in Austria. According to this compromise Austria retained
her independence but had to recognize her essentially Germanic
character. She must contract no agreements with third powers
likely to injure the Germanic conception of Central Europe.
Germany promised not to interfere with Austrian measures against
the domestic National Socialists. The agreement normalizing the
relations between Berlin, Vienna and Rome was concluded on
July 11, 1936. On July 23 a meeting was called of the Locarno
powers to discuss the substitution of a new arrangement for the
abrogated one, but neither Italy nor Germany made their appearance. When the Czechoslovak Premier Hodža and Chancellor
Schuschnigg endeavored to include Austria within a bloc of the
Little Entente and France, they met Mussolini's strong objections.
In March 1936 the Duce called the Vienna and the Budapest governments to Rome to remind them of their obligation to refrain
from negotiating with third powers without his knowledge and
consent. Additional protocols were signed on this occasion to
forestall any separate moves. A permanent council was created
on the lines of the Little Entente and the Balkan Pact, and independent discussion of Danubian problems with third powers was
prohibited. This meant the frustration of the last plan to organize
the Danubian Europe as a system of small nations outside the
control of great powers. The next stage was the compromise about
Austria.

On November 1, 1936, Mussolini delivered a speech at Milan
in which he indicated that another reversal was practically consummated. The speech followed on the return from Berlin of the
Duce's son-in-law, Count Ciano, recently appointed Foreign Minister. The Berlin meeting between Ciano and the German leaders
brought the series of preliminary talks to fruition. The Axis
policies were by now formulated in sufficiently safe terms to be
set in motion. "A clean sweep was to be made of all the com-
monplaces, of all the conventional lies which still constituted the

relics of the great shipwreck of Wilsonian ideology," said the Duce. He denounced the League of Nations, disarmament, collective security, and struck with a new vigor upon his favorite theme of Hungarian revisionism. "Justice must be done to Hungary for otherwise there can be no final order on the Danube."

At the October meeting Italo-German policy toward Eastern Europe was formulated in concrete terms. The Hitler-Mussolini arrangement provided for the disruption of the Little Entente. Italy was to take care of handling the Yugoslav flank, while Germany would work on Rumania. Czechoslovakia was to be isolated from outside, and undermined from inside. This last objective was to be reached through the nazification of her German minority. The German-Polish Declaration of 1934 had already served its purpose by demonstrating to France the futility of attempts to secure Polish assistance in the event of German aggression against Czechoslovakia. The Rumanian Foreign Minister Titulesco was one of the first victims of this new Axis pressure. His strenuous exertions toward rapprochement with the Soviet Union and loyalty to the principle of collective security won him displeasure not only at the Axis capitals but also at Warsaw among the sworn enemies of any too close collaboration with the Russians. The detachment of Yugoslavia from France and the Little Entente took a more spectacular form. Very suddenly Italy offered Premier Stoyadinovich a new treaty of friendship which, when signed in March 1937, had far-reaching significance for all Eastern Europe. Yugoslavia, most severely hit by her cooperation in the sanctions, recognized the conquest of Ethiopia and the Italian protectorate over Albania. She promised to be neutral in case Italy became involved in a European war. Italy undertook to increase Yugoslav trade, and to withdraw support from Croatian Oustachis, the same terrorist organization which was responsible for the murder of King Alexander. Harassed by the Croatian demands for more rights and federalization of the country, Stoyadinovich welcomed the understanding with the Axis. An admirer of strong methods, he deliberately chose the Berlin-Rome orientation in preference to the traditional friendship of the Yugoslav people for the Czechs and the western democracies. His treaty with Italy weakened French influence in Eastern Europe just as the German-Polish agreement had done in 1934. The Axis also induced Hungary to concentrate her revisionism against Czechoslovakia rather than against Yugoslavia and Rumania. The Paris-Geneva-Prague-Moscow system was to be attacked at its most sensitive and strategically most desirable point.

On the whole, March 7, 1936, the day of the remilitarization of the Rhineland, was the turning point in the relations between the western powers, particularly France, and Eastern Europe. All small nations east of the Rhine expected action but all that France and England managed to produce were platonic protests. When in the autumn of 1937 French Foreign Minister Delbos returned from his visits to the Eastern European capitals he had to tell the French Foreign Relations Committee that France had still friends in Eastern Europe but except in Czechoslovakia her credit had sunk so low and her strategic position was regarded so weakened that the statesmen wondered whether any effective help could be expected from her. Colonel Beck would not listen to Delbos' urgent advice to improve his relations with Czechoslovakia. Beneš offered Poland a pact of eternal friendship as early as 1933, and repeated it in 1934, but the offer remained unheeded. When Prague proposed to lay the question of the Polish minority of Teschen before an international tribunal, Beck refused to be bothered by "artificial procedures and useless diplomatic bargaining." He made the improvement of Polish-Czechoslovak relations dependent upon "a spontaneous gesture from Prague," failing to disclose, however, what kind of gesture would satisfy him. In the middle of 1936 preliminary exchanges of views took place between Paris, Belgrade and Bucharest as to the possibility of a mutual assistance pact between France and these two Little Entente states, a pact which would complement the Franco-Czechoslovak relations. The inability of France to make a better show in the west, the new German trade offensive in Southeastern Europe, and the coolness of the Yugoslav and Rumanian ruling classes toward the French leftist government of Leon Blum worked as a combined deterrent against the efforts to revitalize the loosening bonds. The subservience of the Quai d'Orsay to the unproductive diplomacy of the British government was taken as an additional proof of France's weakening position. Moreover, the Franco-Czechoslovak-Soviet treaty system frightened the timid Balkan rulers by its red hue and the umbrage it gave to Germany. Like Beck they cherished no illusion as to the efficacy of Anglo-French help to Austria and Czechoslovakia, and having been taken into confidence by the Reich leaders they had little desire to tie their fate to countries which they regarded as too great a risk.

Blind as they were in their parochial realism they hoped that somehow the crisis would leave them intact and that the expansionist lust of Italy, Germany and their satellites would satiate itself elsewhere. On these false hopes they founded their policy of retreat.

Relying too much on the false security behind the Maginot line France indulged in the luxury of more than twenty serious cabinet crises within less than two decades. She permitted economic maladjustments and social strife to undermine the productivity of her defense industries at a time when the productive energies of Germany and to a lesser degree of Italy were immensely heightened under the direction of determined and ruthless leaders commanding absolute obedience. The Italian-Yugoslav treaty of 1937 showed that the actual state of French affairs did not fail to affect the less farsighted leaders among the small states. The treaty ignored the League and the Little Entente, and when asked what action Yugoslavia would take in case of an attack on Czechoslovakia, Stoyadinovich gave the typical reply that he was for peace.

German Aims in Eastern Europe

Economic interests of France and Great Britain in Eastern Europe have not been important enough to influence the general policies of the two democratic powers. Their inability and unwillingness to make substantial purchases from debtor countries was one of the weaknesses of the Eastern European postwar economy. In the 1929 year of prosperity the United Kingdom bought from Czecho-slovakia, Austria, Hungary, Yugoslavia, Rumania, Greece, Bul-garia and Turkey only 1.46 per cent of its total imports, and sold them 2.13 per cent of its exports. The German share amounted to 7.97 and 9.78 per cent respectively. In 1938 the German trade rose to 14.35 per cent on the import side and 15.75 per cent on the export side. England's position did not materially improve, and the trade between the eastern regions and France was as small as that of the United Kingdom. The importance of German trade becomes even more apparent if measured in terms of the economic structure of the Balkan countries. In 1933 Yugoslavia, Bulgaria, Greece and Turkey exported 25.4 per cent of their products to Germany. In 1938 this trade rose to 40 per cent. Germany also supplied 40 per cent of the aggregate imports to these states.

At the same time per capita trade of the Balkan peoples was low. In 1937 it reached only 21.4 marks on the import and 24.4 marks on the export side. German economists liked to speculate on the rise of the purchasing power of their smaller clients. If their capacity to buy could be raised to the 1927 figures of Austria, for instance, the aggregate Balkan exports would increase three-fold, and imports four times. If southeastern European trade could be developed as rapidly as that of Japan since the turn of the century, it would reach in forty years ten times its present volume. German experts believed that in 25 years the yield per hectare of land could be increased by 50 per cent. The 26 million hectares at present under cultivation should thus through better exploitation produce the equivalent of 39 million hectares. Germany's demand for agrarian products has been calculated as requiring the output of about 10 million hectares of intensely cultivated land outside the Reich in addition to the 23 million hectares of arable land which Germany had at home. A fifty per cent increase in the agricultural yield in the Balkans would therefore give Germany more than she actually needed, with the exception of tropical products.

This objective could be reached according to the German point of view only if the smaller states were not permitted to develop as independent units, and if Germany established her economic hegemony in the sector. The problem transcends the domain of mere adjustments of commercial policies. It asks for complete regulation of the conditions of production, distribution and consumption. The smaller economic units must be made subordinate to the needs of the German economy. They must be merged into one regulated system, of which the Reich would be the center. As the largest and industrially strongest country Germany would be the principal supplier of manufactured goods for the whole area. The smaller countries must concentrate on intensifying agricultural production of foodstuffs and industrial plants. The industries built in prewar and postwar years must be scrapped with the exception of those which are complementary to the industries of Germany. The mark would thus become the international unit of payment throughout Eastern Europe. Mark balances in any one country would be used for the settlement of claims in all other countries by means of clearing arrangements. Currency would not depend on gold but on the value given to it by the state. Throughout this German living space stable rates of currencies would be maintained together with rigid price control. Farmers and workers would not be free, but organized under government supervision and assured of stable prices for their products and wages. The liberal conception of exchange would have no place in the living space. It would be replaced by the system of organized economy maintained by force. All economy would serve the policy of military defense of the space. Willingly or by coercion the individual peoples would have to limit their freedom, not only in the field of economic initiative, but also in political questions. The whole internal political life would be so organized as to guarantee the smooth operation of the plan. A life like this, of course, could not exist in a democracy with its principle of opposition. It could only be maintained under totalitarian conditions of unquestioned authority, blind obedience, and the surrender of the democratic moral code which accepts as its basis the recognition of the principle of human dignity, equal opportunities and the four freedoms.

To a degree Southeastern Europe represented a suitable area in which these practices could be gradually imposed. Because of the heavy indebtedness, high taxation, low productivity of labor and the high cost of transportation the prices of Eastern European agrarian products were often much higher than those existing in the mass-producing nations overseas. The economic sanctions which followed soon after the world depression had also a share in increasing trade difficulties in the Balkan countries. The only way in which the western democratic nations could have prevented Germany from extending her grip over this area would have been the extension to them of sufficient commercial and financial credits, which would have strengthened their resistance. The credits would have probably never been fully repaid, and it may be questioned whether their political effect would have met the expectations. Yet in the absence of any such assistance Germany had entire freedom and could easily offer terms that looked attractive. She bought agricultural surpluses in large quantities at prices exceeding those in the world markets. Her purchases were made on credit but when the time came to pay she lacked foreign exchange and offered manufactured goods instead. The Balkan governments had to finance the whole transaction through government controlled agencies and convert commercial credits to public loans. In order to obtain payment from Germany and release frozen assets, the purchases from other countries had

to be shifted to Germany, thereby giving her an even stronger
grip on their national economy.

The German economic aims have always been intimately connected with political objectives. The two have become indistin-
guishable. He who had economic power could also exercise political influence. Those acquainted with the development of the
Great Germanic conception entertain no doubt as to the ultimate
goal of German policy in Eastern Europe. Its aims have been
repeatedly referred to by authoritative spokesmen whether they
represented the Reich of the Hohenzollerns, the Weimar Republic, or the National Socialist Greater Germany. The Drang nach
Osten dates back to the middle of the nineteenth century. Lorentz
von Stein wrote then that the Danubian and the Balkan countries, the territories bordering on the Black Sea and Asia Minor,
were the natural fields of expansion for the densely inhabited
Germanic lands. Friedrich List attacked the Continental System
of Napoleon but he himself recommended an Anglo-German
alliance for the domination of Europe to the exclusion of Russia
and France. Germany was to reach the Adriatic, the Euphrates
and the Persian Gulf, while England would take care of the more
distant regions inclusive of the United States. Somewhat later the
Pan-German Association adopted some points of this program,
and gave it an anti-English interpretation. England was asked to
give Germany a free hand in European affairs and let her expand
overland. During the World War the Mittel-Europa of Pastor
Friedrich Naumann was conceived as a closed economic system
of the Habsburg Monarchy and the Balkans together with Holland, Belgium and Switzerland, all under German domination.
In 1918 the Brest-Litovsk peace opened the way to expansion in
the direction of the Ukraine. The defeat of the Central Powers
rendered all these plans impracticable, but they continued to constitute the program of the pangermanic elements throughout the
short lived period of postwar experimentation with democracy.
The National Socialists borrowed from all these various schemes.

After Versailles the expansionists assumed of necessity a position of defense. The Weimar Republic consistently endeavored to prevent the idea of an all-inclusive alliance between the Danubian states and the Balkans from maturing. Each constructive attempt was taken as directed against German vital interests. The Eastern European political settlement of 1919 was the chief object of German criticism. It was attacked on nationalist, historical and economic grounds as "the dismemberment of Europe." The German critics were not entirely intellectually honest and had as little moral right to stand up in defense of European unity as Napoleon had in his later years of the struggle for the domination of the Continent. The way in which the Prussian mind confused unity with uniformity had been the source of endless troubles and one of the chief obstacles of European consolidation. What Germany in reality objected to was not the alleged "dismemberment" of Eastern Europe but the recognition of the basic fact of European diversity. In terms of politics Germany opposed the establishment of free nations within the region which she had grown to regard quite unreasonably as her natural area of expansion.

From the point of view of nationality the German element amounts to only a fraction of the Eastern European population, less than one tenth. The German writers stress the point, however, that no other people has penetrated the whole belt, and that the Germans can therefore rightly claim the title to omnipresence. From this they deduce a historical mission to organize the region to the exclusion of all other nations, whether indigenous or not. It would not be right to deny that through the example of German labor and organization Eastern Europe has benefited in many directions in the past. Through Germanic mediation important elements of western civilization had been communicated to Eastern Europe. Germany's own contribution and the work of numerous pioneers scattered throughout the east inspire equal respect. Yet there is a price which no nation is willing to pay, the price of freedom. The idea of "the organization" of their life lost all its attractiveness once they realized that it involved Prussian uniformity and domination.

The 1919 settlement placed three independent countries in the path of German eastern drive: Austria, Poland and Czechoslovakia. Most of the postwar agitation was therefore concentrated on "the bleeding frontiers" of these three neighbors. It is through the eyes of military strategy that a thorough grasp of the background of this agitation can be obtained. The ethnical map shows that German penetration eastwards proceeded along three main tentacles projecting in the direction of East Prussia, Silesia and Austria, with the Sudeten fringe belonging partly to the Silesian and partly to the Austrian pincer.

According to "Mein Kampf" the sword had to clear the way for the German plough. In 1919 this base of the drive, extending from the Baltic to the Adriatic Sea, was politically broken. Austria was to stay independent and thus be in control of the important railway and waterway system of the Danube. Czechoslovakia with her highly developed industry competed with Germany in Southeastern Europe, and held the strategically important bastion of the Bohemian Mountains, the Moravian Gate and the Carpathians. Poland stood at the Prussian border as a constant reminder of the "dismemberment" of the "German east." The cardinal point in the German program was taken up by the determination to dispose of these three countries in whatever order expediency would warrant it. Throughout the Weimar republic this program was merely in temporary suspense. Officially it was repeatedly announced from Berlin that the limited rectifications of boundaries could be secured by peaceful methods. It was realized, however, that mere rectifications would not satisfy the real ambitions. To destroy three countries of more than fifty million people involved risks which could not be met without the presence, if not the use, of overwhelming force.

The right to rearmament was a precondition toward attaining this goal. The abrogation of the Versailles Treaty was the immediate objective. The reference to the right of self-determination was the most plausible means. The plan it was hoped would be achieved with the help of Italy, the connivance of England, and if necessary with the elimination of France, or rather France's position in the east. In order not to alarm England the colonial issue would be left in abeyance to be settled amicably later, once Germany made herself strong on the continent. If the French were reasonable, a reconciliation with them was not out of practical possibility, provided that they understood that they had nothing to seek in what was Germany's natural sphere of action.

The Roman Lebensraum

Italy looks with pride on the former greatness of the Roman Empire. The historical complex is as strong with Fascism as it is with National Socialism. The cultivation of the sense of the glorious past fills a good part of the educational work of both ideologies. It was therefore comparatively easy for Mussolini and Hitler to find common delight in drawing a new map of Europe which would be reminiscent of the ancient Empires. The origin of the Axis goes back to the moment when the two dictators agreed on the blueprint of expansion. The year 1936 marked an important date in the history of Fascism for it brought the German recognition of its specific Lebensraum.

The notion of living space is comparatively new, although its substance is as old as human nature. As a principle of foreign policy it began to be practiced whenever a powerful nation assumed the right and possessed the coercive means to subject alien peoples to its political, economic and military needs. What is new about the concept is the attractive attire into which it has been dressed in order to be made more palatable to modern taste. Its real aspect is sinister, for it implies a state of affairs in which one nation conceives its own expansion as a legitimate expression of its natural force while the simple manifestation of other peoples' will to live their own national existence is branded as artificial,

impudent and aggressive. A typical product of the geopolitical
thinking, the term living space had not been known to Italian
diplomatic vocabulary. It is only since the birth of the Axis partnership that the term has been adopted to define the political idea
of expansion. Imperium would be a much more suitable term to
be employed by Italians as the self-declared heirs to the Roman
Empire.

Judging by what has been divulged of the Axis arrangements,
the Italian Lebensraum dream includes the whole of the Mediterranean basin adjacent to the peninsula. In Europe it extends to
the Balkans and takes in Yugoslavia, Albania, Greece, and partly
Hungary and Bulgaria. Thus it comprises most of the coastal area
lying between Guarnero in the Adriatic and Istanbul. According
to the Italian point of view it is along this coast and in its hinterland that the Roman political, economic and cultural influence has
been exercised since the Roman days, during the period of the
medieval city states, and in our own time.

The essential element inherent in the concept of this Lebensraum, as described in 1936, is its exclusive character. No other
great power has anything to seek there. Neither England, nor
France, nor the Soviet Union. Germany promised not to interfere
with Italy's freedom of action in the sphere. In exchange Italy
promised not to conspire against the somewhat more extensive
Lebensraum of the Reich, comprising the rest of Eastern Europe
down to the mouth of the Danube. The Soviet Union must at all
events be excluded from the Italian sphere, for Russia does not
respond to the voice of occidental civilization which is essentially
Latin and Mediterranean. According to the fascists, Russian culture is a hybrid of Slav and Byzantine contents with only a
western veneer. Italy will not permit any of the nations lying outside this space to interfere with her liberty of movement. In this
respect she regards herself as the first among equals. Similarly
she can not acquiesce in any agreement which the nations within
her Lebensraum would enter into against her interest or without

her consent. The Yugoslav army or the Greek fleet must not, for instance, be placed at the disposal of any third power. The international policy of the states of the living space is limited, and they must abandon all outside entanglements. Should their policies collide with those of the Fascist Empire, they would expose themselves to the grave risk of having their liberty placed under a much more rigid control. This means that they could also be deprived of freedom of action in internal policies. The states of the living space must not be related in any way to any other outside power. Only then can Italy rest assured that her supremacy is unreservedly recognized as a fact open to no equivocation.

Summary

The economic crisis which at the turn of the first postwar decade aggravated the situation of the Eastern European agricultural countries was overshadowed in political consequences by the ascendency of National Socialism. From 1933 onwards Germany was going to dominate again the diplomatic scene as the one supreme factor. No longer the Weimar Germany, defiant and restless, but militarily weak and amenable to compromise, but the Germany of Hitler, moved by the militant spirit of extremist nationalism of the exclusive brand. She was still defiant and restless, but with the unopposed growth of her military machine she soon demonstrated a hardening attitude of non-cooperation and cooperated only on her own terms. The objectives of her foreign policy remained the same: expansion in and control of Eastern Europe.

At the end of World War I five great nations of Europe, Asia and America were given virtual carte blanche to write a new world order, a world in which a cooperative society of nations would be gradually substituted for the free-for-all policies of the recent past. It took only a short time, however, to realize that practical chances of such a transformation were limited. The failure of the United States to assume the responsibilities for both

the positive achievements and the shortcomings of the Peace Settlement showed that the League of Nations could never become
the universal body which its authors intended to make it. There
still was the possibility for Europe to save a good deal of it by its
own means if it faced the task with courage, determination and
unity of purpose. For instance, it would have made a great difference if Germany had been won, at the very early stage, for the
idea of rebuilding the shaken continent as an equal among equals.
Europe might have been spared the spectacle, fourteen years later,
of another Germany, one permeated with an accumulated feeling
of deep resentment. It could almost be proved statistically how
this resentment went up and down in inverse ratio with the
extent to which the ex-enemies were drawn within the common
orbit.

German ability to cooperate was as much a precondition of the
success of the new world as was the intelligence of her former foes
to create and expand the opportunities for such collaboration.
Equally important was the third precondition, namely, the preservation and strengthening of a united stand of England, France
and Italy, or, alternatively, of England, France and the Soviet
Union. The fact that France was never certain of the extent of
British support would go a long way to explain some of the most
uncommon successes of Berlin diplomacy. British detachment
from continental affairs was not the only cause of France's worry.
Even if she had enjoyed consistently British support she would
still have been handicapped by the lack of broad domestic unity
and endurance of effort. The gravest errors committed by the
western democracies were two: negligence of national defense and
missing the great opportunities inherent in the existence of the
League of Nations. When eventually Italy joined Germany
France's and England's combined debility in the air amounted
to national and European calamity. As early as 1937 Germany
alone outbalanced the Anglo-French air fleet in the proportion
of 3 : 2.5. With Italy the Axis balance rose to 4.2 : 2.5. It was

indeed incredible that the two western powers with such great material and financial resources at their disposal and such distant empires to defend should permit their defenses to lag behind countries with far less resources and infinitely smaller responsibilities. The peaceful intentions of the French and the British peoples explained but did not justify this fateful misjudgment of the realities of European evolution. They had to draw logical conclusions from the fact that internally uniform Germany was rearming at the average rate of fifteen billion marks a year.

The remilitarization of the Rhineland in 1936 to the tune of verbal protests but against no effective counter-move shifted the balance definitely against France. Nowhere was it felt more strongly than in Eastern Europe. The diplomatic disorganization which had begun there in 1934 by Hitler's gesture toward Poland proceeded from now on at accelerated speed.

The opening phase of National Socialist diplomacy moved along the road of selective temporization. While holding fast to their ultimate goal, the German leaders embarked on a precautionary policy of preventing Europe from consolidating itself before they felt sufficiently powerful. Separate non-aggression pacts such as the one concluded with Poland were to serve the purpose of placing each neighbor in an isolated position. The naval treaty with England in 1935 was calculated to drive a wedge between the western powers. The bulk of the German revitalized energy was spent on undermining the cohesion of the Paris-Prague-Moscow alliances. This combination, imperfect as it was, contained in itself the potentiality of giving Europe the proverbial two fronts, in the west and in the east, against which Germany would have hardly risked a fight. For that very reason German political strategy spared no effort to make effective collaboration between these three countries unlikely. In this connection the weapon of National Socialist propaganda was employed to its best advantage. The most violent outbursts were directed against Czechoslovakia, strategically an important and at the same time the most exposed member of the system. The typically middle-class Czechoslovak society was pictured as the salient of Bolshevism and the disturber of general peace. No efforts were spared to estrange from her the sympathies of western public opinion. In Germany, Poland, Italy and Hungary publications were disseminated, alleging that Prague was the bridge which would open the passage for the east to invade the west. Partition of the country was suggested in literature published at the expense of or with tacit agreement of official quarters. In England and France powerful sections of the social élite were skillfully cultivated until the view prevailed among those in power that the issue was between fascism or communism rather than between nazism and democracy. The stage was set for the diplomacy of appeasing the irreconcilables.

Part Four

From Appeasement to War

The Case of Austria

The entry of Hitler's troops in Austria on Saturday, March 12, 1938, marked the first territorial revision of the Versailles Treaty. It had been staged so as to produce the impression of a peaceful change, but it had all the elements of an act of force. This initial move toward the execution of the National Socialist program of the domination of Eastern Europe illustrated also the new German technique of conquest. The preliminaries had for their object the undermining of the victim's morale and internal unity. In order to achieve this end the country to be trespassed upon had been previously isolated internationally and duly impressed by the general hopelessness of its position. The third powers were cajoled into believing that they had no reason for anxiety, for the incident about to happen was only of limited local importance and would be dealt with efficiently by mutual agreement so that international peace be not disturbed. To remove any doubt in the outside world as to the righteousness of German action, a case had been elaborated in advance to give the move an appearance of plausibility and reasonableness. In the Austrian instance the right of the people to dispose of its own destiny had been duly invoked. The Nazi propagandists exploited amply the peaceful nature and

abhorrence of war on the part of the democracies, and assured
them by means of skillful, continuous and aggressive propaganda
of a long period of tranquility to follow once this incident was
settled. In all this the defeatists, sympathizers, gullible pacifists
and paid agents in the victim's own ranks, the "reasonable" elements, performed knowingly or out of naïvetè highly useful
services.

Behind the barrage of minute planning and long scientific
preparation the perfectly co-ordinated military and economic machine was ready to be set in motion as soon as the order should be
given. Owing to the constant readiness of the totalitarian powers
to live and to act dangerously and gloriously, the old-fashioned
and alarm-provoking procedure of mobilization could be conveniently dispensed with. This was a new method of military
diplomacy. Even Mussolini was surprised when with the swiftness of lightning the decision emerged out of the dark and was
thrust upon the numbed world. In addressing a Genoa audi-
ence on March 14, just one day after the Anschluss, and sixteen
months after he had publicly assured the world that the 1936
compromise gave Austria a reënforced guarantee of independence,
the Duce confessed his embarrassment. The peace of Europe depended on the decision of Italy, said he, which once again stood
at the crossroads. And recalling the determined stand taken by
him on behalf of Austria at the time of the 1934 putsch, the Fascist
leader declared that Italy could not afford the luxury of mobiliz-
ing every four years to prevent the inevitable epilogue of the
National Socialist revolution. "Fascist Italy could not permanently
take upon herself the ignominious and futile role of the late Habsburg Monarchy of stifling the movement of nations aiming at
union."

Dissatisfied with the way in which the 1936 compromise
worked, and apprehensive lest a united front of Austrian Social
Democrats and Christian Socialist peasantry indefinitely post-
poned, if not frustrated, National Socialist designs, Hitler decided

to forestall the Schuschnigg plebiscite which would have ascertained the attitude of the Austrian people toward the union. On Friday, March 11, 1938, a German ultimatum was sent to Vienna demanding the cancellation of the plebiscite and implying the threat of enforced entry of German troops into Austria. As the result of the ultimatum Schuschnigg resigned in favor of Seyss-Inquart, the Berlin supported leader of the Austrian National Socialists. Seyss-Inquart appealed to Hitler to send troops to maintain order. Early the following morning the German army crossed the borders, and the same day Hitler appeared at Linz in the Upper Austrian province. Before resigning Schuschnigg stated that he had been authorized by President Miklas to disclose the contents of the ultimatum, and that he was yielding to superior force to avoid shedding German blood. The Austrian soldiers were ordered not to offer resistance. The German government subsequently rigorously denied the charge, insisting that it was not Germany but the Austrian government itself which brought in troops. The facts of the situation were that there was no unity on the issue inside the Austrian government. The earlier inclusion of Seyss-Inquart and of two other National Socialists in the government at the insistence of Hitler served as an insurance that unity could not be reached unless the opponents of the Anschluss left the stage.

How many Austrians would have voted against the union with Germany can not be estimated with accuracy. Chancellor Schuschnigg entertained no doubt, however, that he would have had the backing of a solid majority of the electorate. Only the rightist nationalistic groups had favored the Anschluss all throughout the two decades of Austrian independence. Their numbers dwindled down, however, to about one-tenth of the voting strength. The Social Democrats, who had ruled Austria immediately after the World War, were for the Greater Germany until the rise of National Socialism to power. After 1920 they had no share in the government which was largely in the hands of the Christian

Socialists, representing the peasantry and the middle class. Under the leadership of Seipel, Dollfuss and Schuschnigg, the Christian Socialist party was gaining in numbers, and the Anschluss fever showed a steadily falling off. In spite of this any attempt to evaluate the depth and the durability of separate Austrian nationalism would be a guess. Among the Austrian unionists there were many who were moved by the emotional appeal of the national idea of the unification of the German people. On the other hand, Reich big business viewed the issue from a far less sentimental point of view, their chief interest having been in seeing Austria converted to an annex of their industry as an important jumping off ground for further economic conquest in Eastern Europe. The fear of becoming a colony of Prussia kept alive the desire of an important section of the population to support the conception of a small but independent Austria.

There were two alternatives for Austria to decide upon: either to join Germany or to seek close cooperation with other small Central European states. The indecision of the Austrian people as a whole and the internal feud between the Social Democrats and the Christian Socialists in the teeth of their common foe, must be blamed to a large degree for the existence of the Austrian problem. The rest of the blame fell on the international situation. Austria was bound by international treaties not to alienate her independence, but beyond the general provisions of the League Covenant no really effective international guarantee had been extended to her to enable her to withstand the outside pressure. In February and September of 1934 Italy, France and England issued declarations in support of Austrian independence within the existing international obligations, but they made no promises of active assistance. Austria was told to demonstrate her will to independent life in order to merit international assistance. The problem of her guarantee was actually discussed at length early in 1935 at Stresa in connection with the proposed Danubian security pact.

As the zero hour was approaching the Austrian government did offer evidence of carrying out a policy of independence. Yet under German pressure, and partly because of the surviving loyalty to the pangermanic ideals, Austrian public opinion could not be won in its majority for a Danubian system of small states except, perhaps, on the lines and in the tradition of imperial control from Vienna. The Legitimists aimed at the restoration of the Habsburg dynasty to the throne, but they represented only a small fraction of the population, which on the whole was indifferent to the personal fate of the Habsburg heirs. The monarchical idea was even less popular among the other nationalities formerly subjected to the Habsburg rule. Early in 1938 Austria was indeed the most talked of, but at the same time the most isolated country in Europe.

In 1919 Austria accepted her independence as a punishment. In 1938 she wanted to be free, but those who had given her freedom when she did not desire it, lost their interest when their help was badly needed. Prime Minister Chamberlain publicly discouraged Vienna from being too recalcitrant. In February 1938, less than a month before the Anschluss, he found it expedient to warn the small nations that they must not be deluded into thinking that "they will be protected by the League against aggression when nothing of the kind can be expected."

Whether Mussolini made a virtue of necessity when he definitely abandoned Austria to her own fate, or whether he hoped that the sacrifice was worth while considering the advantages which he would reap from close cooperation with his superior Axis partner, the Anschluss was a great moral and strategic victory for Hitler. The encirclement of Czechoslovakia and her separation from France was completed. Europe began to revolve around the Axis which had cut the continent into two halves. If Austria was a liability in regard to her lack of foodstuffs, her industry, timber and iron ore were an asset. But the strategic element overshadowed all other considerations. Hitler struck at the

Versailles Europe at the point where the attack was the easiest and the least expensive. By encouraging Italy's ambitions in Africa, Germany's diplomacy concentrated her attention on Europe, and made herself the master of Central Europe. By annexing Austria Hitler uncovered the most vulnerable southern border of Czechoslovakia, placing that country between half-open pincers.

In line with the National Socialist technique Goering twice assured the Czechoslovak Minister in Berlin that Czechoslovakia had no reason to feel endangered. This was at the height of the Austrian crisis when the German troops, marching to Vienna, were given the order not to approach the Czech borders within the distance of ten miles. This assurance, offered as propaganda to lull Europe to more inactivity, could not be disassociated, however, from Hitler's remarks made only three weeks earlier. In his speech on February 20 he referred to ten million Germans in Austria and Czechoslovakia as having been denied the right of self-determination, and since "they could not by their own strength secure their human, political and ideological liberty, it was the duty of Germany to protect them." Marshall Goering's Air Force "stood one hundred per cent behind the words of the Führer." If in preceding years the Sudeten question had been regarded at least by official Germany as an internal problem of a neighboring state, the two pronouncements indicated that from now on it was a problem for Germany to settle. Despite the assurances, the Czechoslovaks felt that while Austria was being overrun their own fate was already entering upon the decisive stage.

In commenting on the Austrian coup Hitler stated in the Reichstag on January 1, 1939, that his own mind with regard to the Anschluss had already been made up in January of the preceding year. In January 1938 he resolved to win the right of the Austrian people to self-determination "one way or another." Yet on February 12, 1938, he was still assuring Schuschnigg that he would respect the independence of Austria in the spirit of the agreement reached in July 1936. It may also be useful to recollect Hitler's earlier statement in May 1935, when he told the Reichstag that Germany neither intended nor wished to interfere in the internal affairs of Austria, to annex Austria, or to conclude an Anschluss.

The "Peaceful Change" of Munich

On March 7, 1938, the French and British governments instructed their ministers to Prague to recommend to the Czechoslovak government a solution of the problem of its German minority in a manner "that would be compatible with the integrity of the state." This was the beginning of French and British interference in an internal problem of Czechoslovakia. Simultaneously France hastened to give repeated assurances to her Czechoslovak ally of "immediate, effective and integral aid," even if she had to march without Great Britain. On April 5, of the same year, the French ambassadors and ministers to Poland, the Soviet Union, Rumania and Czechoslovakia were summoned to the Quai d'Orsay. They were told that France stood firmly behind her alliances, and were instructed to find out what help could be relied upon to be given by the governments to which they were accredited. They were also asked to ascertain how these governments would bring into harmony their treaties with France with those they had concluded with the Axis powers. The inquiry applied particularly to two countries: Poland, which since 1934 had played an independent hand and had showed more friendliness to Berlin than to Prague, and Yugoslavia. Since 1937 the Stoyadinovich cabinet had flirted quite openly with the Axis, and it became doubtful that Stoyadinovich would do anything which might provoke displeasure of his friends at Rome and Berlin. The inactivity of western powers in the face of German coups in the past, the strategic separation of France from Eastern Europe, and the growing knowledge that the French armies would hardly do more than stand behind the Maginot Line, combined to make the prospect of an eleventh hour's unity look uninspiring. The installation of George Bonnet in the French Foreign Office made the chances even more remote. True enough, his first act in office was to assure the Czechoslovak Minister of the continuity of France's policy, but there was no secret that his real views were substantially different.

The so-called Czechoslovak crisis turned technically around the problem of the German minority. In reality it was a new challenge to postwar European society, and was destined to mark one more step toward the realization of the idea of pangermanic domination. Sometime later Goebbels confessed that it was just a trick which worked, but at the time of the crisis there were few people in western Europe among the governing classes, who understood the true nature of National Socialism. Only a handful of men in high places grasped the full implications of the Nazi challenge. Such circumstances made it possible for Germany to let England and France do the greatest part of preliminary spade work on her behalf. While keeping officially aloof she let London and Paris work on Czechoslovakia. Most ingeniously Hitler pretended to regard the issue as a domestic affair for the Prague government to settle. Between 1934 and 1937 on three occasions Hitler offered Beneš a bilateral agreement between Germany and Czechoslovakia on somewhat similar lines as that which he actually concluded with Poland in 1934. Representatives of Hitler came to Prague several times to discuss the understanding between the two countries. The German negotiators themselves suggested that the minority issue be excluded from the agenda as purely an internal affair. Incidentally, they also intimated that the French and Soviet alliances, being of defensive character, should not stand in the way of an understanding. According to one version the agreement would adapt the German-Czechoslovak arbitration treaty of Locarno to the newly created circumstances and declare that the two countries desired to live in friendship and cultivate close economic relations. The attitude of Beneš was that without the League of Nations and the allied powers Czechoslovakia could do nothing. Personally he never believed Hitler's word and had no illusions as to the value of his signature. From the very nature of the Nazi régime Beneš deduced that the Hitler régime would inevitably lead to war which alone could preserve it, if victorious, or which would bring it to an end.

Prior to the rise of National Socialism peaceful co-existence of the Czechs and Germans in Czechoslovakia was well on its way. For many years the strongest German parties were represented in the cabinet. In 1937 an agreement was reached between the German activists and the Czechs to settle gradually all the outstanding issues, particularly those created by the economic crisis in the Sudeten industrial districts. In 1933, however, the Sudetendeutsche Heimatfront was founded by Konrad Henlein, with a program which resembled the National Socialism of Germany and Austria. The party was based on the principle of leadership and totality, which contrasted with the democratic party system as it existed in the country. At the start, Henlein, the head of the German gymnastic society Turnverband, accepted the Czechoslovak state as the home of the Germans, approved of democracy, condemned fascism as "unbearable for the highly civilized and individualistic peoples of Central Europe," and stressed the dignity of the individual in relation to society. He accepted National Socialism with reservations. Similarly he dismissed the idea of a revision of the frontiers. He even admitted that in Slovakia the Germans were better off than before World War I when under Hungary. With these ideas he later traveled abroad, particularly in England, where he was well received by people with close connections with the government.

In 1935 the Sudetendeutsche Partei received one and a quarter million votes, i.e., 44 seats in the Prague parliament. It thus embraced two-thirds of the German electorate, the remaining third belonging to the activists, recruited from farmers, workers and Christian Socialists. The activists favored democracy, and a feud

soon developed between them and the Henleinists, since these
were becoming more and more totalitarian. National Socialist
domestic and foreign successes turned the Henleinists to ever
growing radicalism. The Anschluss was accepted by them as the
signal for an intransigent attitude of open negation of the state.
The Anschluss caused also many activists to switch to the nega-
tivist group, which at the municipal elections on May 21, 1938,
obtained 85 per cent of all German votes.

Immediately after the elections the Government began to negotiate with the Henleinists. The discussions were carried on
upon the basis of the so-called Carlsbad demands, formulated in
April at a meeting of the Sudetendeutsche Partei. The government at first refused to consider territorial autonomy as impractical and tending to weaken the unity of the state, for it would
lead to the division of the country into a Czech part governed by
a democratic constitution and a German part ruled by totalitarian principle. The other significant demand concerned the acquiescence in National Socialist doctrine and practice in the
Sudeten area. Yielding to the increasing pressure by England
and France Czechoslovakia eventually accepted all the demands
in the hope that she would thus placate the Henleinists and Germany, which stood behind them. There was no direct reference
in the Carlsbad program to foreign policy, but this issue loomed
constantly in the background of the negotiations. Henlein asked
the Czechs to revise the conception of constituting a Slav barrier
against Drang nach Osten, to relinquish the alliances which allegedly placed them on the side of Reich's enemies, and to form
a close union with Germany.

The Czechs were eager to solve this crisis by making concessions to the utmost. They realized that the idyll of the fifteen
postwar years was ended, that Europe was entering a period of
grave decisions, and that they must make their own contribution.
At the same time they were equally determined to fight for the
country if need be. Prime Minister Milan Hodža announced the

negotiations in a speech which could leave no doubts as to the seriousness of the situation and the will of the Czechs to solve it. "We envisage an integral solution that will cut deep into the whole structure of the state. The principles on which our policy stands are autonomy and proportionality. We cannot rely solely on our allies as a sufficient guarantee. No country has yet been placed in a situation like ours. We find ourselves in the immediate propinquity of a unique and elementary process in history. It is the culmination of the nationalism of a nation of seventy-five million, which embarked on a period of evolution which transcends the roots of rationalism and passes to the domain of revolutionary emotionalism. A tremendous process like this cannot be disposed of by mere administrative measures."

The true nature of the conflict was in a way unique. Technically it concerned a domestic Czechoslovak problem. In reality it represented a phase of the clash between the Europe of Versailles and a Reich dominated Europe in the making. England believed that the occasion offered her one more opportunity to act as arbiter between two continental factions. She hoped that by exercising pressure on both Berlin and Prague she would exact reciprocal concessions and bring about a peaceful solution. Soon she had to realize, however, that the days of her influences as continental arbiter had gone. Czechoslovakia was gradually giving in, because she was small and had no other choice. But Germany was strong and did not allow herself to be a party to bargaining. Poorly led Great Britain eventually sank to the role of waiting upon her potential enemy against her friend. For some time the tug of power-political rivalry between London-Paris and Berlin-Rome took the indirect form of anemic negotiations between Henlein, speaking for National Socialism, and the Prague government, ostensibly representing Czechoslovakia, but in fact bending to the will of its allies. In August Chamberlain sent his personal representative Lord Runciman to Prague, and in September he took direct charge of the negotiations, assuming thus the grave responsibility for interfering with the freedom of a country which his government was in honor bound to respect, and for bargaining away the territory which France was under treaty obligation to defend. Rarely had a people been squeezed in a cornered position by the combined pressure of its foes and allies. The more concessions Prague was induced to make by the western powers, the higher was the price Germany set for settlement. The more Germany claimed, the more France and England were willing to give, at Czechoslovakia's expense. In desperation the Czechs appealed to the true democrats in the west. However, democracy, so it must have seemed, was not a principle of international politics.

From ambassador Sir Neville Henderson we have learnt that his principal task in Berlin was to prepare Anglo-German friendship, and that the solution of the Austrian and Czechoslovak problems was regarded in London as the most urgent prerequisite of the success of his mission. Consequently, after January 1938 he applied himself to removing these two obstacles. He had simplified his work considerably by identifying himself largely a priori with the National Socialist point of view. Czechoslovakia was to him an artificial creation of Versailles, and should not stand in the way of Anglo-German friendship. Accordingly, he and the circles which he represented favored one after another all the variously formulated methods of a Germanic solution. At first it was genuine autonomy, then a Swiss cantonal system, self-determination, Germany's natural aspiration for unity and expansion, and finally the amputation of the Sudetenland. The only condition the British set was that everything should be accomplished peacefully. Should Czechoslovakia be obstinate, Germany might attack. France might come to the rescue, and involve England on her side. It was therefore of utmost importance that Czechoslovakia be not permitted to fight for her life, and that things be arranged in a way which would in advance release France from her treaty obligations. Hence, the French and British pressure and threats to Prague to yield to the German demands, hence Chamberlain's three visits to Hitler, and hence his message of September 28, in which he assured the Chancellor that he would get "all essentials without war and without delay."

Down to the middle of May 1938 the real British attitude was kept secret within the inner cabinet. It was first communicated to the British and Czechoslovak public by a roundabout way through the American Press. On May 18 a group of American newspapermen were invited to lunch with Lady Astor, the occasion on which Chamberlain confided that his government favored a drastic solution by annexing the Sudetenland to Germany. On September 7 the London Times mooted the same scheme. The Foreign Office disclaimed the responsibility, but two weeks afterwards Chamberlain recommended it as his and France's plan. The Runciman report to Chamberlain recommended both the separation of the Sudetenland and the alignment of the rest of Czechoslovakia with Germany, which in practice would be virtual vassalage. The report was delivered on September 21, i.e., eight months after ambassador Henderson had received the instruction to work in Berlin for "a peaceful solution," more than four months after the American newspapers printed semi-official information from the Astor meeting, six days after Chamberlain had seen Hitler at Berchtesgaden, and three days after the French and British governments committed themselves to the policy of partition. The report could not but produce the impression of a solicited after-the-event document to justify before public opinion a course of policy which had already been decided upon.

As to the real position of Germany, light was thrown on it by Chancellor Hitler himself in his speech on January 30, 1939, i.e., four months after Munich. Hitler stated that he had made up his mind as early as May 28 of the previous year, when he decided "to solve the problem radically and once for all," and had given orders that military action against Czechoslovakia be prepared for October 2. He arrived at this decision after the "unbearable

provocation" committed by Czechoslovakia on May 21 in mobiliz-
ing one year of reservists. In view of this decision the fifteen
month negotiations with Henlein must have indeed been doomed
to failure. Between May and September 1938 the Prague government produced four successive plans for the solution of the crisis.
Each of them had been refused on the flimsiest of pretexts as soon
as it had been made. The last one was characterized as generous
and acceptable even by Runciman, who believed that "non-
acceptance of the plan would certainly stir the British government to stand with all its might behind Czechoslovakia." The
Foreign Office in London informed foreign newspapermen on
September 11 that the concessions made by Prague went even
too far. The most radical Germans themselves referred to it as
satisfying seventy per cent of their demands. According to Runciman, "nobody in the world could have asked that Czechoslovakia had done more for peace."

On September 12 Hitler made a speech which had most far-
reaching repercussions throughout Europe. It was up to Czechoslovakia, said he, to come to one or another agreement with the
Sudeten Germans, but it was Hitler's job to see that right would
not turn to be wrong. The immediate consequences of the speech
were local riots of the Henlein party, seizure of public buildings,
and fatal shooting of Czech policemen. The Sudeten Partei which
four days earlier accepted the fourth plan as the basis for final
settlement, on September 14 withdrew its delegates and broke off
the negotiations for good. France, which since February 1938 had
given Czechoslovakia ten official assurances of assistance through
her three successive governments, became suddenly weak and
panicky. Daladier turned to London for either an unconditional
pledge of military aid or for direct negotiations with Hitler. The
fact that on September 13 France decided against mobilization
indicated that she was climbing down from her previous position
and throwing herself into the arms of the British inner cabinet.
This amounted to acceptance by her of the Chamberlain concep-

tion of Germanic Mitteleuropa, and incidentally the open surrender of her twenty years' postwar policy. Instead of coming out with a calm restatement of her traditional policy, of her loyalty to the given pledges, of the re-affirmation of her view that the independence of Czechoslovakia was essential to her own security, France offered the humiliating spectacle of a disunited, defeatist and demoralized people, whose bourgeoisie and intelligentsia, with notable exceptions, were subservient to the German propaganda, haunted by the ghost of communism, and permeated with the feeling of instability that had persisted since the devaluation of the franc in 1936. Only recently the most powerful military nation, she now found herself overbalanced by the rapidly built German machine, while her aircraft industry had been permitted to sink into a state of deplorable deterioration.

To London fell the task of extricating France from her treaty obligations, and thus of relieving her of the consequences of the policy which she had been promoting with such zeal ever since the end of the Peace Conference. A remarkable coincidence of events followed upon Chamberlain's sudden decision to fly to Berchtesgaden. On September 14, the day when the decision was made, Henlein told Runciman that no further negotiations would be carried on with Prague. On the following day, when the meeting took place between Chamberlain and Hitler, Konrad Henlein declared in a manifesto that further co-existence of Germans and Czechs in one state had become "definitely impossible." Hitler told Chamberlain that nothing but an outright cession of Czechoslovak territory would satisfy him. Hence "the Anglo-French plan" of partition of the country, offered with a sugar coating of an Anglo-French guarantee of the reduced borders of what would remain. Czechoslovakia protested and refused the plan, saying that it would cripple her and subject her to complete German domination. Only parliament could decide on the cession of territory.

She suggested that the conflict be submitted to arbitration provided for in her treaty with Germany signed in 1925. However, neither parliaments nor international arbitration machinery were allowed to interfere with a cold diplomatic bargain. At 2 A.M. on September 21 the British and French Ministers woke up President Beneš and declared that their governments insisted on unconditional acceptance. The French Minister Lacroix stated verbally that should hostilities break out, France would not take action and Czechoslovakia would be held responsible for having provoked war. Newton made a written statement. After having consulted the cabinet and the army Beneš accepted under irresistible pressure and with a protest, on condition that the proposed guarantee would form an inseparable part of the settlement, that the territory to be ceded would remain Czechoslovak until after the new frontiers were definitely drawn, and that she would be a party to the commission charged with the delimitation of the boundary.

With this answer Chamberlain flew on September 22 to Godesberg. There to his surprise he was told by Hitler that the acceptance was no longer of much use, for Germany's price for peace had in the meantime risen. It now included some purely Czech districts, and went far beyond the original demand of areas inhabited by a simple German majority. Prague refused this second plan which she officially described as an ultimatum to a defeated nation rather than a proposal addressed to a country which had proved in the greatest possible measure its willingness to submit to sacrifices in order to preserve peace. In response to Chamberlain's inquiry Czechoslovakia expressed willingness, through her London Minister Jan Masaryk, to settle the dispute at an international conference in which she would participate. Since September 23 her army had been fully mobilized, and even the French and English made some preparations. On September 27 Sir Horace Wilson brought this new proposal to Hitler. He informed him that should France, in pursuing her treaty obligation, become engaged in hostilities, the United Kingdom would feel obliged to support her. Hitler was not fully convinced, but probably not absolutely certain. For in a personal letter he urged Chamberlain to continue his good offices with a view of inducing the Czechoslovak government to make further concessions. It was in this letter that the Chancellor offered to give formal guarantees to the remainder of the country. He wrote that he had not the slightest intention of interfering with the life of the Czechs, and that after the loss of the Sudetenland their country would constitute a healthier and more unified economic organism than before.

In his Sportpalast speech of September 26, the most violent of the series, Hitler repeated that "after this last territorial demand in Europe" he would "no longer be interested in the Czechs." But he reminded the world that if Prague "had not ceded all the Sudetenland by October 1, Germany would occupy it that day with himself as the first soldier of the Reich." In the morning of September 28 Chamberlain hastily assured Hitler that however much he, the Chancellor, might have distrusted the Prague intentions, he, the British Prime Minister and the French government would see to it that the promises were carried out "fairly and fully and forthwith." At the same time at the request of Paris Chamberlain asked Mussolini to urge upon Hitler the postponement of mobilization for twenty-four hours. Then, in the afternoon of September 28, "light came after darkness," when Chamberlain received from Hitler the invitation to meet the two heads of the Axis at Munich. The British appeasers had been for a long time in favor of some such conference. Sir Neville Henderson had suggested this course early in the year, and Chamberlain was of the opinion that the peace of Europe must depend upon the collaboration of the four major powers, Great Britain, France, Germany and Italy, with the exclusion of the Soviet Union.

Thus came the celebrated meeting at the Brown House at Munich. It lasted from 1:30 P.M. of September 29 to 2 A.M. of the following day. In less than twelve hours, including the intervals for translation, the oldest geographic, economic and historical boundary in Europe was destroyed by a diplomatic act which has already gone down in history as one of the most ignominious and fateful documents of our time. Czechoslovakia, whose territory and most vital interest were traded by her French ally and British friend for doubtful peace, was refused admittance. Also excluded was the Soviet Union, France's and Czechoslovakia's ally. Hitler and Mussolini could hardly conceal their delight while watching Chamberlain and Daladier selling their little democratic protégé down the river. Rarely indeed had democracy staged a spectacle of so much self-deception, disability and ignorance. The result was the amputation from Czechoslovakia of a third of her territory, a promise of a four power guarantee of the rump state after it had given satisfaction to the Polish and Hungarian territorial demands, and the institution of an international boundary commission under German chairmanship to give effect to the agreement. The deliberations of the commission showed that it was in fact a yes-vote machine. The British and French ambassadors sanctioned all the additional demands raised by the Reich Secretary of State, Baron von Weizsacker, and passed them on to the Czechoslovak Minister to be transmitted to his government for unconditional fulfilment. The Czechoslovak newspapers commented on Munich diplomacy in the following terms: "What might have been achieved in pre-Munich days by enlightened and vigorous diplomacy was now impossible to regain. As in 1914 in the case of Serbia the question at issue was not so much the independence of a little country but who was going to dominate Europe. The crippling of Czechoslovakia could not avert the clash between the Reich and the western powers, but brought it nearer." The most immediate loss was that of forty well trained and well mechanized divisions of the Czechoslovak army, equalling in numbers the troops which Russia, France's pre-War ally, was in 1914 able to place on the eastern borders of the Central Powers. The long term result was the elimination of

western influence from the European continent. By diplomacy
of threats, intimidation and blackmail Germany thus was brought
nearer to the realization of the plan which the world had tried
to prevent her from achieving at the cost of World War I. Opin-
ions have since been expressed by various foreign writers that it
would have been wiser for Czechoslovakia to have refused the
Munich dictate and have waited for actual German attack, the
implication being that a heroic, even if futile, stand of a betrayed
and wronged little nation would have made French, English and
other democratic people rise and demand that their governments
intercede. In view of the political, moral, psychological, and military conditions of Europe in the autumn of 1938 it is very doubtful
whether such a reaction would have taken place. For Czechoslovakia to proceed alone would have been an act of desperation or
a vain gesture. This was the view of Beneš and the majority of the
Czechs understood it. The capitulation to England and France,
coupled with the invasion of Prague in 1939, revealed the true
character of Nazi Germany and enabled public opinion in the
democracies to mature morally and to prepare seriously for
defense.

The Last Mile of Appeasement

The "solution" of the Austrian and Sudeten issues was to pave
the way toward the major objective of the Chamberlain diplomacy: enduring rapprochement with Germany. Having helped
Hitler to his greatest diplomatic victory, the appeasers hoped to
reap the benefit of their labors. Consequently, discussions took place
between Hitler and Chamberlain at Munich with a view to capi-
talize on what was erroneously believed to be everybody's victory. These discussions led to the signature of the Anglo-German
declaration of September 30, 1938, "never to go to war with one
another again." In government circles in London and Paris it was
assumed indeed that from this moment on the outstanding issues would be settled à la Munich. It was the kind of diplomacy

which Mussolini had in mind in 1933 when he proposed the Four
Power Pact. However, conditions in Europe had changed materially between 1933 and 1938. In 1933 England and France were
stronger than Germany and Italy. In 1933 Mussolini was amenable to a more genuine compromise with the democracies than in
1938, when the totalitarian powers had gained material superiority. They also had superiority in morale, for throughout the
Czechoslovak crisis London and Paris behaved as if they had
already been beaten. Their constant pleas on behalf of peace could
not fail to be interpreted by the dictators as a symptom of weakness. Hitler and Mussolini found it to their advantage to accommodate the democracies without going to war, provided they
could get what they wanted.

Chamberlain was at the time profoundly convinced that world
peace had once again been saved by ingenious and honorable
diplomacy. The German leaders saw the situation in a different
light; as far as they were concerned it was the superiority of
totalitarian military diplomacy that saved the peace of Europe.
France and England could but submit to superior force, particularly to the Luftwaffe. According to the interpretation given
to Munich by the "Frankfurter Zeitung" in November 1938, Germany became aware of the force which resided in a united
German people. The solution of the Czechoslovak crisis reinforced
the German position to an extraordinary degree from the political,
economic and strategic points of view. The dangerous Czechoslovak wedge thrust into the southeastern flank of the Reich
had been eliminated. On the Rhine an insurmountable wall of
fortifications had been erected. Even the experts saw that the
strategic situation in Europe had been fundamentally reversed.
No increase in armament in England, France, and less so in the
United States would be able to overthrow the new situation.
By seizing the Bohemian bastion and thus crippling economically
her principal competitor in Eastern Europe, Germany had
widened the base of supply of food and raw materials in

Southeastern Europe. Germany looked towards the east. Her position might in time become indeed enviable. "It was not sentiment, emotion or conciliation that set the pace of Europe. All these things failed shockingly. It was the brutal reality, the weight of crashing facts, which set the pace. Nothing could stop Germany in her march. At Munich it was admitted by implication that Germany, acting in full agreement with Italy, had a definite hegemony in Eastern Europe. France had to realize that the new power factors could not be reversed by alliances. The previous status quo made room for an entirely different state of affairs. Interior conditions and psychological obstacles that prevailed elsewhere prevented other countries from asserting authority and making clear-cut decisions. It devolved therefore upon the courageous and upon those who see their goal clearly to push forward the evolution of Europe by their own might."

It had become a longtime habit in democratic countries to attach less significance to German propaganda than it deserved. Even the reading of "Mein Kampf" had been regarded as the somewhat luxurious diversion of the over-curious. It was not surprising, therefore, that the real meaning of Munich escaped the notice of the democracies, and that several post-Munich months passed amidst diplomatic squabbles between Paris and Berlin as to exactly what France meant to concede, and what Germany actually conceded to herself.

One of the Munich provisions concerned the Polish and Hungarian borders with Czechoslovakia. It was provided that should the revision of these borders not be agreed upon by direct negotiations between the interested governments within three months, the problem should form the subject of another meeting of the heads of the four great powers. The Poles settled their part of the problem by their own means. When the distress of Czechoslovakia was at its height, they sent an ultimatum to Prague and marched their troops into the Teschen district. In the case of Hungary no compromise could be reached as to the extent of the territory to be sliced off from the Slovak and Ruthenian provinces. There was an opportunity for the Munich diplomats to meet again and repeat the experience. Hitler, however, brought pressure on Prague and Budapest to avoid a four-power settlement, and instead to submit to arbitration to the two Axis powers.

The procedure took place in Vienna on November 2, 1938, without consultation of England and France. The omnipresence of France in Europe, insisted upon by M. Coulondre at the Wilhelmstrasse, received thus another serious blow. In consoling the French Ambassador, as he mildly protested against this oversight, Hitler told him that all he wanted to do was to avert the peril of a conference which would have placed the four powers in front of two opposing theses. "Whatever was my personal opinion," said Hitler, "I would have to favor the Hungarians and the Poles because of the political ties which united us. Mussolini would have acted similarly. The French and the English would have supported the Czechoslovaks for analogous reasons. Thus in three weeks after Munich we would be confronted with a conflict which could not be adjusted." In fact, Hitler was telling the French that he would have none of the limited expansion in Eastern Europe, for Munich had placed him in a position to exercise full freedom of independent action.

On December 6, 1938, Joachim von Ribbentrop went to Paris to sign a Franco-German Declaration similar to that which Chamberlain brought home from Munich. The conversations with French Foreign Minister Bonnet disclosed, however, that behind the commonplace assurance of mutual good will, the same fundamental differences stood between the two countries which had divided them ever since 1919. According to the German interpretation the Declaration was strictly bilateral, having nothing to do with Germany's or France's relations with a third country. The French argued that the new document had value only in conjunction with other contracts France still had with Eastern European states. The Munich guarantee to Czechoslovakia was one of them, and the treaties with Poland, the Soviets, Rumania and Yugoslavia were the others. Ribbentrop answered that had he known that this was the French conception he would have never signed the Declaration. The French policy of checking the omnipotence of a single European power by the association of all the powers, in so far as they faced common danger, was once again confronting the German diplomatic precept of reserving full freedom of action in all problems of Eastern Europe as the exclusive sphere of its interests. Prior to Munich the French point of view was cautiously scrutinized in Berlin. After Munich the Berlin diplomacy began to draw a distinction between French words and French capacity to perform.

The French ambassador was told at the German Foreign Office that, given the Reich's material predominance in Eastern Europe, its guarantee to Czechoslovakia should be sufficient. The inspired Press echoed the view and pointed out that the Franco-German Declaration had value only if France recognized that Germany's natural position gave her the right and the duty to carry out a constructive policy east of the Rhine. On January 30, 1939, Hitler told the western powers in a public speech that they had nothing to look for in Eastern Europe. And, finally, in replying on March 2, 1939, to identical notes presented on February 8 by Sir Neville Henderson and M. Coulondre, the German Foreign Office informed the western powers that their guarantee to Czechoslovakia was in fact an attempt at intervention in Eastern Europe, and that it would do more harm than good. "The extension of the guarantee would not contribute to the appeasement of the region, but it would strengthen only the unreasonable tendencies as had been done in the past. In the last analysis the general evolution of Eastern Europe belonged in the first place to the sphere of the Reich's essential interests." The diplomatic struggle of the western powers for influence in Eastern Europe was virtually lost. The way in which the promise of international guarantee to post-Munich Czechoslovakia had been disposed of indicated how far the Munich scale moved against the French and the British.

In the meantime the Czechoslovak Foreign Minister Chval-kovsky was summoned to Berlin to be acquainted with the con-ditions after the effective fulfilment of which Germany might eventually consider extending the guarantee. Hitler and Ribben-trop explained to Chvalkovsky that they were seeking to establish a bloc of anti-Semitic states, and that they could not treat as friends any states in which Jews would retain any influence what-ever in economy or public life. The conditions included full neu-trality of Czechoslovakia, conformity of her foreign policy with that of the Reich, eventual adhesion to the Anti-Komintern pact, abandonment of the League of Nations, transfer to Germany of a part of the gold reserve and of foreign exchange, suppression of new industries competing with the industries in the Sudetenland, introduction of the Nürnberg anti-Semitic laws, dismissal of all civil servants against whom Germany might raise objections, granting to the remaining German minority the right of wearing National Socialist insignia and standards, and reduction of the Czechoslovakia army below the ratio of the ceded territories.

Among the pretexts on which the German government refused to join the international guarantees were the alleged difficulties between Poland and Hungary on one side, and Czechoslovakia on the other side. This was a tacit confession that the much praised Vienna arbitration award was not, after all, such a master stroke of the Axis diplomacy. The difficulty arose in connection with the status of Carpathian Ukraine (Ruthenia), a mountain-ous little province of three-quarters of a million inhabitants, of which more than half were of Ukrainian nationality and belonged to the Greek Catholic Church. The Vienna arbitration award gave the capital Užhorod and the town Mukačevo to Hungary cutting off the rump province from the rest of the country. Hun-gary claimed the whole province and was supported by Italy, which desired to compensate her for her alliance and non-partici-pation in sanctions. Germany favored the ethnographical division, for such a settlement fitted in her scheme of using the province as a corridor to Rumania and the Soviet Union. Poland claimed the territory for Hungary in order to wipe out the little autonomous Ukrainian state, the autonomous status of which she disliked, as it might serve as an example and inspiration to her own dissatisfied Ukrainians. For a time the new village capital Hust became the center of National Socialist and Ukrainian Nationalistic propaganda which planned, rather naïvely, to use the province as a sort of Piedmont, around which the forty million Ukrainians of the Soviet Union and of Poland might rally under German protection.

In Moscow the German scheme of separating 35 million Soviet Ukrainians was ridiculed. Joseph Stalin referred to it as a dream of madmen wanting to annex the elephant to the gnat. "If there really are such lunatics in Germany, rest assured that we shall find enough straitjackets for them in our country," said he to the eighteenth congress of the Communist Party. "Imagine: the gnat comes to the elephant and says perkily: 'Ah, brother, how sorry I am for you. Here you are without any landlord, without any capitalists, with no national oppression, without any fascist bosses. Is that a way to live?' "

In January 1939 Hitler decided to abandon for the time being the Ukrainain project. He told Beck and Hungarian Foreign Minister Czaky that Hungary could seize the whole of the Ukrainian province at a propitious moment. Officially nothing had been said of the reasons for this change, but there were indications that a total reversal of German policy toward Russia was well under way. It was also explained that the incommunicable Carpathian region offered no easy route eastwards. The growing anti-appeasement feeling in western Europe and England's rearmament prompted the mobile National Socialist strategy to leave the project in abeyance and to attend to the Danzig and Corridor issues.

The winter of 1938-1939 demonstrated clearly the porous fabric into which the appeasement policy resolved itself. It revealed the house-of-cards nature of both the Munich deal and the Anglo-German and Franco-German Declarations. The wishful thinkers of appeasement believed naïvely enough that the National Socialist revolution could be stopped where it would suit them. The basic, dynamic, driving nature of National Socialism escaped them completely. Having unified the Germanic people within one Reich and under one leadership the new Napoleon dropped the doctrine of limited expansion within ethnic bounds and substituted for it the more extensive policy of expansion within the unlimited sphere of living space.

The first non-Germanic territory to form a part of the living space of the rising Reich was Bohemia and Moravia, the two westernmost provinces of former Czechoslovakia. The technique employed in the annexation of their territory was that of an attack from within, just as in the case of Austria. The clockwork precision with which the invasion of Prague was engineered corroborated the view that the final destruction of Czechoslovakia had been planned well ahead, and completely invalidated the theory advanced by Sir Neville Henderson, that Hitler's foreign policy was a work of chance.

Already long before Munich German propaganda lent attentive ear to a numerically small but vociferous group of Slovak separatists and later on the Vienna radio urged the Slovaks to sever their relations with Prague. The vigilant German minority at Bratislava and a few other Slovak towns helped to incite the local population against the Czechs. Provincial Premier Josef Tiso performed the part played by Seyss-Inquart in Austria. After being deposed by the Prague government he asked Hitler for protection. On March 14, 1939, the Provincial Diet at Bratislava proclaimed the separation of Slovakia from the rest of the country behind closed doors. Four days later the new "independent" Slovakia was put under the Reich protection. In five more days a German-Slovak agreement was signed which gave the

Germans the right to establish their military bases in Slovakia, chiefly at the southern borders of Poland, and made Slovak foreign policy subject to German approval.

The same day, March 14, 1939, the Czech President Emil Hacha was summoned to Berlin to sign on the dotted line the death warrant of his country. To give it an appearance of legality, a document had been prepared for signature in which Hacha and his Foreign Minister Chvalkovsky "placed the destiny of the Czech people and of their lands in the hands of the Führer," and the Führer in turn "decided to take the Czech people under his protection and to assure them autonomous development conforming to their proper character." The two Czech representatives were told plainly that this decision had already been made, and that every resistance would be crushed by the German Air Force and Army surrounding the Czech state. Before Hacha returned to Prague on March 15, the capital was already in the German hands. The following night the status of the annexed provinces was made public. Bohemia and Moravia were placed under the Reich protector, who "could change the degree establishing the Protectorate and thereby the nature of the status of the provinces whenever common interests warranted." The Gestapo was rounding up all liberals, democrats, refugees, Jews and the "unreasonable" elements of the old régime.

Simultaneously Hungarian troops invaded the rest of the Carpathian Ukraine. The creation of separate Slovakia had already isolated her from Prague. Its new Ukrainian premier Vološin proclaimed the independence of the province after having been assured from Berlin that the little territory was still regarded as indispensable to the Reich for the creation of the Greater Ukraine out of part of Poland and the Soviet Union. Vološin ordered the Ukrainian nationalist troops, the "Sech Sharpshooters," cooperating with the Nazi units, to defend the country against the Magyar invaders, believing that such was the wish of the Nazi leaders. To his surprise he soon learnt that the instructions no longer applied and that he had better give in and make of his short-lived office an example of self-sacrifice. The independence of the Carpathian Ukraine was one of the shortest on record. It lasted twenty-four hours.

Rarely in history had a state been put under the knife in such an arbitrary manner as was Czechoslovakia. At Munich her German inhabited regions were carved out in the name of the principle of self-determination, but 800,000 Czechs were incorporated into the Reich in defiance of this principle. At the same time Poland "liberated" 77,0000 Poles, but she took also 123,000 Czechs. On November 2, the Vienna arbitration award gave 272,000 Slovaks and Ukrainians to Hungary, also in the name of self-determination. Soon afterwards Hungary seized 102,000 more. On March 14, the Slovak province of less than three million was made a separate state, while seven million Czechs were annexed to Germany the following day. At the time of the Munich crisis the separation of the Czechs and Germans was insisted upon by Hitler, Henlein and Runciman because "of absolute incompatibility of their character and political systems." In March 1939, less than six months afterwards, "the co-existence of the two peoples was perfectly natural and desirable." The solemn word of the four great powers had not turned out to be worth very much.

The German soldiers on entering Prague could find no burned houses and mal-treated persons of German nationality. The city was hostile but quiet. One might recall the description of Prague, given by the German war observer Fontane at the time of the invasion of Bohemia by the Prussians in 1866: "Our flags did not descend to a land of misery and barbarism, but to a smiling garden resembling a park. Everything around us evoked the impression that the inhabitants went around in soft socks, while our Prussian behaviour reminded one too much of cavalry boots and spurs." One might also recall a passage from Goebbel's description of modern propaganda methods: "It is not the business of propaganda to be respectable or mild or tender or humble, its business is to lead to a result."

The annihilation of the Czechoslovak state served as a signal for several more aggressions by the Axis in Eastern Europe. On March 22 the German government sent a note to Lithuania demanding the cession of the autonomous territory of Memel to the Reich. Seeing that she had nothing to hope from the western powers Lithuania gave in.

The following day an economic convention was signed between Germany and Rumania which turned the latter country into a virtual economic protectorate of the Reich. The conclusion of the convention followed after a sort of ultimatum in which Germany demanded extensive privileges in exchange for the guarantee of Rumanian frontiers. The implication must have been that should Rumania refuse to be guaranteed Germany would be compelled to enforce her submission. Rumanian production, trade, the exploitation of her natural resources and her transportation were *gleichgeschalten*, completely integrated, into the Reich economy. The timing of the Memel and the Rumanian moves immediately after the coup at Prague illustrated well the National Socialist lightning diplomacy. The convention brought the German penetration eastwards to a new milestone, the Black Sea coast and Rumanian oil.

Eager to prove to the Italian people the worth of the Axis partnership, on the following Good Friday Mussolini let his guns shell the Albanian harbors. Formal assurances given by the Duce to London on April 6, 1939, that Italy had no intention of violating Albanian territory, had been set aside with singular unconcern. King Zog fled the country, and the state which began in 1913, fell into eclipse.

The western powers were perplexed at the audacity of these aggressions. France, England, the United States and the Soviet Union refused to recognize the seizure of Czechoslovokia de jure.

Nevertheless certain acts indicated that had Germany stopped there and had she refrained from further territorial designs, the great powers would have acquiesced in the Prague coup. No mention of Czechoslovakia was made, for instance, in the message of April 16, 1939, which the President of the United States addressed to Hitler and Mussolini. In this message Roosevelt asked for guarantees of the integrity and independence of 31 states, specified by name, in exchange for similar guarantees for Germany and Italy. The message also suggested that an international conference be called to deal with disarmament and the problem of access to raw materials. Mussolini's and Hitler's replies produced no constructive plan, except that Hitler reiterated his willingness to conclude strictly separate non-aggression agreements with those states which cared to. Besides Denmark, only Latvia and Estonia availed themselves of the offer. Europe's mind was no longer on peace through appeasement. War with Poland loomed on the horizon as the next reality.

Descent to War

The April of 1939 marked a rapid rise of war fever throughout Europe. The House of Commons passed the conscription bill, in France the working week was extended to 45 hours, military budgets everywhere jumped to unprecedented figures, and new years of conscripts were called to colors for training. The aggravating relations between Germany and Poland furnished the chief stimulus for these measures. The disappearance of Czechoslovakia, to which Poland made not an insignificant contribution, converted over six hundred miles of the former peaceful Czechoslovak-Polish borders to a German military base for a thrust against the Polish state at its weakest point. Poland was encircled by the two mightiest great powers of Europe, Germany and the Soviet Union, each of which had some claim on her territory. Hitler's plan of dividing the Eastern European nations before defeating them moved one more decisive step forward,

while the democratic and quasi-democratic powers offered a piti-
ful picture of indecision and cross-purposes.

The plan had begun to materialize in Austria a year earlier.
By directing Mussolini's ambitions to an empire to be created in
Africa, German diplomacy immobilized his intentions in Europe
and secured his lack of interest in the fate of Vienna, once his
protégé. By annexing Austria, Hitler had opened the most vulnerable southern frontier of Czechoslovakia, forced that country between half closed pincers, which England and France, as well as
Poland, helped him to close. Now it was Poland herself which
became the principal target of concentrated German pressure.
Distrust of Hitler's true intentions, poorly screened for the time
being by the Germany-Polish Declaration of 1934, now burst into
the open.

The immediate strategic objectives of Germany were the Free
City of Danzig and Polish Pomorze, the Corridor, but the real
aim of Hitler's diplomacy was to eliminate the Polish state as a
European power. The struggle for the control of the mouth of the
river Vistula and adjacent Baltic territory had been going on for
nearly a thousand years. In that endless struggle between land
and sea the Prussians sought to prevent the rise of a strong Polish
state by cutting off the Poles from the Baltic seacoast. The Poles
on the other hand endeavored to reach and maintain the outlet to
the sea which in their mind symbolized their independence and
national greatness, and in addition offered them strategic and
commercial advantages. From the tenth century to 1309 they enjoyed that contact with the sea. The Teutonic Knights conquered
it from them, and held it until 1454. Then Poland became again
a maritime nation until her first partition in 1772. Since 1360
Danzig had belonged to the Hansa League; it administered itself
and lived as rich middleman on the expanding trade with the
Polish hinterland and the Baltic towns. From 1772 to 1919 West
Prussia and Danzig were again a part of Prussia and the Reich
respectively. The Versailles Treaty reëstablished the autonomous

position of Danzig within the Polish customs area, and gave Pomorze to Poland. Thus East Prussia was separated on land from the rest of Germany, a provision which no government in Berlin seemed to be willing to accept as permanent. Gustav Stresemann refused to sign non-aggression treaties with Czechoslovakia and Poland, for "they would have seriously obliged Germany to abstain from all initiative." By the Locarno Pact he accepted that undertaking in the west but not in the east. He fought the eastern "bleeding frontiers" with diplomatic formulas. Had Germany been strong he would have probably fought with military weapons.

It was therefore with great relief that Pilsudski in 1934 entered into an arrangement of apparent friendship with Hitler. Of all the German leaders it fell to the National Socialist Chancellor to break the ancient tradition of enmity. Instead of aiming at the elimination of Poland with the consent of participation of Russia, Hitler suddenly embarked upon a contrary policy of friendship with the Poles. At least so it seemed to some Poles who hated the Russians more than they hated the Germans and who were disposed to believe in the sincerity of National Socialist assurances. In point of fact the Poles could argue for several reasons that no real cause existed why their relations toward Germany could not be placed and remain upon a friendly footing. Thanks to transit arrangements the Corridor could become and to some extent had already become invisible. Furthermore there existed the cheaper and more convenient sea communication between East Prussia and the rest of the Reich. Pomorze had never changed its preponderantly Polish ethnic character despite the ruthless Prussian policy of forcible colonization. Danzig had no commercial importance for Germany since it was preëminently a trading post for Polish exports and imports. The Polish government was not changing the ethnic character of the German populated Free City whether it tried to do so or not. In 1910 there were 308,000 German Danzigers to 16,000 Poles as compared with 387,000 and

15,000 respectively in 1929. It seemed as if even the Germans saw the point. Such was the impression conveyed by their ace spokesmen during the heyday of the German-Polish fraternization.

Hitler himself referred directly to Danzig and the Corridor in a way which could not fail to inspire confidence. He told Ambassador Lipski that "a rapprochement with Poland was more advantageous to Germany than uneasy relations with Russia. Russia is Asia ... Germany faced the problem of finding areas for economic expansion, or room for her population. Poland had not and could not provide either ... In the face of greater problems the Corridor was of no importance whatsoever. How could the Reich be prejudiced provided good German-Polish relations existed, by this short journey of a few dozen kilometers across Polish territory? In a few years given the continuance of good relations in Germany they would forget all about the Corridor. And in Poland the question would cease to be acute."

On November 5, 1937, Hitler spoke on the occasion of the agreement concerning the treatment of German and Polish minorities and said again that "there would be no change in the legal and political position in Danzig." By that time the Danzigers were pretty well nazified, a development which the Polish government undoubtedly regretted but made no effective attempt to hamper. The last time Hitler publicly praised German-Polish relations was in his pre-Munich speech in the Sportpalast on September 26, 1938: "A people of 33 millions will always strive for an outlet to the sea. A way to understanding then had to be found. It has been found, and it will be continually extended."

This was the last of the reassuring statements that came from Germany. With the Munich victory in their pockets and Poland's acquiescence in the Czechoslovak partition the National Socialists were hastily bringing the Poles down to the earth of reality. At a luncheon with Ambassador Lipski at Berchtesgaden on October 24, all of a sudden von Ribbentrop put forward a proposal for "a general settlement" of all issues between Poland and Germany.

Lipski was told that the Declaration of friendship and non-aggression signed under Pilsudski implied that the problem of Danzig and the Corridor would be solved within the framework of that instrument in a peaceful manner, and that in no way could it be interpreted as having removed the existence of those issues. Lipski was also reminded of the alleged persecution of the German minority and of the strangulation of Danzig economically, both of which called for "a prompt solution." There had indeed been a reduction in the volume of transit trade through Danzig with the corresponding increase in the traffic through the government sponsored harbor of Gdynia, located in purely Polish territory, but it was not certain whether this was the cause or the effect of the anti-Polish attitude of the 400,000 Danzig Germans. The proposal included the reunion of Danzig with the Reich, while Poland would retain her railway and economic facilities there, the construction of an extraterritorial motor road and railway line across Pomorze, a twenty-five year guarantee of Polish frontiers, and the possibility of joint action in colonial matters, in the problem of the emigration of Jews, and in a foreign policy toward Russia on the basis of the Anti-Komintern Pact. The Carpathian Ukraine problem could eventually also be settled in a manner to satisfy Poland, by the creation of a common Polish-Hungarian frontier, at the expense of post-Munich Czechoslovakia.

The Polish reaction to these suggestions was completely negative. First of all, the Warsaw government had a different conception of the Declaration of 1934, interpreting it as a re-affirmation of the Versailles territorial provisions in so far as the Polish frontiers were concerned. Moreover, the timing of the proposals, coming as they did after the breakup of Czechoslovakia, put the Poles on the alert. All that Colonel Beck was willing to concede was the replacement of the League protectorate over Danzig by a joint German-Polish guarantee of the existing status and further facilities across the Corridor. Pilsudski's postulate that "the Danzig question was a sure criterion for estimating the Reich's intentions"

still held good. "Any attempt to incorporate the Free City into
the Reich would lead to a conflict." On January 5, 1939, Beck had
a talk with Hitler from which he returned "for the first time in
a pessimistic mood." Hitler had told him that "as a German city
Danzig must sooner or later return to the Reich." There would
not be any fait accompli however, for a strong Poland was still
a necessity for Germany on account of the Russian menace. "Every
Polish division engaged against Russia was a corresponding saving of a German division." There followed a brief reference to
the German-Polish relations in the Chancellor's speech to the
Reichstag on January 30, but it dwelt upon the past only, and was
conspicuous for the absence of any reassuring note as to the future.
As prior to Munich the scene was being shifted to Downing
Street.

At the height of the Munich crisis Prime Minister Neville
Chamberlain in a national broadcast made the following remarks:
"However we may sympathize with a small nation confronted
by a big and powerful neighbor, we cannot in all circumstances
undertake to involve the whole British Empire in a war simply on
her account. If we have to fight it must be on a larger issue than
that. Armed conflict between nations is a nightmare to me; but
if I were convinced that any nation had made up its mind to
dominate the world by fear of its force I should feel that it must
be resisted." In March, 1939, i.e., six months after Munich, Chamberlain became convinced that Germany was the power seeking
domination. At Munich he believed that Hitler's objectives were
limited to the unification of the territories with predominantly
Germanic population. He visualized himself as a crusader right-
ing what he regarded as a serious blunder of the Versailles treaty.
By March he saw that he had been duped, that the objectives of
the Axis partners were limitless, and that by forcing Czechoslovakia into submission he had destroyed whatever balance might
have existed between the democratic forces and the aggressors.
To be exact, on March 15, the day of the annexation of the first

non-Germanic territory, the British Prime Minister did not yet
feel strongly on the subject. In fact he implored the House, partly
alarmed by what had just occurred, not to be deflected from the
course of appeasement. "Although we may have to suffer checks
and disappointments from time to time, the object we have in
mind is of too great significance to the happiness of mankind for
us lightly to give it up or set it to one side."

It was three days later at Birmingham that Chamberlain announced a change in his attitude towards Hitler, by implication,
and a change of England's policy in Eastern Europe. The inner
history of those three days deserves a careful analysis with Chamberlain's mind as its chief subject of study. No evidence has so far
been made public on the doings of Sir Neville Henderson at Berlin on the fateful days of mid-March, except a German record of
the meeting between the British Ambassador and the Reich State
Secretary held on March 14. From this record, the final judgment
of which must be delayed until the British version is known, we
learn that Henderson, while inquiring about the future German
policy toward Czechoslovakia, wished to make it clear that he
was neither making a démarche nor did he wish to create the
impression that his government was interested in the Czechoslovakia affair, for it was accepted in London that Germany had
preponderant interests throughout Czech territory. No reliable
conclusion can be drawn at present as to the nature of Henderson's reporting, and to the influence which his reports, if any, may
have had on Chamberlain's immediate and somewhat evasive reactions to the Prague coup. However, strong anti-appeasement
outbursts were heard in the House of Commons and throughout
British liberal, labor and conservative circles, which coincided with
the opinion held by several influential professional diplomats in
the Foreign Office. This and Chamberlain's own personal disillusionment formed the background of the historic speech at
Birmingham.

The change of British policy toward Eastern Europe took the

form of an attempt to elaborate "an anti-aggression front" to stop Hitler's advance. Coming as it did after the elimination of Czechoslovakia, the main prop of postwar Eastern European structure, the attempt was bound to encounter great difficulties. The chief of them was the unsatisfactory relationship between the Soviet Union on the one hand and Poland and Rumania on the other. The plan was an ambitious one, and had it been resorted to before, instead of the Munich negotiations, the chronicle of Eastern Europe for the past two years would have to be written much differently. It included the creation of a diplomatic barrage, which in wartime would develop into a military front, extending from the White to the Black Sea. There it would be joined with the nations of Near and Middle East and projected to the Eastern Mediterranean, the Balkans and Egypt, all member states bound to one another through non-aggression or mutual assistance pacts of security under the protection of England and France. As at Munich, England took the lead, while France, torn by inner dissension and without initiative, rather haltingly followed suit.

The first link in this chain was the Anglo-Polish understanding made public on the last day of March. Great Britain assumed the obligation to assist Poland in the event of any action which threatened Polish independence and which the Polish government considered it vital to resist with her national forces. The British government had originally in mind a collective declaration by France, England, Russia and Poland providing for mutual consultation. The Soviet Government was prompt in answering the British request in the affirmative, provided France and Poland accepted the proposal. Poland opposed a collective declaration in which the Soviets would occupy a place of importance, however, and in the British Cabinet influences eventually prevailed which did not favor full and direct Soviet participation. Poland feared that once the Red Army entered her territory in fulfilment of the collective obligation, it would permanently occupy the Ukrainian and White Russian provinces. For the same reason the Soviet proposal of a four-power conference was frustrated. Officially this modification of the British method was explained by the urgency of the Polish situation "which permitted no delay." The Prime Minister assured the Labor opposition that the switch had not been made "behind Russia's back," and that Moscow had been informed of the nature of the Anglo-Polish negotiations. A military alliance between the four powers, or at least between France, England and Russia, had apparently not been officially contemplated, even though it found favor among some Laborities. England also abandoned her earlier project of Anglo-Franco-Polish collective consultation, yielding to the Polish preference for bilateral pacts "in order to avoid waste of time." On April 6 the unilateral guarantee was converted into a reciprocal agreement, England and Poland obligating themselves to render one another assistance in case of aggression. On April 16 similar guarantees were offered by Great Britain, and also by France, to Greece and Rumania, without, however, obligating these two smaller powers to reciprocal assistance. The pro-Axis Yugoslav government of Stoyadinovich refused British guarantees in order not to displease Rome and Berlin. Personally Stoyadinovich had little faith in effective Anglo-French assistance and hoped that he would keep out of war if it actually came.

In Germany, the British and French activity in Eastern Europe was resented as "another policy of encirclement." The German people were told that the Polish affair was only a pretext for curbing the Reich at any cost. England was pictured as attempting the repetition of "the bloodthirsty game of Queen Elizabeth against Spain, of Cromwell against Holland, of Pitt against Napoleon, and of Edward VII against Germany. Now to forge the ring around Germany, England stretched her hand also to Moscow."

In Warsaw the Poles, armed with the British guarantee and French assurance, adopted from the start a firm attitude, refusing to compromise on the main issue of the growing conflict. On

March 26 Ambassador Lipski told Ribbentrop that "any further pursuance of German plans meant war with Poland." On April 28 Hitler spoke to the Reichstag. He was still willing to come to a peaceful solution, but on his own terms, and no longer considered himself bound by the Declaration of 1934. In his view Poland unilaterally infringed upon the Declaration by entering into an agreement with a third power. Replying to this charge Colonel Beck declared on May 5 that Hitler's argument, assuming the premise that the Anglo-Polish agreement was incompatible with the German-Polish Declaration, was untenable, for neither England nor Poland had any aggressive intentions. The German offer of the recognition of Polish frontiers after the separation of Danzig was defined by Beck as in reality a unilateral demand, for Hitler offered to recognize what had already been de jure and de facto indisputable Polish property. He, too, favored further negotiations providing they were carried out on the basis of peaceful intentions and procedure. This was the last direct exchange of official views between Berlin and Warsaw. From May to September, 1937, no contacts of any consequence were maintained between the two Governments. As in the case of Czechoslovakia, the British Government interposed itself as intermediary between the disputing parties. Its policy was a complete reversal of its earlier tactics. If in the Czechoslovak crisis Chamberlain overexerted himself against the weaker side, in the case of Poland he gave the smaller party virtually a blank check.

Without some sympathetic collaboration of the Soviet Union the Eastern European diplomatic barrage was doomed to be incomplete and ineffective. There was no doubt that London wanted Russian participation, if only to preclude a closer Russo-German rapprochement. But neither England nor France wished to bind themselves too closely to a régime, on the interpretation of which official and the public opinion was anything but united. A certain section among the British conservatives, the liberals and labor, all envisaging the inevitability of war and all convinced of the futility of further appeasement, saw in the Soviets large reserves and resources of man and material power, and favored a real entente with Moscow. In France, people wavered between the traditional policy of looking toward the small Eastern European nations as complementary to French security, and the policy of coming to a direct agreement with Hitler at the cost of cancelling all continental alliances except that with England and of developing the colonial empire. There were also what might be called the psychological difficulties between Moscow and the western democracies. Stalin mistrusted Chamberlain, and the mistrust was reciprocated. The Russians did not believe too much in the revolutionary change of English policy, seeing that it was in the same hands which brought on Munich. Was Chamberlain really taking the sword? If so, then it was up to him to pay the price by reciprocating the Soviet assistance which he solicited.

Stalin's speech to the Eighteenth Congress of the Communist Party on March 10, 1939, was indicative of the difficulties which the inclusion of Russia in the planned Eastern Peace Front was to be confronted with. Systematic concessions from the non-aggressive encouraged the aggressors who had already seized Manchuria, Ethiopia, Austria and the Czechoslovak Sudetenland, said the virtual Soviet Dictator. "The majority of the non-aggressive countries, particularly England and France, have rejected the policy of collective security and have taken up a position of non-intervention, of neutrality . . . Caution did not allow the Soviet Union to be drawn into conflicts by warmongers who are accustomed to have others pull the chestnuts out of the fire for them."

In England and France it was presumed that a strong Poland and Rumania, as buffer states between Russia and Germany, were of the same value to Moscow as they were to London and Paris, and that Russia should therefore see advantage for herself in supporting the Anglo-French sponsored alignment. Moscow, on the other hand, could not see how any useful purpose would be served in co-guaranteeing Polish and Rumanian eastern frontiers to which she had consistently and repeatedly made objection. Moreover, the Polish policy since 1934 was viewed at the Kremlin with utter displeasure. It was pointed out that Warsaw vetoed every attempt at a collective system in Eastern Europe in which Russia would be included as one of the guarantors. It was also noted that Colonel Beck went out of his way on the eve of the Munich crisis to plead with the Scandinavian and Baltic small countries not to adhere to automatic sanctions should such be invoked in connection with the German-Czechoslovak conflict. The Polish refusal, up to the very last minute, to permit the Soviets to fight Germany through Poland presented another practical difficulty. Moscow feared that the defeat of Poland would bring the German military machine right to the Russian western borders with the result that the gravity of the war would be shifted to the Soviet lands, an eventuality Stalin was determined at all costs to avoid.

Some light was thrown on the protracted Anglo-Franco-Soviet negotiations by Foreign Minister Molotov in his address to the Supreme Council on May 21. By that time the rest of Czechoslovakia, Memel and Albania had been added to the list of the victims of aggression, and Rumania had been turned into a virtual German economic protectorate under the terms of an agreement concluded earlier in March. On the whole, European diplomacy was assuming very realistic shapes. The dropping of Litvinov, the man of Geneva, was illustrative of this general tendency. Molotov laid down the minimum conditions on which Russia would be willing to support actively the policy of combating aggression. They included a defensive pact between France, Britain and the Soviet Union, guarantees by these great powers to all Eastern European and Baltic states without exception, concrete military agreements regarding the extent of assistance to be effectively rendered in the event of aggression, and quality and reciprocity of obligations. Russia wanted to be sure that she could count on

British and French assistance should she become the object of an attack. Eventually the western powers recognized this principle of reciprocity, but Molotov complained that this recognition had been hedged around by such reservations that it might prove to be a fictitious step forward. The Soviets were asked to give assistance to the countries to which Britain and France had already extended their guarantees, but according to Molotov, nothing had been said about Britain and France assisting Estonia, Latvia and Finland should these small neighbors of Russia be unable to defend their neutrality and be used with or against their consent as a territory of passage for German troops against Russia, as had already happened at the end of World War I. By the inclusion of the Baltic states within the Eastern Front, Moscow sought to restrict the diplomatic activities of these three neighbors and to prevent them from choosing their own protector in case of emergency. From the practical point of view, the guarantees of the Baltic region would have been of small significance unless military bases were permitted to be established within its territory and along its seacoast. Neither Britain nor France was willing to grant any such concessions, and the Baltic states themselves were opposed to it. Estonia and Latvia preferred German offers of non-aggression, while Finland declared strict neutrality. Under such conditions the only justification for continuing the Russian negotiation was the anxiety to keep Moscow away from incalculable maneuvers of the diplomacy of Hitler and Ribbentrop.

The impression had been created in English labor circles and abroad that though the London government desired some kind of agreement with Russia, it was far from anxious to make the necessary effort and sacrifice. For several preceding years many Englishmen in high positions felt that a German-Soviet war would not be so bad for the democracies. If Germany was to be given a stronger position in the world, her direction eastwards should not be unduly blocked. We know from Ambassador Dodd that Lord Lothian, for instance, subscribed to this view in 1935.

After Munich the circumstances changed greatly, and after March 1939 the British were shorn of many illusions about the Nazi intentions. Yet they were farther than at any time from elaborating with the Russians a really comprehensive system of collective security. Sir John Simon was still referring to the impossibility of entering into extensive and general commitments on behalf of long and varied frontiers, not realizing that the struggle Great Britain was about to embark upon transcended most of the obsolete notions of political boundaries and traditional warfare.

Attempts to secure Soviet participation in the eastern front by a roundabout way by taking advantage of the comparatively friendly relations between Turkey and the Soviet Union were also far from satisfactory. By virtue of the Montreux Convention of 1936 Turkey was the sovereign guardian of the Straits. Ever since 1920 she had been on good terms with the Soviet Union except for occasional differences which had been kept under control. At the same time the British made every effort to wipe out the reminiscences of the World War and put their relations with Ankara on the basis of solid collaboration. They could point back to the Crimean crisis when they had stood behind the Ottoman Empire. Why should not the new Turkey, purified from the rotten heritage of the nineteenth century, have every right and chance to be treated as an equal entitled to full measure of reciprocity? For England Turkey represented both a strong point of support in the Near and Middle East and a barrier against the expansion of both the Soviets and Germany. Consequently the position of Ankara in regard to the anti-aggression front was as important as it was delicate. For some time negotiations had been afoot with Moscow for the conclusion of a pact of non-aggression which would bring stability to the Black Sea region. One of the Russian conditions was that Turkey should close the Straits in all circumstances to vessels hostile to the Soviet Union. The granting of such a concession would probably entail the necessity of revising the Straits Convention. Turkey was not disposed to do so.

Nor were the British in a mood to touch the instrument which served well their Eastern Mediterranean purposes. As before, the British did not consider justified the Russian fear of being bottled up in the Black Sea by the German fleet. If the Russians considered the Black Sea as an inland sea leading nowhere except to the shores of the rich Ukraine, the British had always regarded it as an open sea which should not be exempt from the application of the principle of reciprocity and the freedom of the seas.

After the August agreement with Hitler the Soviet government lost much of its interest in continuing the negotiations. England and France on the other hand attached even more significance to Turkey's position. Their mutual assistance agreements with Ankara, signed on May 12 and June 23 respectively, were extended to fifteen year formal treaties in October 1939. These treaties provided for mutual and reciprocal help but relieved Turkey from her obligations in the event her assistance should involve her in a conflict with the Soviet Union. In practice that meant that Turkey's hands were tied by Russia, and that her freedom of action was conditioned at the Kremlin as much as in London. By a concurrent protocol England and France gave the Ankara government 25 million pounds credit for war material to be bought from the English and French armament factories and an additional loan of 15 millions in gold.

While the Anglo-French Eastern Front was being laboriously worked out, the Axis powers were not idle. On May 22 the Milan agreement was dressed into a definite military Rome-Berlin alliance, which Molotov characterized as "an offensive alliance." As far as Mussolini was concerned there would be "no more waltzes" in Italian foreign policy. Even if Mussolini wished to turn around, as he had done with regard to Austria, Hitler would see to it that no reversal should happen in the future at the southern extremity of the Axis. If a volte face were ever necessitated by the revolving diplomatic circumstances in Europe, it was to be in line with Germany's needs. In fact, such a turn was already in process.

After the break-up of Czechoslovakia, involving as it did the dissolution of the London-Paris-Prague-Moscow quasi-system of security, Hitler's main efforts were directed toward bringing about a rapprochement with Stalin. On no condition would he place Germany in a position of having to fight on two fronts, i.e., against France and Britain in the west, and Russia in the east. Stalin, too, remembering that each major war Russia had been engaged in during the past hundred or so years had ended in a domestic revolution, found satisfaction in being able to put on record the continued symptoms of good German-Soviet relations: "The hullabaloo raised by the British, French and American press over the Soviet Ukraine was intended to incense the Soviet Union against Germany, to poison the atmosphere and to provoke a conflict with Germany without any visible ground." The German-Soviet agreements which many people feared, in which the wishful thinkers did not believe, and which the English and French fascists, deceived by Hitler's formula of fighting for the capitalistic cause, refused to contemplate, on August 23 became a reality. At the time when the Anglo-French negotiators at Moscow held before the Kremlin "barbarians" the vision of a peace imposed by a coalition of peaceful powers, the Soviet government was carrying on an entirely different series of negotiations with Germany, the second bidder.

Taking into account all the antecedents of European diplomacy during the past few years and months, and paying due attention to the state of the Soviet Union, it was not difficult to predict the final choice. England and France offered a peace, not altogether certain, at the cost of the loss or postponement of the recovery of the provinces Russia coveted. The two distant democratic powers, militarily no match for Germany, also offered qualified assistance, the effectiveness of which Moscow doubted. Moreover, they might implicate the Soviet Union in war. Germany, on the other hand, asked for no military assistance, offered peace at the convenient price of neutrality, and gave the Soviet Union, whether expressly

or by implication, a free hand in the Baltic. The more resolute
the British attitude toward Germany grew, and the more apparent
it became that this time Britain meant business, the more vacillat-
ing grew the Kremlin stand. Russia was out to conduct a Russian
policy, no longer obligated by any collective ideology, which had
cost her so dearly and left her isolated. The agreement was based
on the non-aggression and neutrality treaty of 1926. The Soviet
Union and Germany bound themselves to refrain from any act of
force, both singly or jointly with other powers, and promised not
to participate in any grouping of powers which aimed directly
or indirectly at the other party. This amounted to the collapse
of the grandiose scheme of the eastern barrage against aggression.

The position of Poland became extremely precarious and, compared with 1914, France and England were to enter the war under
much less auspicious circumstances. When all facts are known
history will no doubt divide the direct and negative responsibilities
among the powers according to due shares. The published documents do not give as yet a reliable picture of what was going on
behind the closed doors at the moment when the to be or not to
be question of the second World War was being decided. The
uneasiness of French diplomacy derived from the incomparable
advantage of the German power position. At the time of Munich
France had about one-sixtieth of the strength of the German air-
force in the first class fighting category. In Germany 150,000
workers labored 50 hours per week in the aircraft and auxiliary
factories. In France only 50,000 men worked 45 hours a week.
The Germans produced in a week what France could produce
in a month. Although the defenses of France had increased, her
obligations also increased. She was committed to assistance to
Poland and Turkey, and guarantees to Rumania and Greece.
Officially the government promised to stand by all these alliances.
But behind the official mask there was a worry as to whether the
country would be able to discharge its duties when the time came.

In fact, on several occasions suggestions had been to the Quai d'Orsay to convert the hard and fast alliances to mere pacts of consultations which would have permitted the government at the critical moment to avoid the dilemma between capitulation and war. Some diplomats favored such a retreat, but the military usually opposed it on grounds of strategy. The Franco-Soviet pact was doomed to become ineffective partly owing to the opposition of the Poles to granting permission to the Soviets to move their armies across Polish territory.

Geography proved to be a hard nut to crack. The only way to fight Germany was through Polish or Rumanian territory. The Soviet spokesmen insisted that France should extract from Warsaw and Bucharest concessions to that effect. Colonel Beck divined, rightly or wrongly, that behind the demand of transit loomed the menace of another partition. In any event he was adamant in his stand to refuse such a grant before the actual outbreak of warfare. This proved to be the greatest stumbling block to any coordination of military policies of the Franco-Soviet treaty. There were other difficulties which eventually brought the Anglo-French-Soviet negotiations to naught. One of them was the refusal of the Soviets to guarantee the borders of Holland and Belgium unless the proposed tripartite agreement rested on iron-clad reciprocity.

The news of the German-Soviet pact was intended by the Wilhelmstrasse to stun the world, and particularly the British. Germany reckoned on localizing the inevitable war. Hitler's plan had always been to conquer by stages, in a series of isolated local wars, and he calculated that England would shrink from fighting him on a single western front. However, it was Hitler's turn to be surprised. England and France decided not to be intimidated. The Anglo-Polish agreement of April 6 took the form of a definite alliance signed in London by Lord Halifax and Ambassador Raczynski. It covered implicitly also the Danzig menace.

The French government, too, signed a protocol with the Poles reinforcing thus the alliance of 1921. All signatories undertook the obligation not to conclude a separate armistice except by mutual agreement.

The Critical Days

The historians of the first World War have criticized Sir Edward Grey for not having made his position clearer in 1914, and have expressed the view that had England declared her determination to fight in the event of the invasion of Belgium, Germany would have refrained from attack. The historians of the second World War will have no such ground for criticism. As early as August 22 Prime Minister Chamberlain in a personal letter to Chancellor Hitler stated that on this occasion no such tragic misunderstanding would be permitted. It would be a mistake to take the announcement of the Moscow-Berlin agreement to indicate that the intervention by Great Britain on behalf of Poland was no longer a contingency to be reckoned with. Hitler accepted the explanation by stating that Germany had no intention of attacking either France or England, but that she possessed in Eastern Europe certain interests, viz., Danzig and the Corridor, which she would not renounce. Should the British announcement of assistance to Poland be carried into effect, he, Hitler, would order immediate mobilization to counter the contemplated threat against the Reich. Two days later, on August 25, in a supplementary communication, Hitler informed Sir Neville Henderson, that should England forego her support of Poland, and be willing to settle the colonial problem peacefully, he would be willing to accept the British Empire and even support it. Reacting to what in the Downing Street was taken as an attempt at bribery and blackmail, Henderson gave Hitler the answer within three days in the course of a personal interview. England would not, despite any advantages offered her, jeopardize the independence of a state to which she had given her guarantee. The British government recommended direct negotiation between Berlin and Warsaw on the basis announced by Hitler on April 28, and international guarantee of the Polish settlement.

On the evening of August 29 the Reich government accepted in principle direct negotiation, provided that a Polish representative, authorized to negotiate and to sign, should come to Berlin within twenty-four hours, i.e., before midnight of August 30. As to the guarantees, the Soviet Union would have to agree to them, a point whose precise meaning was rather vague. The German government was sceptical about Polish acquiescence, the answer ran, and did all this only because of the prospect of the German-British alliance.

At midnight on August 30, Henderson brought the British answer to von Ribbentrop. He recommended abstention from border incidents, and a modus vivendi at Danzig for the period of direct German-Polish negotiation. Since Germany had received no answer from Poland, Ribbentrop told Henderson that the question of further proposals no longer existed. In order to show, however, what proposals Germany had intended to make if the Polish representative had come, Ribbentrop read to Henderson the much discussed sixteen points which had been allegedly prepared by the German Foreign Office for Polish signature. This was the first time that they had been made known to anyone outside the inner German circles. The proposals included the cession of Danzig to Germany, and a plebiscite in the Corridor to be arranged within twelve months under international supervision. The port of Gdynia was to be left to Poland without a plebiscite. The party which should be outvoted would have the right to build an extra-territorial *autobahn* and a four-track railway line, e.g., either Germany to East Prussia, or Poland to Gdynia, according to the outcome of the plebiscite. Both Danzig and Gdynia would be mercantile harbors without any military installations. Nationality rights (*Volkstum*) of minorities would be reciprocally protected, damages inflicted on Poles in Germany and Germans in

Poland since 1918 made good, and, in the event of an agreement, both countries would eventually demobilize.

A controversy arose as to whether the abortive German proposal was a virtual ultimatum or not. Ambassador Henderson, to whom the sixteen points seemed "altogether not too unreasonable," interpreted it as such, because of its time limit. Hitler justified its urgency by the fact that "two fully mobilized armies were standing face to face within firing distance of each other, and that at any moment some incident might lead to serious conflict." Another controversy concerned the delay in the delivery of the proposal. The German government accused Halifax, "the dishonest broker," of duplicity, for the proposal, which had been made in the evening of August 29, was allegedly communicated to the Polish government through Sir H. Kennard, the British Ambassador at Warsaw, sometime between August 30 and 31, that is, after the expiration of the period in which a Polish emissary was expected. Moreover, the German argument went, instead of applying pressure upon the Poles to induce them to send their plenipotentiary, the British government discouraged them from taking this sole peace-saving course. The British government explained its position to the German Foreign Minister on August 30, when Henderson told Ribbentrop that his government was not in a position to advise the Polish government to accept this procedure. Great Britain suggested that the normal diplomatic way should be adopted, i.e., that the German government should hand their proposals to the Polish Ambassador in order to set matters in motion and to make it possible for the Polish Ambassador to cooperate with his government preparing the direct negotiations. If the German government would also communicate these proposals to the British government and the latter were of the opinion that the proposals constituted a reasonable basis for the solution of the dispute, it would use its influence in Warsaw to achieve a settlement.

Had the general political situation in Europe been similar to that in the summer of 1938, the British government would have exerted itself to produce a Polish emissary at short notice. This time the circumstances and the experiences were different. In London there was no inclination to map out another Munich, and to help Hitler to another easy victory by succumbing to one more display of force. The Polish government instructed Ambassador Lipski to hand the German Foreign Minister a declaration that it was favorably considering the British suggestion of direct negotiations, received during the night of August 30, but not to accept any text relevant to the German proposals. The instructions came to Berlin soon after 12 o'clock on August 31. At 6:15 P.M. Lipski was received by von Ribbentrop "to establish direct contact," but without full powers to negotiate. "On my return to the Embassy I found myself unable to communicate with Warsaw," wrote Lipski, "as the Germans had cut the telephone lines." In the early hour of September 1, the German wireless announced that German armed forces had entered Polish territory. Chancellor Hitler delivered a speech to the Reichstag on that day telling the members that since 5:45 A.M. the Germans had been returning Polish soldiers' fire. Said he: "I will carry on this fight, no matter against whom, until such time as the safety of the Reich and its rights are secure. As for the rest of the world, I can assure them that November of 1918 shall never occur again in German history."

Later in the morning of September 1 Ambassadors Henderson and Coulondre informed the German Foreign Minister that, unless satisfactory assurances were given to their respective governments of the suspension by Germany of all aggressive action against Poland and of her readiness to withdraw her forces promptly from Polish territory, England and France would without hesitation fulfill their obligations to Poland. Mindful of the success that his last minute intervention achieved at the time of the Munich crisis, Mussolini hoped, though with less optimism, that he might be able to isolate the war in Poland, and prevent its spread to the west. On the last day of August he suggested to

France and England through their Ambassadors in Rome that they meet at a conference of the four great powers on September 5. The conference would first arrange for an armistice between Germany and Poland in which each army would retain the position which it had reached, and then examine the clauses of the Versailles Treaty which caused the crisis. As matters stood, the military position would under such circumstances favor Germany. Both England and France accepted Mussolini's suggestion in principle, France with a more ardent desire and hope of their acceptance by Germany, perhaps, than England. They laid down the condition, however, that the German troops withdraw to the Reich's frontier, a condition which Hitler was unlikely even to consider. Mussolini therefore decided on September 2 to abandon his project. The following day at 9 A.M. the British Ambassador in Berlin informed the German government that unless not later than at 11 A.M. that day satisfactory assurance had been given by the German government concerning the withdrawal of its forces, a state of war would exist between the two countries as from that hour. At 11 A.M. a state of war actually began. Under identical circumstances French Ambassador Coulondre delivered a note to the German Foreign Minister in which the French government declared itself duty bound to fulfill its contractual obligations towards Poland. Following the two declarations, nothing occurred that might give a more favorable turn to the precipitating course of fatal events. The second World War was on. It was just eleven months and three days after Chamberlain and Hitler signed the Anglo-German Declaration "never to go to war with one another again."

Part Five

The Maelstrom

Hitler's "Last" Offer of Peace

The military conflict between Germany and Poland was the first test of the total blitzkrieg method. From the military point of view the victory of the overwhelming Reich forces had been a foregone conclusion, but the swiftness of the German drive and the occupation of Warsaw as early as September 27 surpassed expectations. The reasons were not far to seek. The attacking army was three times superior to the defending army in respect of infantry, thirty times superior in motorized units, especially tanks, and many more times in aviation. Each German infantry division had on the average twice as many guns, machine guns and anti-tank guns. Of the 52 Polish infantry divisions only 22 were mobilized on the first day of the hostilities. Most of the German forces were sent to Poland for a swift knockout, and only eleven infantry divisions and some specialized units had been left on the inactive western front. War in Poland would have been longer and more costly to Germany had France taken a vigorous offensive in the west. All that General Gamelin would do was to stage a few minor "symbolic" skirmishes in front of the Maginot Line which had no military importance. Yet in the opinion of the German General Staff an offensive on the western front offered the only chance of a Franco-British victory.

The systematic espionage undertaken in Poland by the German intelligence service, including many Polish citizen of Germanic blood, made the task of the invading forces and particularly of the air force comparatively easy. Centers of communications and airfields were rapidly destroyed, the mobilization of the Polish army and the concentration of troops made almost impossible, and the civilian population was terrified by incessant devastating flights. In three days all the lines of communication behind the Polish line were destroyed, and the air was cleared of the Polish air force. Most of the land installations had been rendered useless. In the air, on land and at sea German forces worked in perfect coordination, wresting all initiative from Polish hands. According to German expert estimation, the Polish soldiers fought bravely, but they had to perish because of the inadequacy of the leaders and faulty organization. The absence of seasonal heavy rains was also one of the factors working to Polish disadvantage.

The last but in no way decisive factor which sealed the fate of Poland was the invasion of her territory by the Soviet troops at the dawn of September 17. The invasion followed closely on the unilateral denunciation by the Soviets of the Polish-Soviet non-aggression pact of 1932, which had been extended in 1935 to last until 1945. Vice-Commissar Potemkin announced the abrogation to Ambassador Grzybowski at the early hour of 3 A.M. He motivated the action by the alleged abandonment of Polish territory by the government. The Poles refuted the charge by pointing out that it was the Soviet invasion which prompted the government and the High Command to move to neutral Rumania. On September 22 the German and the Soviet High Commands agreed on a line of demarcation of the occupied zones, running roughly along the rivers Narva, Vistula, Bug and San. On September 28 a treaty of friendship and boundary was signed, which fixed the new borders "of mutual imperial interests." The Governments of the Reich and of U.S.S.R. considered it "as exclusively their task to restore peace and order in these territories and to assure to the

peoples inhabiting them a peaceful existence which would correspond to their national characteristics." As in the case of the
Bohemian and Moravian protectorate the national characteristics
and the needs of the subjected peoples would be laid down by the
conquerors.

The Soviet Union acquired the eastern Polish provinces the
majority of whose inhabitants were White Russians and Ukrainians, with a Polish minority. Germany absorbed the "liberated
provinces" peopled by about twelve million inhabitants, most
of whom were of Polish nationality, language and culture. The
remaining Poles were included in the newly created Government General of Poland, which comprised some 44,000 square
miles, or little more than one-fourth of the former state.

The Soviet-German boundary agreement marked the fourth
partition of the Polish state. The years of 1772, 1793, 1795 and
1939 told the grim story of the ancient vigorous and gifted nation
which had been trying to maintain itself between the Germanic
and Russian juggernauts. As in the past Polish independence
ended the moment the two great powers came to an agreement.
In his speech of October 6 Hitler summed up the situation
in the following terms: "So long as Russia and Germany
mutually respect their divergent régimes, no reason longer exists
why they should be hostile to one another. It had been established
in long historical periods that the peoples of these two largest
European states have always been happy when they were friendly.
The World War which set them against each other became a
misfortune for both. The conclusion of the non-aggression pact
marked the turning point in the whole German foreign policy,
and the two countries will now together deprive the most dangerous part of Europe of its menace. The agreement proved that
all the assumptions as to Germany's aims in the direction of the
Urals, Ukraine and Rumania, and so on, were only a figment of
the morbid imagination of the worried advocates of freedom."

In the same speech Hitler made "the very last" peace offer on the basis of the territorial acquisitions achieved so far. He declared that Germany's aims were strictly limited, that Germany and the Soviets guaranteed that the Poland of the Versailles Treaty would never rise again, and made a strong plea for the sanctioning of the new status in Eastern Europe. He was also ready to discuss disarmament, to guarantee general peace and to remove obstacles to freer trade. The Chancellor then defined Germany's aims in the space which he had designated as her Lebensraum. The Reich was to have frontiers which corresponded to historical, ethnic and economic realities. The living space would be regulated according to the nationality principle. He would solve the Jewish problem, reconstruct economic life and communications to the benefit of all who lived in the Lebensraum, and guarantee the security of the new empire from within and without. He also promised to establish a new Polish state which "in its structure and leadership would guarantee that neither a new base of attack against Germany be created, nor a focus of intrigues against Germany and Russia."

The mention of Russia in Hitler's speech created the impression abroad that the Soviet government associated itself with the Nazi peace offer. The Communists went so far as to refer to Hitler's terms as the Soviet proposals for peace. What actually happened was that the Nazis endeavored to associate Moscow with their peace maneuvre in order to make it appear as a concerted effort likely to attract more attention. The Soviets had probably little to do with it, except that they reiterated their customary formula that peace was in the interests of the working class everywhere and of Russia in particular.

The National Socialists regarded the Fuehrer's speech as a magnanimous peace-offer by a victorious nation. They could not understand why England and France met it with flat refusal. The voices that came from the west and spoke about the impossibility of peace based on the exploitation of Eastern Europe as a colonial domain, on condoning aggression and on letting the wrongs done to Czechoslovakia and Poland go unrighted, had a sound which the German mind had little capacity to perceive. Used to seeing only their own point of view, and to judging the smaller neighboring peoples in terms of their own German good, the Germans thought it incomprehensible that their magnanimity should be ignored. The voices from the west spoke also of the impossibility of attaching any value to the words of the Chancellor by reference to similar assurances he had given in the past. Hitler reacted to these refusals on October 10, when he addressed the Winter Relief campaigners. He said that the western powers started the war for ridiculous reasons, and that nothing would stop the German people from claiming the space to which they were entitled by virtue of their greatness and numbers.

Two weeks later Foreign Minister Ribbentrop elaborated further on the German foreign policy in a speech at Danzig. He declared that the process of consolidation of the Reich had been terminated, and that in the new Eastern European order Germany had acquired territory for colonization sufficient for generations. Germany would unite within this space German elements disseminated throughout Europe in order to create a neat state of affairs and ethnic frontiers. By mass transfers of population the possibility of future conflicts would be eliminated. "The Reich borders in the north, east, south and west are henceforth definitive. The folly of Versailles has disappeared and a stable situation has been created in Europe."

The announced plan of resettlement of minorities marked a radical departure from previous National Socialist policy. Hitherto Germanic minorities were valued as outposts of Germanism and missionaries of expansion. The idea of moving population from one region to another was not new. Long before Christ the Assyrian and other rulers settled people of their own race in strategic centers in conquered lands and forced out the native population. After World War I the exchange of population between Greece and Turkey, and between Greece and Bulgaria was agreed upon by the respective governments and executed under the auspices and with the financial help of the League of Nations. The scheme undertaken by Hitler was designed to serve two purposes at the same time. One was connected with the new orientation of his foreign policy, the other concerned the strengthening of the inner safety of the inflated empire. The Germans from the Baltic states, Russian occupied Poland, Bessarabia, Bucovina and other territories assigned to the Soviet sphere of influence were to be moved to the conquered Polish Pomorze, Posnania, Upper Silesia, Bohemia and Moravia to impress Germanic character on these preponderantly Slav lands. In particular the region between East Prussia and Upper Silesia, where the pre-War policy of Prussian colonization had been reversed under the twenty years of Polish rule, was to be speedily re-Germanized so as to make the new political boundary coincide with the ethnic frontier. Some six million Poles were earmarked for removal. Considering the fact, that Pomorze had 171 inhabitants per square mile, Posnania 207, and Bohemia and Moravia 150, as compared with 140 in Germany proper, few Germans could be brought in unless the native Polish and Czech population was evicted.

The resettlement program was set afoot with customary National Socialist thoroughness. Europe was to be brought before an accomplished fact with no chances left to procrastination. A series of agreements had been signed with Italy, the Soviet Union, Estonia, Latvia and Lithuania, providing for the transfer of local Germans to the Reich. The Italian citizens of the Upper Adige region had to declare themselves either Germans and leave Italy, or Italians and be Italianized. The Italian government would compensate them for the property left behind through the liquidation of Italian businesses in the German annexed Austria and Czechoslovakia, and in kind. About 70 per cent of South Tyrolians voted for the Reich out of the total of 268,000, the value of their property amounting to five billion lira. In Latvia 62,000 Baltic Germans were removed within fourteen days involving the transfer of 12-15 billion francs. In Estonia the transfer involved over 16,000 persons. They were permitted to take with them movable property, their immovables having been disposed of by the Estonian government. The proceeds were transferred to German consular officials. The 30,000 Germans of Lithuania, living in more modest social circumstances than the Germans of Estonia and Latvia, were to be exchanged for Lithuanians from East Prussia and the former Polish district of Suvalki, now in German hands. The repatriation of 118,000 Germans from the Soviet occupied Poland was completed early in 1940.

It would be idle to pretend that these measures were popular with the individuals and families subjected to mass movements. In many cases it was only from fear of consequences that people obeyed the order. Considering that hundreds of thousands of Jews were moved from Eastern Europe to extra-European countries, and that many more Poles and other Slavs were uprooted, this device of reshuffling people by forcible means introduced into Eastern Europe an element of violent change such as it had not experienced since the Thirty Years' War. It was to be noted at the same time that the repatriation of Germans was restricted to Italy and the Soviet sphere of interests. The Germans living in the smaller states of the Central European and Balkan regions as minorities were to stay at their posts to serve as carriers of German Kultur. No exchange of population was envisaged with regard to Slovakia, Hungary, Rumania, Yugoslavia, Bulgaria, Greece and Turkey. This resettlement policy indicated clearly the extent of German ambitions; it revealed the Mitteleuropa in the making.

The Soviet Counterpoise

It was at this junction that the Soviet Union set out to do its bit of unmaking and remaking. Whether Stalin was given free hand in the Baltic region as a part of his agreement with Hitler, or not, the war in the west offered him the opportunity to realize some of his long outstanding desires. He had already recovered two-fifths of Poland. As the next step the Soviets brought within their orbit all the Baltic states with the exception of Finland. In quick succession Estonia (September 29, 1939), Latvia (October 5), and Lithuania (October 10) signed with Moscow pacts of mutual assistance, agreeing to render one another every assistance, including military, in the event of aggression by any European power. They also undertook not to conclude any alliances with third powers, and not to take part in any coalition directed against each other. In order that the Soviet Union might effectively protect its partners, it demanded and was granted the right to build at its expense bases at the Baltic ports of Libau, Windau and others, and to install artillery along the coast. It could also maintain land and air forces at selected inland points. The pacts were signed variously for a period of ten to fifteen years, and rested on the principle of independent state existence and non-interference in internal affairs. Lithuania even received back the city of Wilno, which the Russians took from Poland, with 57 small towns, 220 miles of railway and 425 square miles of forests. Schools in Lithuania were closed to celebrate the occasion. The Lithuanians won the city, not realizing probably, that in less than ten months they would be losing their whole country. In the early summer of 1940 Moscow advanced charges against the three Baltic states of plotting against the Soviet Union.

As the result of the revitalized local communist groups, of whom little had been heard in the preceding years, political power passed to the hands of the new people's parliament, under the Soviet pressure. The new parliaments of Latvia, Lithuania and the Estonian State Duma proclaimed the establishment of the dictatorship of the proletariat. In the following August the parliaments constituted themselves as provisional supreme soviets, applied for entry into the Soviet Union, and after admission adopted constitutions which were in complete conformity with the constitution of the Soviets. The Baltic constitutions noted that the power of their Soviets resulted from the overthrow of capitalists and large landed proprietors, and that the abolition of private ownership would lead to abolishing completely the exploitation of man by man and to building the socialist society. Banks, railroads, water transport and the means of communication were fully nationalized. Small industries were temporarily exempted from nationalization. Personal property of peasants was placed under protection and peasants could not be forced against their will to organize collective farms. In these and several similar provisions the Baltic constitutions reflected the conditions which had existed in the three countries previously. The framers of the new constitutions realized that Baltic socialism constituted an objective rather than an accomplished fact, and that a certain transitional period should be allowed before the same kind of socialism could be established as had developed in the Soviet Union proper during the twenty-three year period of inner struggle and building. Since the Baltic republics were in a more advantageous position than were the Russian Soviets in 1917, the process of overcoming the remnants of capitalism was expected to proceed at an accelerated pace.

The extension of Soviet rule to the three little Baltic states was effected without serious difficulties. Poland was no more, and Germany, the only other power which would otherwise have to be reckoned with, viewed at that time her Baltic interests as inferior to Russian neutrality. In Finland the Soviets encountered opposition, however, which required a war to break. In the past few months it had become the diplomatic practice to invite the governments of the smaller Eastern European countries to Berlin "to settle all the outstanding problems." The outcome was almost uniformly the same. Imbued with the ardent desire to preserve peace, the Reich offered protection to the small nations in exchange for the surrender of freedom with some incidental costs such as military bases or trade monopolies. To Americans the workings of these international protective arrangements should not be unfamiliar. Examples of them can be found in the operation of some pseudo-protective organizations whose extortionist methods can be studied from the records of court proceedings.

Fearing that Finland might be used by a foreign power as a base for attacking the Soviet Union, and especially Leningrad, lying within the reach of long-range artillery from the Finnish border, Moscow requested the cession of five islands in the Gulf of Finland, a lease of the port of Hango, surrender of a part of the Karelian Isthmus adjacent to Leningrad, and the rectification of the Petsamo frontier on the warm Arctic coast. In exchange Finland would receive twice as large, though strategically less important, territory inhabited by racially kindred Karelians. Moscow would also abandon her objections to the fortification of the Finnish controlled Aland Islands, provided Finland herself carried out the work. In addition Finland was asked to strengthen the 1932 non-aggression treaty with the Soviets by the inclusion of a clause forbidding either party to join any hostile group of powers.

These demands were handed over to the Finns four days after an analogous request was accepted by Lithuania. After some thinking the Finnish government showed willingness to accept or compromise on all issues except the port of Hango, which it refused to lease or sell. On November 26 an incident occurred at the Russian village Mainila, in which four Russians were killed and nine wounded, allegedly by Finnish artillery operating from the other side of the frontier. The Finnish government repudiated the charge, suggested that the accident might have been caused during Soviet artillery practice, and asked for joint investigation. To Molotov this communication "reflected the deep-rooted hostility of the Finnish government toward the U.S.S.R., the real cause of the tension." After repudiating the non-aggression treaty the Soviet government ordered the Red Army to open hostilities. At 8 A.M. on November 30, 1939, the Russo-Finnish war broke out.

The Finns appealed to the League which in turn appealed to the Soviets to open peace negotiations. The Moscow government denied, however, that a state of war existed between the Soviets and Finland, and refused therefore to recognize the League's competence. On the contrary, the Soviet Union maintained peaceful relations with "the popular government of the democratic republic of Finland." This "phantom government," as the Finns called it, was planted by Moscow at Torijoki, a village in the Soviet occupied part of Finland, in order to take over the power after Finland collapsed under the strain of war or as the result of inner revolt. The war continued until March 12, 1940. In spite of brilliant resistance the Finns could have no illusion as to the final outcome, particularly when Norway and Sweden barred the transportation of outside aid. The Russians on the other hand miscalculated the inner conditions in Finland where no signs appeared of slackening morale or communist opposition, in spite of heavy bombing of all but six cities. The treaty of peace gave the Soviets more than they originally asked for. Finland surrendered all the five islands, the whole of the Isthmus, parts of Petsamo, and she agreed to lease the Hango cape for thirty years, without any territorial quid pro quo. The inhabitants of the ceded area, about one-tenth of the total population, fled to the interior, and had to be taken care of. The Finnish delegate accepted the terms as unexpectedly hard. Yet he could hardly fail to admit that they might have been much more onerous. The Soviets showed more leniency towards the Finns than did the Nazis towards the Czechs or Poles. They limited their acquisitions to areas regarded as strategically essential in anticipation of the clash with Hitler. Finland retained her independence, and still had sufficient opportunity and land for work. On March 31 the Karelian-Finnish republic was received as the twelfth member of the Soviet Union.

Two days earlier Foreign Commissar Molotov stated in a speech that no international agreement existed which recognized the status of Bessarabia as Rumanian territory. Considerable Soviet forces stood all along the Rumanian frontier. Hard pressed by the concurrent revisionist demands of Hungary and Bulgaria, both of which had Axis backing, King Carol ceded without resistance both Bessarabia and the Ukrainian part of Bucovina. Among the three million ceded inhabitants more than a half were Rumanians. Thus June 27, 1940, brought to an end the twenty year old dispute and put Russia at the mouth of the Danube.

In reviewing this latest phase of Soviet foreign policy Molotov was able to announce in his speech on August 1, 1940, that "in less than a year the Soviet Union has added more than 23 million people," so that the population of the country increased from 170 to 193 million. "Nineteen-twentieths of the population of these areas formerly were parts of Russia," said Molotov, "but had been forcibly torn from the U.S.S.R. by western imperialistic powers when it was militarily weak. The addition of the Baltic states will greatly increase their strength and safety, and at the same time still further enhance the might of the great Soviet Union." By the method of bargaining by means of its neutrality, through the use of diplomatic pressure supported by the threat of force, and by resorting to "preventive aggression," the Soviet Union profited territorially and consolidated its western borders from the Arctic to the Black Sea at the comparatively small price of the Finnish campaign.

The surrender of Bessarabia did not mean that Rumania's troubles were over. On August 21 she reached an agreement with Bulgaria for the cession of Southern Dobrudja, recreating the status which had existed there prior to the Peace of Bucharest at the end of the second Balkan war in 1913. Bulgaria was to repatriate about 50,000 Rumanians living in the ceded province. The most important loss however was that of Transylvania to which the Bucharest government was forced to consent by the Vienna arbitration award of August 30, 1940.

The Vienna conference on August 30, 1940, attended by the Foreign Ministers of Germany, Italy, Rumania and Hungary was called by the Axis for the ostensible purpose of avoiding a possible Hungaro-Rumanian war. Any such local diversion would have interfered with the major Axis undertaking against Great Britain.

Rumania was put to the wall, having to choose between saving her existence at a great territorial cost, or disappearing completely. She chose the former alternative, surrendering to Hungary, the Axis protégé, 16,000 square miles of territory with two and a half million people, three-fifths of whom were Rumanian by nationality and loyalty. The Rumanians were given the right of option within six months, after which period those who opted for Rumania were to leave the country within one year. They could take with them movable property and sell the immovables. Unwittingly the Axis created a precedent which could be taken as an example by the Rumanians or the other victims of the Italo-German-Hungarian aggressions should the fortunes of war turn definitely in their favor. Throughout Rumanian Transylvania the peasants gathered to oppose the arbitrary decision, but under duress their government accepted it as final. The Axis powers undertook to guarantee the new borders of the rump state. The guarantee was imposed with an eye on Russia. After the signature of the partition award Ribbentrop described the affair as the solution of the last remaining territorial issue in Southeastern Europe. As after Munich congratulatory messages were exchanged between the great powers on this new success of their diplomacy. Only in Rumania the people could not believe and clenched their fists in humiliation.

David versus *Goliath*

Ribbentrop's statement to the Vienna Press on August 30, 1940, on the occasion of the partition of Rumania, that "the Fuehrer and the Duce had solved the last remaining question in Southeastern Europe," proved as unconvincing as most of the Nazi assurances given earlier. Keeping one's word has never been among the strong points of diplomacy but with the Nazis self-repudiation has been developed into an almost perfect technique. The same day the Duce's troops in Albania, numbering several divisions, were on the move against Greece. Mussolini had already entered the war actively on June 10, 1940, when France was on the point of collapse. He did not fare according to expectations, however, and each of his advances ended in a retreat. The formidable deadlock in the west after Dunkirk made it imperative for the Axis powers to resume the war on some other front where chances of an easy victory seemed assured. There had been a long standing agreement between Hitler and Mussolini on the division of their sphere of influence and combat. Each of them retained a degree of autonomy within his assigned sector. The Greek campaign was to be Mussolini's contribution to common victory.

In line with the totalitarian pattern of war-making the Italian Press and radio opened the hostilities by accusing the Greeks of the alleged persecution of Italian-protected Albanians. Moreover, the Fascist argument ran, Greece held unjustly the Yanina region and the Epirus coast. The time had now arrived for this problem to be definitely solved. The imperial safety of Italy depended on this solution. In the future new order the Eastern Mediterranean was to be placed under the control of Rome. For reasons of both prestige and economic expansion Greece must be taken out of the British orbit. Selfish ambitions of territorial nationalism run amok were wrapped up in high sounding slogans envisaging a world of unlimited glory. At the same time a more realistic aspect mingled with the flamboyant visions. The holders of gold were reminded that should they refuse to recognize the new order the Axis would refuse to recognize the gold standard. "This war is a war of revolution," declared the Fascist organs. "After being put into effect at home this revolution has been transferred with arms to the imperial sphere, for it is not possible to achieve the highest form of social justice unless we win back the means to give it to the Italian people. The Italian people are conscious of this mission, and live their war, thus following with enthusiasm the glorious exploits of their sons." Encouraged by Germany's successes in Central Europe, Italy set out after her share of the new Lebensraum in the south.

On October 28, 1940, General Metaxas of Greece was handed an Italian ultimatum demanding that the Greek Government permit Italian forces to occupy certain strategic points in north-western Greece for the ostensible purpose of preventing this Greek territory from being transformed into a British military base against Italy. Any resistance would be crushed by force of arms, and the responsibility for the conflict would fall on the Greek Government. The Greeks were given three hours to answer the request. They decided to fight against "the power which refused to recognize their rights to live as a free people." The struggle for Eastern Europe switched to the Balkans, just one year after Germany had destroyed Poland in the Baltics. Facing an adversary inferior to the Germans, and with the substantial aid of the British air force, the Greeks not only held their own, but made consider-able advances into Albania. Outnumbered in men and equipment they cleared their country of all Italian troops and seized one-third of Albania. Incredible though it might seem, after six months of warfare the chances were that given increased aid from Great Britain the Greeks would have brought Mussolini's attempt to a stalemate or to complete frustration. In order to save Italy from threatening defeat and to forestall internal collapse which might follow the misfortunes on the battlefields, Hitler decided to come to the rescue of his weaker partner.

Economically Germany had little reason to march against Greece. In the last four years her trade with the little Balkan nation was relatively more extensive than with any other country. The declaration of war was therefore hardly justified by urgent economic needs as in the case of Rumania. The real motive be-hind German action was to cut off from England one more of her Eastern European friends. Like Denmark, Norway, Holland and Belgium, Greece clung scrupulously to her neutrality. She tried to keep a strict neutrality even after Italy's attack. But she stood in the way of the Axis plan of an onslaught against the British power in Eastern Mediterranean, the Near and the Middle East.

Greece and her islands represented a strategic obstacle which had to be removed so as not to obstruct more important ventures. In the words of Turkish Foreign Minister, Saracoglu, Greece was thus "the most innocent state to fall a victim to unjust aggression."

Since 1934 Greece had been one of the four members of the Balkan Entente. With the elimination of Rumania, Turkey and Yugoslavia were the only other partners. The member states were under no obligation to assist one another in the event of aggression from a non-Balkan power. They were bound not to become parties to any movement directed against any other state of the Balkans. The Entente was conceived as a diplomatic instrument for preventing wars between the small nations themselves. It did not cover the more real danger to the Balkan peace on the part of outside aggressors. Had the Balkan states formed a union and pooled their separate potentials, they might have been in a stronger defensive position.

The Balkans became once again the scene of diplomatic contest between the great powers. Germany held the trump card of force, which she was ever ready to use in order to obtain a free passage for her troops south. The occupation of Rumania opened to her the way to the mouth of the Danube and to Rumanian oil. These were the only important oil wells of Europe, the geopoliticians in Berlin and Rome explained, and should be the common property of all European people, and no one had the right to monopolize them. The presence of German troops in Rumania was to be a guarantee that the oil was "safeguarded for Europe." Before the war the Rumanian wells produced about nine million tons of oil or slightly more than four per cent of the world output. Most of the oil area was held under private concessions, one-third Dutch-British, and the rest British, French, Belgian and American, with a share held by Rumanian nationals. Why the wells had not been made useless, even if only for some time, when the danger of their falling into the hands of the Axis was imminent, remains one of the many mysteries of this war.

Hungary proved herself to be most cooperative in facilitating the German drive to the Balkans. She shared with the Axis powers the hatred for the Slavs, and her postwar policy, bent on a territorial revision of the World War settlement, made her a natural ally of German and Italian revisionism. As early as 1923, the year of the Munich beer cellar putsch, her onetime premier Gömbös wanted to come to an understanding with Hitler. In 1927 another Hungarian premier, Count Bethlen, signed a military treaty with Mussolini, the first such treaty concluded by fascist Italy with a foreign state. Systematic opposition by Hungary to any comprehensive Danubian arrangement made her a willing instrument in the Rome-Berlin hands. Richly rewarded for her services at the partition of Czechoslovakia and Rumania, the Budapest Government was expected to reciprocate, and thus it placed itself in even greater indebtedness and dependence upon the Axis. On November 20, 1940, the Government signed the Berlin-Rome-Tokyo military pact. Hungary undertook to let the German armies use her territory and to adjust her economy to the Nazi pattern. Compared with Austria, Czechoslovakia, Poland, Rumania and all other Nazi-occupied countries, Hungary of today can probably claim to be the least dependent of the German dependencies, with the possible exception of Italy. Should Hitler's new order become permanent, however, she would fall into complete oblivion with the rest of the smaller nations.

On November 23 and 24 respectively the series of signatures of the Berlin-Rome-Tokyo Tripartite Pact was extended to include the puppet states of Rumania and Slovakia. The two countries were under German occupation or, as Rumanian Premier General Antonescu put it, stood "within the orbit of the brilliant military civilization." According to Ribbentrop, the purpose of the Tripartite Pact was to establish a just world order and its stabilization, "to offer a challenge to the warmongers and to those powers that stood for the expansion of the war, instead of peace, and to create an alliance directed to the speedy restoration of world peace." In reality, the aims pursued by the pact were those which the Germany of the ex-Kaiser had set out to reach in the World War, namely, world domination. Italy's part in the Nazi scheme of things was to take care of the conquest of a subsidiary empire in Africa, while Japan's mission was to cover the Asiatic continent. Eventually both Italy and Japan together with their conquests would serve German interests. Specifically the Tripartite Pact was directed against the Soviet Union, and even more against the United States. In the words of Virginio Gayda, American aid to China was an ostentatious challenge which it would be the role of Japan to handle. The incorporation of Hungary, Rumania and Slovakia within the orbit of the pact was intended to impress the Soviet Union, particularly should Moscow be found intractable.

Bulgaria came next on the list of Nazi expansion. Hitler endeavored for some time to impress on King Boris the opportuneness of taking action in order to realize the territorial claims against Greece, especially the outlet to the Aegean seacoast. The King shied from taking the risk of involving a small country "in the battle of giants." However, the revisionist feeling in Bulgaria ran high. Nazi influences penetrated into the economic, military and cultural life of the little nation to such an extent, that the problem was not how Bulgaria could bar Germany from using her as a step to the south, but how to meet the German demands without aggravating her relations with Turkey, Russia and the Balkan neighbors. There was an undercurrent of traditional Russian sympathy among Bulgarian peasants and laborers, and a latent resentment against Britain dating back to the Congress of Berlin and Versailles. German pressure was, however, the strongest factor in influencing the Bulgarian official course. The government introduced the anti-Jewish laws, permitted entry of large numbers of Nazi "tourists," curtailed pro-Russian and pro-Ally activities, and gave its neutrality a decidedly pro-Axis bias. The official denials of the reports of German preparations for crossing the country were in contrast with the warnings in the press that any resistance to the Germans would be useless and disastrous.

The preoccupation of Berlin diplomacy was now directed toward making certain that Turkey would not rise if German troops attacked Greece through Bulgaria. On February 17, four days before Field-Marshal List set up his headquarters in Sofia, the Bulgarian-Turkish declaration of non-aggression was signed. The two countries reaffirmed that they would abstain from mutual aggression. Confusing interpretations were given to this one more short-lived declaration, but it could not be doubted that it was the work of German diplomacy. On March 1, Bulgaria finally signed the Tripartite Pact "in view of the pressure of events and the changed situation around." Premier Filoff officially announced in the Sobranje that Germany had asked for and Bulgaria had agreed to the free passage of Nazi troops. He explained that the German government had not asked anything that would clash with Bulgarian peaceful policy or her true obligations to her neighbors, and promised that the country would refrain from any attack and from any measures that might threaten the interests of anyone. On March 3, the Bulgarian people celebrated the independence of their country. At the same time, German mechanized forces crossed Bulgaria and reached the Greek frontiers to administer a stab in the back of Greek independence.

Bulgaria, having been disposed of, the only remaining Balkan country which had not yet been brought to her knees was Yugoslavia. Militarily, the country was now surrounded on all sides by the Axis. The next step was to bring her to submission. In dealing with Yugoslavia the Germans used the same method as in the case of Czechoslovakia. Ever since their rise the Nazis and the Fascists had been working up discontent among the Croats and also among the Slovenes with a view of preventing a united Yugoslavia. There had always been a degree of tension between the constituent peoples of the kingdom which had its origin in the inequality of cultural development resulting from long political separation. The somewhat over-centralizing tendency of the Serbs tended to accentuate these differences. This tension was exploited to the utmost by the Nazi propagandists.

Like most other nations, the Yugoslavs desired to stay outside the war. Their policy during the years preceding the conflict was to keep aloof from the growing international entanglements. It was a diplomacy of passive defense which could be carried out as long as it was also profitable to the Axis. Officially Yugoslavia tried to be neutral, but stressed that hers was an armed non-belligerency. The fateful hour came when early in March the Germans extended an "offer" to the Belgrade government inviting it to adhere to the Tripartite Pact on somewhat qualified terms. Yugoslavia would receive guarantees of her frontiers and the Axis armies would refrain from crossing her territory. She would have to allow the free passage of German war material without any right of control. Moreover, she was asked to check all anti-Axis activities (the vast majority of the people sympathized with the democracies), to bring herself into harmony with the Reich's economy, i.e., to place her production of raw materials and foodstuffs under Nazi export supervision, and to demobilize the army. The Germans promised to take account of Yugoslav aspirations in Salonica at the expense of Greece. Previously Hitler suggested that Yugoslavia might even be compensated at the expense of Italy in Fiume, Istria, and northern Albania.

The shortest route to the Eastern Mediterranean follows the valley of the Morava and Vardar rivers through Yugoslavia. The seizure of the port of Salonica had been one of the aims of Austria-Hungary. It was to be expected that Hitler, in pursuance of the traditional Germanic policy of the Drang nach Osten, would try to occupy the port as a naval and air base against the British Mediterranean fleet. Taking Salonica from Greece and giving it to Yugoslavia and taking over the control of Yugoslavia as a

whole, was a plan which admirably suited Hitler's purpose and
fitted into his diplomatic strategy.

The Cvetkovich government, endeavoring to strike a bargain,
was willing to permit transit of German hospital trains and accept
Nazi economic supervision. It was reluctant to accept the other
terms, still clinging to the fiction of being somehow able to preserve neutrality. Whether Hitler agreed to these terms or not, no
doubt existed at Belgrade that he would enforce the passage of
troops as soon as found expedient. After the occupation of Bulgaria by the German troops early in March, Prince Paul finally
put his trust completely in German promises. Against the advice
of Prime Minister Cvetkovich, the army leaders, the Orthodox
Patriarch and many patriotic Serbs, he agreed to the signature.
This move had far-reaching reaction. It was so repugnant to
the people that it provoked a veritable revolution. On March
27 the Prince Regent was deposed as the result of a speedily
executed coup at night led by General Simovich. The seventeen-
year-old King Peter assumed the throne. The change was declared to be a matter of home policy. Yet the Germans knew very
well its true meaning. They immediately pressed for the ratification of the pact, demobilization of the army and an apology for
"maltreatment of German nationals." The new government without committing itself still tried to appease Hitler by any sacrifice
short of the loss of national independence and integrity. Yet they
had no other choice than to allow the inevitable to take its course.
The nation was mobilized for the worst. On April 6, 1941, Germany invaded both Yugoslavia and Greece, facing resistance. Had
the Belgrade Regency joined Greece at the start of Mussolini's
campaign in Albania, a course suggested by the military,
much valuable time might have been gained. With the Italians
driven out of Albania, the Greek and Yugoslav armies would
have been able to join hands and maintain themselves much
longer. As it happened, the Regency committed the same blunder

that had been committed by the other nations since the beginning of Hitler's march across the continent. With the Nazi machine of conquest at the high gear, isolation and neutrality by means of diplomatic bargaining was no longer an effective substitute for direct preventive military action.

The determination of the Yugoslavs to fight rather than to surrender was hailed by the democracies as an event which might give the war a different course. Exaggerated hopes were placed in the military potential of the defenders and in the ability of Great Britain to extricate her new ally from the precarious, if not hopeless, situation. It was recalled that in 1914 five million Serbs stood against fifty million Austro-Hungarians, keeping them at bay for fifteen months. It was overlooked that the strategic position of Yugoslavia was incomparably worse, and that the determined policy of Prince Paul to allow no military preparations that could give offense to the Germans made the country militarily weakened and politically confused. The Croat question was settled to some extent in August 1939 when the Croat leader Matchek assumed the newly created post of the vice-premier. But the Serbo-Croat understanding was not allowed sufficient time to give the country that perfect unity which it needed to deal firmly with the approaching Nazi assault. Although Matchek identified himself with the external and domestic policies of the new Simovich cabinet, his party would have gone to the extreme limits of cooperation with Germany. Like the majority of the Croats he refused, however, to join the Axis sponsored regime of Pavelitch, the Croat Quisling, and retired. Some of his aides escaped and joined the government in exile, others were put in jail.

The new order in the Balkans was inaugurated from the same formula from which the Axis propaganda had been uniformly brewed. Yugoslavia was partitioned in the same crude and arbitrary manner as Czechoslovakia and Rumania had been previously. Acting under the protection of German-Italian troops, Pavelitch, whom the French courts had condemned to death for the assassination of King Alexander at Marseilles in 1934, pro-claimed "the independent state of Croatia." Among the members of his cabinet are pro-Nazi leaders of the terrorist organization Ustashi as well as several fascists of the group called Frankovtsi. In accordance with an arrangement reached with Mussolini and Ciano in 1940, Croatia entered the Italian empire as a vassal state with the Duke of Spoleto as her King. Having taken up from where the incompetent Regency left off, Pavelitch contributed to the country's destruction. In addition to Croatia proper the new state incorporated the old provinces of Bosnia and Herzegovina. Rumania was the only neighbor which did not share in the spoils. Italy annexed all but three Adriatic islands, the whole of Dalmatia with the ancient city of Dubrovnik, Montenegro, the southern part of Slovenia and a slice of the hinterland of the Fiume harbor. Germany installed a governor at Belgrade to rule over Serbia, annexed the best part of Slovenia, inclusive of the province of Styria and a section of Carniola. She took over the iron works of Jesenice and the copper mines of Trepcha. Hungary, whose late Count Teleki signed a treaty with Yugoslavia in 1940 "to live in constant peace and perpetual friendship," seized the Vojvodina with the important towns Novi Sad and Subotica. The Bulgarians have taken the southern, Macedonian part of Serbia, with Skoplje, and a generous slice of eastern Serbia. In fact, Bulgaria has been raised by Germany to the status of the largest and the most influential state in the Balkans, a kind of counter-balance to Italy and Russia. Yet the Bulgarians seem to be asking for more. In addition to Thrace which they have taken from the Greeks they aspire to Salonica and to a section of Albania, both policed at present by Italy.

On the whole, Germany has taken some of the best agricultural and industrial regions, and since she does not regard the present distribution of the occupying forces as final, places such as Salonica may eventually drop in her lap. The next beneficiary, Hungary, increased her territory through the partition of Czechoslovakia,

Rumania and Yugoslavia by over eighty per cent and her population by three-fifths, to more than fourteen million. Since more than a third of these are Slavs, Rumanians or Germans, Hungary has thus become a more truly mixed state of nationalities than any post-Versailles country of Eastern Europe. Her acquisitions are largely agricultural regions. She is now an industrial country to the extent of only one-third of her economy instead of one-half as before her expansion. This is where Germany wants to have her. Italy satisfied most of her close-by historical ambitions, but economically her new territories are largely inferior, of low fertility and with a population half of which had been unable to earn its own living. The rich Banat basin of pre-World-War Hungary is held by the Germans. Finally, the map is not definitely fixed for each party entertains claims which the arch-spoiler, Germany, is willing to meet only so far as they do not interfere with her own war economy and do not preclude her from emerging in the end as the sole master over the whole peninsula.

The much-advertised inadequacies of Versailles were pale by comparison with the arbitrary way in which the people of Eastern Europe have been disposed of by the pretended creators of a juster world.

With the fall of Crete, all of Eastern Europe fell under direct domination of the Axis. Eastern Thrace, protecting the Turkish Straits along the European overland approach, is the only portion of the Balkans which has not yet been occupied when these lines are written. Factually, however, Turkey, in pursuance of a so-called realistic policy, has immobilized herself to such a degree that no diplomatic maneuvring will be sufficient to help her to escape from the grip of the Germans, once they feel that she stands in their way. The course Turkey has been steering through the vicissitudes of World War II is most instructive for the appreciation of the difficulties with which a small nation is beset in trying to escape the dangers of an armed conflict with a powerful foe. Temperamentally, the Turks are to a considerable degree pro-British, largely anti-Soviet, with an important element which sympathizes with Germany. In the last twenty years the Ankara government concluded alliances of various kinds with all neighbors in Europe and Asia. During the supremacy of the League the Turks supported collective security and were ready to practice it within the Balkan region. In October, 1939, they perfected their treaty of mutual assistance with France and Great Britain. After the fall of France in June, 1940, the government renounced the French alliance and stressed its status of non-belligerency. During the Italian campaign against Greece and later when the German threat of marching into the Balkans became ever more real, Turkish diplomacy was constantly reinterpretating its position. It denounced both Fascist war on its Greek ally and the Nazi march into Rumania. At one time southern Bulgaria was declared to lie within the Turkish security zone. The foreign minister stated in February 1941 that the country could not remain indifferent to foreign activities within the zone of security, and the official press wrote that Turkey would regard her security as being endangered if a non-Balkan power obtained a lodgment in the Balkans. The struggle of Greece was regarded by many Turks as their own struggle.

Even after the Rumanians were liquidated, efforts were made from Ankara to bring about a defensive alliance between Turkey, Greece, Yugoslavia and Bulgaria. As the war in the Balkans was reaching its peak, the "no-change" attitude in the foreign policy of the Republic was continually stressed and faithfulness to the British alliance reiterated. In reality, a change had already been occurring. Erstwhile a military ally of Great Britain, a nation which declared itself non-belligerent, but not neutral, had gradually passed into neutrality, until on June 18, 1941, four days before the German invasion of the Soviet Union, it signed a treaty of friendship with Germany by which it undertook to take no measure aimed directly or indirectly at the Reich. The treaty was to be non-prejudicial to the Turkish alliance with Britain, and while the Turkish press took a less outspoken tone in regard to the new German friend, no doubt was intended to be left as to the resistance which would meet any aggression against Turkish soil.

Summing up, the Turkish government has successively failed to give effect to the Treaty of Ankara with Britain. It also failed to take action in the Balkans, particularly when Greece was invaded, when by its verbal diplomacy the impression was given, intentionally or not, that it would act. The surrender of France changed the circumstances under which the British Treaty was signed, and Rumania's submission to Germany altered the picture in the Balkans as drawn up at the time of the Balkan Entente; the show of British forces in Eastern Mediterranean probably did not give the Turks full satisfaction. The uncertainty of the Soviet policy between 1939 and 1941 may have also directed them along the path of caution. Moreover, the technical equipment of the Turkish army leaves much to desire. It is remembered that out of a million and a half of Yugoslavs liable for mobilization only about one-third could be properly armed. The Turks could also make much of the argument that their staying out of war was more advantageous for Great Britain than precipitating a war in which they might succumb to superior forces. Only ample aid from abroad would prolong their capability of sustained resistance, aid which England has not been so far in a position to guarantee. Whatever exterior and domestic factors shaped Ankara's conduct, her maneuvring has been one of the most subtle diplomatic activities of recent years. The immediate future may prove its wisdom or its ultimate unfruitfulness.

Holy Crusade against Bolshevism

There had been numerous indications during the twenty-two months of the operation of the German-Soviet pact of non-aggression that the agreement was not a genuine expression of a harmony of interests. An eloquent testimony of the divergent

policies of the two armed Titans was furnished by the head of
the Soviet state planning commission in May 1941, when he said
that the Soviets had been keeping their powder dry and had continued to build up their defenses. All along the German-Russian
borders large armies had been maintained on both sides in watch-
ful readiness, and every move on the opposite flank had been
anxiously scrutinized. The divergence of policies was deep, basic,
and in the long run intractable. By signing the pact in 1939, at a
time when collective security seemed dead beyond revival, the
Soviets desired to remain out of the coming war and to prevent
its spread in the east. The Germans on the contrary condescended
to soliciting a treaty with "the scum of humanity" in order to be
better able to start the war and to carry it to whatever part of
Europe they deemed expedient. Both powers had been spending
vast sums on rearmament, with Germany far ahead. In the five
years preceding the outbreak of the war in 1939 Germany spent
25 to 30 billion dollars on military expenditures, i.e., twice as much
as the Soviet Union and six times as much as Great Britain. Yet of
all the non-Fascist states Russia was the only one which had the
foresight to build up systematically her military power to meet the
future thrust. Unlike the democracies she also made the year to
year sacrifices to divert a substantial portion of her income toward
the production of tools of defense. Her foreign policy was substantially that of peace. She armed for self-defense, labored for
collective security, and down to the outbreak of the war observed
all her international obligations, a line of conduct of which few
great powers could boast. Germany on the other hand armed for
the specific purpose of war and offence, fought collective security,
and made unilateral abrogation of international agreements a
principle of her policy. The two attitudes were so widely apart
that they could hardly be harmonized.

Apart from these ideological differences the German and Soviet
interests appeared to conflict almost the very day of their ad hoc
understanding over Poland. It is little relevant whether Stalin

had express or tacit approval from Hitler when he moved into the Baltic area, traditionally regarded as a German objective, or whether he undertook the series of repressive steps against Lithuania, Latvia, Estonia and Rumania, and the aggression against Finland, in disregard of Hitler's feeling and for the sole purpose of obtaining strategic bases when such could be secured at the least cost. To Germany Russian neutrality during the first phase of the war meant a good deal and she had to pay the price. Comparatively safe in the east the German High Command could drive with full vigor against the Low Countries and France in the west, while German war economy was benefiting from the continued supply of Russian resources. It was the Nazi activities in Central Europe and the Balkans, however, that stirred the apparently smooth surface of the Berlin-Moscow marriage of convenience.

In his speech delivered on the occasion of the new Winter Campaign in 1941, Hitler revealed four demands allegedly made by Commissar Molotov the previous year: free hand in Finland, Rumania and the Straits, and a Russian garrison in Bulgaria. Considering the long standing ambitions of German diplomacy in that area, and the gradual economic and military penetration which had been taking place there since Munich, the Russian demands were probably presented in a materially different form. What Molotov most likely demanded was that Germany stop expanding her control over those parts of Eastern Europe which constituted a kind of buffer territory between the two powers, a zone which it would be of mutual advantage to keep neutral. What actually went on was the old game of the balance of power: to create a preponderance of one's own power in order to outweigh the growing power of the potential rival.

In 1941 the signs of Russian displeasure became more frequent. The Kremlin made known its attitude through the official Tass agency in brief comments which often seemed to sound deliberately casual. On March 25, 1941, the Soviets assured Turkey that should she be attacked and forced into war in protection of her own territory, she might count on full understanding and neutrality on the part of the Moscow government. On April 1, "Pravda" denied that the Soviet government congratulated the new Yugoslav government, favoring resistance to foreign aggression, but added that such congratulations would have been in order. On April 6, a treaty of friendship with Yugoslavia was announced. On April 12, Vice-Commissar Vyshinski in a talk with the Hungarian Minister in Moscow disapproved of Hungary's invasion of Yugoslavia, "only four months after she had concluded with that country a pact of eternal friendship."

The tight-lipped Russian diplomacy of that period was responsible partly for the confusing theories which it rekindled both among friends and foes abroad as to its real intentions. Much of the foolish talk of "the Russian sphinx" would have been silenced had Moscow made her stand plain and had she stated her case in unmistakable language. Thus she would not have played into the hands of those who made no distinction between the Soviet and the Nazi foreign policy and who waited for every opportunity to switch the attention of the western nations from the real theater of war, i.e., democracy versus Nazism, to the wishful dreaming of a gigantic battle of self-annihilation between Nazism and Communism while democracy could inactively wait and see. The Russian "enigma" could be explained, if not entirely justified, by the self-imposed restraint to say or do nothing that could give the Germans ground for complaints as regards observance of the pact. We know from Foreign Secretary Eden that "in every phase the developments of Anglo-Soviet relations were always retarded by the attention paid by the Soviet Union to the observance of their pact with Germany." "The Soviet government were not prepared to negotiate in view of their anxiety not to introduce any embarrassment into their relations with Germany." Numerous pieces of evidence could be produced in support of this. The Soviets accepted all Nazi conquests and were anxious to develop their trade relations with the Reich and the conquered territories. Reversing their earlier policy they withdrew diplomatic recognition from Czechoslovakia, and other German occupied nations such as Norway, Belgium, Yugoslavia and Greece. Molotov could point out that "during the operation of the pact Germany had presented no claims to the Soviet Union."

In the end the Russian attempts to appease Hitler were bound to fail as did the earlier appeasements by the democracies. On June 22, 1941, Hitler ordered the drive on Moscow. Four days earlier a German-Turkish neutrality pact was signed, and on the same day Finland called her men to colors. Turkey and Finland represented the southern and the northern extremity of the line dividing the Eurasian continent from German occupied Europe. Not until Hitler was assured that Turkey could be relied upon not to interfere and that Finland would march together did he embark on his most adventurous enterprise so far of knocking out of his path a country covering eight million square miles, one-sixth of the earth, and having a population of two hundred million.

Numerous explanations have been advanced as to the reasons why Hitler chose to attack Russia at that particular moment: to seize the oil of the Caucasus, reach the Iran oil through Russia and thus outflank the British in the Middle East, to replenish his reserves of agricultural provisions from the Ukraine, to make the Greater Reich a more perfect and a more self-sufficient economic unit, to eliminate Russian military strength prior to final attack against Great Britain, to achieve a grand continental victory and then propose peace to England on the basis of the status quo for the British Empire, or, to quote a German thesis, to prevent the Russians from attacking first. Hitler is a gambler for great stakes and in starting the Russian campaign he certainly meant to play a big game.

In the Nazi interpretation of the motives given after the invasion was already in progress, Germany had lived up strictly to

the pact, but the Russians had not. They had attacked Finland,
encouraged the Yugoslavs, stirred up the Czechs, and generally
indulged in systematic acts of sabotage. They had violated the
pact of friendship in deed and in spirit. Both Hitler and Ribbentrop took great pains to stress the point that the Russians had
carried on subversive activities against the Reich, massed their
troops along the borders, and were preparing to attack. According to the Nazis theirs was a war of defense and a struggle "to
save the entire civilized world."

In reviewing the progress of the fifteen weeks long Soviet war
Hitler attempted once again on October 2, 1941, to build up the
atmosphere of a divine mission over the bodies of millions of men
who lay dead in the Russian plains. He admitted that his pact
with Stalin was only a stratagem the signature of which caused
him the deepest humiliation in all his life and that a surprise
invasion of Russia was left to him as the only weapon. Had he
ever hoped that the sudden assumption of the holy crusade against
the Soviet infidels would win for the German cause the favor of
many groups in England and America, such as churches, conservatives and business, he must have become aware that this
time the old trick did not work. This time the democracies and
their allies avoided the mistake of allowing their ideological and
class differences to prevail over their vital interests and they backed
up the Soviet resistance with financial, technical and military assistance. To the majority of common people throughout the continents the Soviet war became the people's war and the battles
for Russian cities, harbors, rivers and factories became the world's
battles. On July 12 the text of the Anglo-Soviet pact was made
public providing for mutual support of all kinds in the present
war and barring the conclusion of separate armistice or peace
without mutual agreement. On July 18 an agreement of mutual
assistance with the Czechoslovak government in London was
signed by which the Soviets returned to their original attitude of
non-recognition of German conquest and consented to the forma-

tion of Czechoslovak military units on their territory. Similar agreement was reached with the Polish government in exile on July 30. The Soviet government did not expressly renounce all the territories taken away from Poland in 1939, but recognized the Soviet-German treaties of that year covering territorial changes in Poland as having lost their validity. The way was thus opened for Soviet-Polish collaboration in the war and for fixing the boundary on the basis of a mutually acceptable settlement. The loan of one billion dollars which the government of the United States pledged the Soviets on November 7, 1941, within the lend-lease program of assisting the nations resisting aggression, united America with Russia in so far as the conduct of the war was concerned. The loan was to be repaid without interest in ten years, the payments to start five years after the termination of the war. The lend-lease program was also extended to include Poland, Czechoslovakia and Turkey, whose resistance was declared by President Roosevelt to be vital to the interests of the United States. This move was expected to swing Ankara definitely to the British side.

The Kremlin answered the challenge of the holy crusade with habitual brevity and characteristic frankness. When German Ambassador von der Schulenburg called at the People's Commissariat of Foreign Affairs at 5:30 in the morning of June 22, 1941, i.e., one hour and a half after the invasion was in full swing and had taken a toll of two hundred persons, Molotov inquired as to the reason of the undeclared war. He was told that the German government had decided to launch war in connection with the concentration of Red Army units near eastern German borders. Molotov stated that until the very last moment the German government had not presented any claims or complaints to the Soviets, that at no point had the Red Army or air force committed a violation of the frontier, and charged Germany as aggressor. In a broadcast on the same day he branded the attack as "perfidy unparalleled in the history of civilized nations." Otherwise neither Berlin nor Moscow had revealed whether any concrete demands had been made at

the very last moment and if so what was their nature. Stalin
ignored the point in his "scorched earth" speech of July 3, in
which he tried to justify the conclusion of the pact with Hitler
twenty-two months earlier. "It may be asked," said he, "how could
the Soviet Government have consented to conclude a non-aggression pact with such treacherous fiends as Hitler and Ribbentrop?
Was it not an error on our part? Of course not. No peace-loving
state could decline a peace treaty with a neighboring state even
though the latter was headed by such fiends and cannibals as
Hitler and Ribbentrop, provided that treaty did not infringe on
the territorial integrity, independence and honor of the peace-
loving state. By concluding the pact we gained for our country
peace for a year and a half and the opportunity of preparing our
forces to repulse Fascist Germany should she risk an attack on
our country despite the pact."

Understandable as it was, Stalin's argumentation in so far as
it related to the appeasement policy could hardly be more con-
vincing than the reasoning by the democracies in the earlier era
of appeasements. Appeasement as a method of solving international difficulties could be justified if it proceeded in the spirit
suggested by analogous terms of conciliation, or to use the German
word, Versöhnung. Such a procedure would imply reciprocity of
good will, mutuality of gains and losses, and bilateral acceptance
of temporary disadvantages for the sake of paving the way for
the attainment of more permanent general benefits in the future.
Neither the democratic-Nazi appeasement nor the Soviet-Nazi
appeasement belonged to that category. To some extent Stalin
could rightly point out that it was the behavior of the democracies
in the crises of Manchuria, Ethiopia, China, Spain, Austria and
Czechoslovakia that pushed him on to the road of dealing with
Hitler. For all that, Hitler was not a bona fide party to any
genuine conciliation. Appeasements were to him nothing more
than a technique of dividing his potential foes and watching them
being battered one at a time, a temporary expedient to score an

advantage over the world he was bent on conquering. His was a long-planned strategy, a total war the true nature of which has only gradually become more familiar to his opponents, a grand design transcending established notions and rendered no less effective by its underlying evilness and improbity. Nothing could better meet his plans than to create situations in which one of his potential rivals would be stalemated into immunity while the other was being subjected to an ordeal. Such were the circumstances of all his victories. The case of the Soviet Union was not different. It could barely escape the notice of the managers of the Nazi war enterprise that the shortest way from England to the Russian White Sea was nearly two thousand miles, while the route from "the arsenal of democracies" between San Francisco and Moscow covered more than ten thousand miles.

Consequently "the holy crusade against bolshevism" was bound to proceed, at least during its initial phase, according to the Nazi schedule, even though the dogged Russian resistance was responsible for Hitler's confessed mistake of underrating his formidable enemy. No one knew for certain in how many weeks or months Hitler supposed he could liquidate the Red Army. This much is certain, however, that after half a year of the campaign he found himself in a grave predicament. German troops had been seizing Russian cities and occupied more territory than the ex-Kaiser's armies controlled in the spring of 1918. But the Soviet army was anything but defeated and behind the deadly defense lines of the Soviet Union could be found almost inexhaustible reservoirs of fresh man power. The war passed to the stage of a war of reserves, characteristic of total warfare. With the arrival of winter the Red Army stopped Hitler's war machine and turned it back. At the same time it became increasingly evident that the final outcome of the Russo-German struggle would depend to no small a degree on the amount of material Great Britain and the United States could add to the domestic Soviet output.

Great Britain and the United States were not slow to realize the unique significance of the Soviet front and the perils that would result should Russia be incapacitated or militarily, economically or morally paralyzed. Even the optimists among the experts admitted that while such an eventuality would not necessarily mean the fall of Great Britain, it would make it incomparably harder to beat Hitler. In any case the war would go into more years and would necessitate even greater efforts on the part of the British Empire and a more effective assistance, including unlimited manpower, from the United States and the Western hemisphere.

Axis Junior Partners

It would seem reasonable to assume that after having subdued all the smaller nations of Eastern Europe, the Germans would give them a measure of freedom which would enable them to adapt themselves to the new political circumstances. It would also seem obvious that any such reconciliation would be facilitated by allowing the conquered peoples to develop their cultural traditions and retain the essential attributes of human dignity. Common reason would seem to dictate such an attitude from any conqueror. Yet reason, self-restraint, magnanimity, moderation, regard for and understanding of other peoples' rights, needs, and psychology are not the qualities recommended in the Nazi primer. The submerged nations are evaluated only in terms of the amount of grain, oil or manual labor their territories can contribute quickly to the successful prosecution of the war at present and to the fulness of their masters' life afterwards. The individual, spiritual element comes up for consideration only as a negative and subversive phenomenon to form the object and the justification of systematic punitive measures and purges intended to intimidate and terrorize the victims and render them impotent. Lebensraum means to the Nazis the Todesraum of the Poles, Czechs, Serbs and all other peoples who happen to be in their way. This is the underlying concept of the simplified Weltanschauung, the way of looking at things through Nazi eyes. Underneath the singleness of this ultimate purpose differences can be noticed both in the hierarchical arrangement of the conquered lands and in the technique of execution. The screw is not applied equally but varies from one people to another. Sometimes persuasion combined with pressure is regarded as sufficient to insure compliance whereas in other instances no attempts at peaceful inducement are made and prostration is produced by ruthless subjection. Bulgaria, Hungary and Rumania were manipulated into submission by economic and cultural penetration and flattering promises of aggrandizement. The Poles, Greeks and Yugoslavs were conquered by overwhelming military force. With regard to the Slovaks and Croats their nascent nationalism had been taken advantage of for the disruption of the states whose unity and strength was a thorn in the German eyes. Local Quislings, Nazified minorities and individuals who counted on Hitler's support of their privileges assisted in the process. Austria was an example of an inside job. To some extent the case of Czechoslovakia was similar, although it was principally the decision of the great democratic powers to offer that country as a lamb at the altar of appeasement that brought about its end. The Baltic states were wrested from the Soviet Union by force. Finland's resentment of the Russian aggression in 1939 and the desire to reconquer the lost fringes of territory, coupled with the anti-Russian and particularly the anti-Soviet bias of the conservative class, made that democratic country an ally of Nazi Germany.

The presence of the Finns among the small nations whom Hitler's diplomacy succeeded in using for the holy crusade against bolshevism was not without strategic importance. They could cut the railway from Leningrad to Murmansk, the only ice-free port for receiving British and American supplies. They also facilitated German operations on the left flank of the two thousand mile long front. Whether Germany actually forced Finland into the war and on what terms will no doubt be revealed in due course. As everywhere else the Germans could not resist the temptation to use the local nationalists and fascists as a shield for conquests. The idea of the "Greater Finland" comprising Russian Karelia, some purely Russian sectors around Leningrad and the northern part of both Sweden and Norway had been freely propagated by the banned anti-socialist and fascist Lapua, operating under the name of the Patriotic People's Movement. This movement dwindled to only six seats in the Finnish parliament out of two hundred and it is unlikely that any large section of the population would endorse its expansionist program. Most Finns desired close collaboration with the Scandinavian nations, but for strategic reasons they might wish to enlarge their territory at Soviet expense. Opposition might come from the Social Democrats, including also certain numbers of workers and landless peasants sympathetic to communism. The leftist front had behind it more than two-fifths of the electorate, and it was this element which after the termination of the Russo-Finnish war in the spring of 1940 worked for an understanding with the Soviet Union.

The German penetration into Finland was made easier for economic reasons. When the blockade cut off the country from Great Britain and overseas markets, Russia and the Scandinavian nations were unable to absorb its exports. Germany could. Difficult as the international position had thus become, it would nevertheless be correct to assume, until sufficient evidence be supplied to the contrary, that the Finnish government was its own free agent when it decided to fight the Soviets alongside and with direct assistance of Germany. Should Hitler win, Finland would probably be built up into an important vassal state in the north of Germanic Europe. Should Germany be defeated, the Finns would regain their freedom, as they did in 1918, thanks chiefly to the democratic powers. The main problem of the Finnish foreign policy, i.e., relations with the Soviet Union, would still require proper attention. Given a durable settlement with Russia, Finland could be counted upon again as a small power supporting international cooperation. It might be remembered that it was Finland which furnished the League of Nations with its first and the last important items of agenda, the Aland Island dispute and the war with the Soviet Union.

Of all the junior partners of the Anti-Komintern pact the Rumanians must have been the most baffled people upon seeing themselves aligned alongside the Magyars and the Germans in the "Christian crusade against the bolshevik menace to Europe." As a farming community they were never communists and there was little need for fear that they might become ones. The wave of communism in 1917 and in the subsequent years stopped before the gates of Rumania whose peasant armies returned home to cultivate the holdings bestowed upon them by the radical land reform laws. The clue to the understanding of the anomalous position the country has found itself in the present war can be obtained by drawing a line between its rulers and the masses, a distinction which in the complex case of Rumania is as important to make as in most other Eastern European lands. King Carol undoubtedly cherished the ambition to unite his country behind the throne. Yet by making constant concessions in foreign matters and by trying to save his personal position at home he arrived at quite the opposite result. The methods he used led not to unification but to isolation of the masses from the throne. Long before he committed himself to cooperation with the Axis in July 1940, he estranged the democratic element, numerically the strongest, though by no means united and capable of action. His totalitarian personal régime, intended to cement the country's unity in the throes of the fourfold thrust from outside, i.e., from Russia, Hungary, Germany and Bulgaria, in reality paved the way for the inflow of Nazi penetration until the country became a virtual protectorate of Berlin. The economic absorption in March 1939 led gradually to military occupation and ended in political subjection.

The geographic fact that Rumania held the mouth of the

Danube and the oilfields was bound to attract the Nazi "guardians of the oil deposits," the military mission and the increasing numbers of "German tourists." Officially Rumania joined the Axis on November 23, 1940, but actually she was sold to it long before that date. Carol's critics, such as Maniu and Bratianu, contested his right to make territorial concessions and recommended resistance if only to upset the timetable of the aggressors. They pointed out that the country had two million soldiers and that resistance rather than concessions would unite the people for come-what-may, disregarding the most immediate consequences of the clash. Whatever merits such a course had, the fact was that the country eventually landed on the side of the strongest and the most insistent power in the hope that collaboration with Germany would save her from utter ruin.

General Antonescu, appointed shortly before Carol's abdication, became the Fuehrer, with the fascist Iron Guard as his chief support. The change toward unreserved collaboration with Germany was by no means popular. It plunged Rumania into a civil war, caused the resignation of thirty high officers and widespread murders of men like Iorga, Madgearu and Argeseanu. The masses, largely inarticulate and uninitiated in the doings of the government, were as bewildered as they were apathetic.

Much of Hitler's success in dealing with his weaker neighbors was due to his insistence on making his own choice of persons with whom he could "collaborate." The collaborative, or "reasonable" elements, as the Nazi Press referred to them, were recruited principally from among the anti-liberals, outright fascists, Jew-baiters, disgruntled oppositionists, long flattered ambitionists, or weaklings. Equally helpful to him was the practice of the Byzantine diplomacy of playing off his rival victims against each other and thus making himself constantly useful in squaring their differences. By raising passions of both Rumanians and Magyars over Transylvania he eventually brought them both under his thumb, and in the end settled the issue in a manner that was most bene-

ficial to himself. Several weeks before the aggression against
Russia Berlin diplomacy promised Antonescu the restoration of
Bessarabia and Bucovina for participation in the Soviet war.
Moreover, more or less veiled promises had been made ever since
the Vienna award in 1940 of restoring to Rumania a part of
Transylvania. This last plan, if it were ever meant in sincerity,
was frustrated when Hungary declared her eagerness of participating in the crusade. Eventually both the Magyars and the
Rumanians found themselves shoulder to shoulder fighting the
largely imaginary menace of bolshevism in the service of their
master.

The case of the Magyars was much simpler, however, than that
of the Rumanians, and more logical. They were indebted to the
Axis for having nearly doubled the size of their country, and for
having conferred upon them the mission of checking the Slavs
in the Danubian basin. Although the Budapest government did
not receive back all it expected—Transylvania was to be shared
with Rumania, and Italy retained Fiume, the only possible Hungarian outlet to the Adriatic Sea—the direct price it paid for what
it did receive did not involve its manpower. A long standing
agreement existed, however, between the German and Hungarian
High Commands providing for full military assistance should
Germany become engaged in war with Russia. In fact, the Hungarian army took a not unimportant part in the German drive
against Yugoslavia in the spring of 1941. Hitler recognized this
service on May 4, when he stressed that he had been able to attack
Yugoslavia all the more calmly as he could rely on the constant
and immutable fidelity of Hungary and Bulgaria. Without Hungary, said he, "it would have been very difficult indeed to carry
out the orders in the short time at our disposal." Apart from the
ideological and class antagonism of the governing caste in Hungary towards the Russians the only territorial consideration that
might justify its part in the crusade was the ultimate fate of the
Slav inhabited province of Ruthenia, which the Magyars seized

from Czechoslovakia in March 1939. The Soviets never made claim to it but the Magyars might have felt that a German defeat would inevitably result in its separation, an eventuality they hoped to prevent from happening.

For the last twenty years, in fact since the Compromise of 1867, the Hungarian ruling class has clung to the formula that the future of Hungary was bound up with the closest collaboration with Germany. Italy was added when Mussolini inaugurated his revisionist policy preliminary to forging the Axis. At the beginning it was only a minority of Magyars that became infatuated with the Nazi doctrine. The Arrow-Cross, the Magyar version of nationalistic extremism, had been split into as many groups as there were would-be leaders, each of whom drew heavily on moral and financial support from the headquarters of the Nazi international. The majority of people did not take them with sufficient seriousness, and the ruling classes, a few thousand families, were too much absorbed in their positions and inherited privileges to allow a popular anti-Nazi movement to crystallize. The country was in any case politically unprepared for such a task. Under the existing oligarchy the political rise of the masses was unthinkable and inadmissible, and every attempt to break through the thousand year bondage was stifled in its origin. While the old clan was inertly sitting on its benches the Arrow Cross grew into a more coherent body which no one dared oppose. Younger army officers supported the Nazi course and those in the government party let things go provided no injury was done to their clan interests. Magyar patriotism of the two decades between the wars was channeled into the one and all-pervading theme of revisionism by which the ruling party hoped to maintain itself in power. In order to recover the Saint Stephen frontiers the protagonists of revision would confessedly join hands even if it were a devil. Only too late did some of the more discriminating among them realize that the country's very freedom might perish in the process. The Russian diversion was only the latest exterior expression of this inner latent confusion. No doubt that the fall of France and the resulting loss of faith in the ability of Great Britain to defeat Hitler clinched the decision of Budapest to make the German alliance a hundred per cent one. The governments of Finland, Rumania and Yugoslavia were similarly influenced when the moment of resolution presented itself. Once again the gap made itself felt in the intricate fabric of Europe that was left by the eclipse of France as a power.

The Slovak participation in the German attack on Russia was ill-fated from the very start. Considerable numbers of soldiers sent to the Russian front were reported to have deserted to the enemy and the rest were soon withdrawn. The reason as officially given was inadequate preparation for technical warfare. While this may have been true, the more probable motive was the unwillingness of the Slovaks to fight with sufficient fervor for a cause that was not their own. There was indeed little Germany could promise them in the way of territorial acquisitions without antagonizing the Magyars. At the beginning of the invasion of the Soviet Union the German governor of the Gouvernment-General also appealed to the Poles to join "the defense of Christian Europe against the arch-enemy of Christianity and western civilization." As a reward the creation of a larger Polish state, under German protection, to include parts of the newly conquered Russian territories was hinted. The appeal found little response. No attempt was made to enlist the Czechs or the Yugoslavs for obvious reasons. The Bulgarian government was reported in August 1941 to have promised Admiral Raeder to participate in German military operations against any nation other than the Soviet Union.

Ever since World War I Berlin had offered hospitality to the Ukrainian nationalists who under the leadership of Hetman Skoropadski carried on propaganda for the establishment, under German tutelage, of an independent Ukrainian state. This would include the Soviet Ukraine, Eastern Galicia (since 1918 under Polish rule), and Subcarpathian Russia (Ruthenia), an autonomous part of Czechoslovakia. Considerable interest was therefore attached to the possibility that on the outbreak of the German-Soviet war Ukrainian troops would make their appearance, or that Ukrainian regiments would be formed on the territories of Poland and Russia as the German panzer divisions rolled eastwards. No evidence has so far been furnished of this occurring. The Ukrainians were somewhat better treated than the Poles and were encouraged to consider themselves as German protégés. With regard to their political status, however, no definite plan so far emerged from the otherwise prolific Nazi laboratory. On the contrary, the incorporation of Eastern Galicia, inhabited by six and a half million people, half of whom are of Ukrainian nationality, within the General Government of Poland would indicate that German policy towards the Ukrainian design changed, or reached a temporary halt. The districts of Lvov, Stanislav and Tarnopol have always been considered by the Ukrainian nationalists as the most natural part of the future state. The official explanation attributed the step to reasons of administration and supply of foodstuffs. The real cause most probably lay in lack of enthusiasm among the "liberated" peasants for the long heralded venture.

Thus of the six junior partners of the Axis in Eastern Europe only the Finns, Rumanians and Magyars were actively engaged on the German side when on November 25, 1941, the Anti-Komintern Pact, concluded five years earlier, was being extended for another five years. The Foreign Ministers of Bulgaria, Croatia and Slovakia attended the meeting on behalf of the countries, all of them incidentally under German and partly Italian military occupation, which undertook to fight bolshevism wherever it was found. All but Hungary were newcomers to the Anti-Komintern Pact, and all but Finland had already been the junior members of the Tripartite Pact between Germany, Italy and Japan, signed on November 20, 1941.

The exact distinction between these two diplomatic documents had never been officially drawn. It is assumed that while the

Tripartite Pact binds its signatories to specific military and other duties under specific circumstances, the Anti-Komintern Pact serves the purpose of aligning nations of identical ideological pursuits. This time attention of the member states was turned by Ribbentrop to eradicate germ cells of bolshevism whenever they could be combatted. Since in most member states communists had been subjected to capital punishment, it was understood that the only tangible purpose of the Pact could be (1) keeping the members immune from bolshevik propaganda and (2) concert on common activities against its spread. Ideological pacts are rarely concluded for abstract purposes, however. They always have a material motivation and as a rule are the prelude and the pretext for foreign military interventions. The near future should demonstrate whether this particular pact was only an innocent gesture for want of something more substantial, or whether it was the signal to more action in hitherto unaffected areas. Ribbentrop's introductory remarks may have meant both. "Ignoring the real danger to themselves," said he, "the western democracies, out of pure egoism and opportunism, have made common cause with Communists, and thereby have become assistants to world Communism." The following countries have so far signed the Tripartite Pact: Germany, Italy, Japan, Hungary, Manchukuo, Rumania, Bulgaria, Slovakia and Croatia. In addition to these countries the Anti-Komintern Pact bears the signatures of Finland, Denmark, Spain and Nanking-China.

Inside the Living Space

Four hundred years ago Machiavelli wrote the classic precept of how to behave in a conquered territory. He advised that the conquered country be turned into a colony, and that, if expediency warranted it, the native population should be exterminated. The Prince-conqueror should particularly get rid of those classes of population who had suffered through the conquest and of those who had previously held important offices. If a subjugated city revolted it was better to destroy it completely, for otherwise it might destroy the conqueror. The Romans had to destroy Carthage first in order to keep her. The Nazi conquerors took to heart most of the evil advices of the Florentine writer. They overlooked that the same "realist" gave also some very excellent counsels of prudence. In particular they ignored the warning that there is no better fortress for the Prince than the affection of his subjects. If he is hated by his people all other fortresses will be in vain.

Following the maxim that enemies are harmless when dead the Gestapo rounded up all "unreasonable" elements as soon as the invading army took possession of the strategic points. Various figures have been issued from time to time of the extent of the violent deaths inflicted on the victims of what has become one of the most terrorizing man-hunts in history. The exact numbers will not be known until the world has returned to normal. It will then be shown that the proportion of the so-called preventive and exemplary executions far exceeded the death sentences passed for the offenses actually or allegedly committed. It will also become evident that by far the greatest number of "liquidations" occurred during two periods. The first followed immediately upon each conquest, and the second coincided with the culmination of the process of the Nazification of the High Command. The process was consummated during the first half year of the campaign in Russia. Dissatisfied with the slowing-down production and the rising revolutionary spirit in the occupied countries, the High Command gradually assumed control not only of the whole economic system but also of the entire state machinery. Shooting of proven and suspected saboteurs and potential revolutionaries became a daily routine and was carried out with mechanical precision by the order of the High Command without regard to any political or extenuating circumstances. If during the Himmler era the Gestapo was left to attend to the dirty work of "pacifying" the civilian population, in order that the army might enjoy the reputation of clean, correct and friendly conduct, during the second phase no such pretense was made and the generals ordered brutal extermination of civilians whenever they thought it militarily expedient. The chief executor of their will was Reinhard Heydrich, Himmler's deputy in the office of the Chief of Political Police. An expert in the "science" of detecting and eradicating nascent revolts, Heydrich filled before the war the post of the president of the International Criminal Commission. In October 1941 he replaced Baron von Neurath as Reich Protector of Bohemia and Moravia. The shooting of hostages for crimes committed by others was the work of the generals determined to quell public discontent by the wholesale display of acts of terror. The sooner the legend is dispelled that the Prussianized army can be used for rebuilding civilized contacts with postwar Germany, the better for political sanity.

The nationalistic extremists among the Eastern Europeans also received their dose of surprise. Having taken the National Socialist propaganda at its face value many of them believed that Hitler was really going to found a new order on the basis of loyal and inspiring co-existence and collaboration between strong and independent nationalisms, cleansed of all leftist, impure and fraternizing influences. Too late did they realize that by its very nature National Socialism was an exclusive affair, opposed to tolerance as an element of weakness, and basically inimical to any multinational partnerships. Under the pretense of likemindedness the Nazi spies and their agents forced themselves upon the misled sympathizers in order to undermine their solidarity and purge their ranks. In the end only a very few collaborationists managed to maintain themselves and to soar to better positions at the price of facing the contempt of the vast majority of their countrymen.

One of the noteworthy aspects of the German "eastern space policy" is the fact that the great concentration of efforts demanded by the continued warfare did not diminish the zeal to organize the conquered territories on a footing of permanency. The conquests had been prepared so thoroughly that the short term objectives of the war period are attended to in such a manner as to fit into the long term policies after the war. There is a good deal of improvization in many respects, but the ultimate goal is never lost sight of and is pursued with singular clarity of purpose and resoluteness. One of the things most difficult to eradicate from the German mind is the master race complex. It is from this complex that the Germans, particularly Prussians, derive the claim to rule the other peoples and to make the Eastern Europeans work for their benefit. This self-assumed attitude of superiority, which many students of German national psychology explain merely as an inferiority complex seeking escape through self-assertion, is the greatest bar to the establishment of reasonably tolerable relationships between the Germanic and the non-Germanic world. So long as it persists Europe, and particularly Eastern Europe, will stay exposed to the restless state of affairs which has been its curse for many past decades, if not centuries.

It is by the example of the Czechs, Poles and the Baltic peoples that the Nazi rule and its effect can be most conveniently illustrated in concrete terms. The changes which have been wrought in the face of the eastern area can be observed from three aspects: political, economic and cultural. Thousands of experts and pseudo-experts are engaged in dovetailing these three activities to make them cumulatively more effective. The world has not yet seen a more elaborate machine for the gradual suppression of whole nations combining fifty million inhabitants. Relentless tempo in creating accomplished facts of permanent subjection marks the process of the total conquest with which hardly any previous occupation known to history can compare.

Politically the Czechs, Poles and the Baltic nations were annexed to the Reich with which they are to form the nucleus, "as hard as steel," of the new German empire, free from all alien elements. Austria had already been incorporated in this "core of steel." The builders of future Germany are chiefly concerned with material technical organization, not worrying about the human factors.

Strategic raw materials, rivers, mountain ranges, industrial centers, etc., are the things that count. In order to make this core exclusively Germanic the Slavs, particularly the Czechs, must get out of Central Europe, partly through dispersion, partly through accelerated Germanization, and partly through outright ejection. "As long as the Czechs remain they will always be a center of Hussite-bolshevik disintegration." The Slavs are told by the Nazi geopoliticians that they had invaded the German space and as undesirable tenants they are subject to the law of eviction. According to Hitler, as quoted by Rauschning, the Reich must not be afraid of unmaking the results of a historical process of fifteen hundred years and to sacrifice the blood of two to three million young Germans to build an empire to last for all time.

Germanization takes two forms. One consists of giving the annexed cities the exterior appearance of old Germanic possessions by means of filling them with German troops, pioneer settlements, staffs of exploiters, imported school children, institutions of various kinds, and by introducing German as the predominant language. The other method follows Hitler's thesis that the only true and effective way of assimilating alien people is through the Germanization of their land and withdrawing from them the economic sustenance of their growth. Publicly owned properties were automatically transferred to the Reich. With regard to private property the technique of the Aryanization was enforced whereby the Jewish owned undertakings were subject to transfer to Aryan hands when one non-Aryan was on the board. The German bidders from the Reich had preference over Czechs and vast properties representing the key industries fell thus within the provisions of legalized plunder. Since in Eastern Europe banks acted as promoters of industry the transfer was made even easier by seizing control over the whole banking system. By resuming the Bismarckian colonizing policy the Nazis began to establish new settlements in strategically situated areas creating zones of Germanic population around cities and in border areas which cut across purely Slav districts.

To give an example of the progress made so far in this systematic extermination of the Czechs and Poles, a few figures are available from a recent account made by the Gauleiter of the Warthegau province, formerly Polish: During the first nine months of 1941 3,116,000 hectares of arable land were taken from the Poles out of the total of 3,900,000. The seizure involved 337,192 farms and estates on which 50,000 German families with 200,000 members were settled. Of the 15,000 business concerns before the war all but 2,000 were permitted to remain in Polish hands. The seizure included large industrial enterprises as well as small artisan workshops, 2,000 of which had been reserved for German soldiers coming home after the war. In the same period 40,000 sentences had been passed on Poles inclusive of 2,000 given by the special "people's courts" which usually inflict the death penalty. The inhabitants of the conquered lands are to be shorn of the industrial structure and reduced to the serving class of wage earners that need not be reckoned with.

In respect of culture the Czechs, Poles and the Baltic peoples are subject to the process of forced de-education. In the Fuehrer's words they are being given the blessings of illiteracy. Institutions of secondary and higher learning were closed, the intellectuals purged, and youth turned into forced laborers. Never should they again rise to reverse their lot. "When nothing can be changed," explained Dr. Goebbels, himself manifold holder of various academic doctorates, to a group of Czech workers during a conducted visit to Berlin in September 1940, "then the existing state of affairs must be accepted willingly or not." And in the true inquisitorial tradition he wanted their "inner and unreserved submission without leaving open any doors, not even in the most secret recess of their hearts." The native population is thus being converted to the status of aliens in their own home and Hitler did not hesitate to call them "the modern slave class." They are at the very bottom of the Nazi social pyramid. Above them will be the anonymous mass of perpetually disfranchized population with no political or cultural importance, kept in line by the middle class of party members, who in turn will be led by the Nazi élite, a military class, created through battles, the only people who will obtain high education in leadership. It is easy to imagine them like the old Prussian Junkers, restored to full glory and bossing the new empire in the old strict tradition. The Junker class has probably been substantially weakened during the nine years of Nazi rule. The Hitler élite will take its place.

Administratively the Czech Bohemia and Moravia were constituted as the Reich Protectorate. The local Czech government with a Staatspresident at its head has no political authority, its only usefulness being that it acts as intermediary between the Nazis and the hostile Czech population. Its supreme task is to impress on the Czechs the immutability of their fate, to re-educate them according to the new status, and to see that they do not indulge in politics but work and keep their mouths shut. On October 2, 1941, Alois Eliáš, the Premier of the government, was condemned to death on charges of high treason. The Protectorate's laws have been gradually replaced or supplemented by the Reich laws, and in every office and community Nazi overseers exercise the real authority. Eight million Czechs were placed in the status of secondary citizens of the Greater Reich, and no exact figure can yet be given of the growing numbers of those who were shot, deported, uprooted or otherwise mishandled, except that it is large and rises continually.

Of the former Polish state twelve million people were annexed to the Reich of whom more than eleven million were Poles, and less than a million were Germans. About ten millions, of whom more than a half were Ukrainians and White Russians, went to the Soviet Union at the time of the partition. The rest of the country, with ten to eleven million inhabitants, was constituted as the Polish Government General with Warsaw as its capital. This rump state was given a German governor general, and it was stated that its future status would be that of an autonomous state under the Reich's supervision. However, in less than a year, on August 15, 1940, governor Hans Frank declared that "the Government General should be regarded not as an occupied territory but as an integral part of Greater Germany." Frank added that "there will never be a Polish state again," for "once again the Polish people had come under the protective rule of the German nation. The Vistula will remain a German river." The atrocities committed by the Germans against the Poles during the post-invasion period were described in an official account issued by the exiled Polish government in London on the basis of German and Polish evidence. The Reich government issued its own book of atrocities committed by the Poles against the Germans. When all the facts of the treatment meted out to the conquered people are known and men are again able to think normally, the world will be astounded at the degree to which the Nazis practiced their theory that in a totalitarian war brutality knows no limits and anything is fair.

The attack on Russia made it possible for Germany to add the conquered Baltic states to the "steel core" of the Greater Reich. Many Lithuanians, Latvians and Estonians cherished the hope that Hitler would grant them some measure of autonomy. In Lithuania an autonomous local government maintained itself alive for a few weeks trying to collaborate with the occupying authorities. Their hopes were definitely shattered when on July 17, 1941, Lithuania together with the two other Baltic states and White Russia were annexed to Germany as a new province called Ostland, with Heinrich Lohse as the Reichskommissar at Riga. The Letts took the opportunity of the German-Russian war to stage a revolt against the Soviets early in July, and after the expulsion of the Red Army by Hitler's panzer divisions they thought of returning to the pre-war practice of holding general elections to establish a national government. They asked German permission which was instantaneously refused. The former president of Lithuania was at the same time accused by the newly established Nazi organ of having conducted an Anglophile policy and thus having enabled the bolsheviks to enslave the country. The case of Estonia was very much alike. The five million Baltic peoples found themselves eventually reduced to the status of aliens within the German orbit. They underwent once again the familiar process of the Nazi tactics: imprisonment of alleged communists, firing squads, the Star of David, requisitions, confiscations, outright expropriations, closing of schools and universities, changing the names of streets and cities, banning national flags and anthems, labor conscription, and the rest of the paraphernalia of terror that had swept from Vienna to Prague and Warsaw during the three preceding years. The task of the administration of the Ostland fell to the descendants of the Baltic barons who for the past eight centuries had already exploited the Baltic peoples in the spirit of racial superiority which Hitler raised to the principle of government.

Around the steel core of the Reich, extended to Austria, the economically richest and strategically most important western half of Czechoslovakia, Poland, Lithuania with White Russia, Latvia and Estonia, altogether over fifty million people, a system of exclusive alliances had been imposed on neighboring nations that tied them so thoroughly to Germany that they lost all freedom of action. Originally thought of as little moons gravitating around the Reich with no light of their own all of them actually became integral parts of the new order not as partners but as subordinates. Slovakia, Hungary, Rumania, Croatia, Bulgaria, Turkey, the Ukraine, the Volga basin and Stalin's own native land Georgia were earmarked to make up this wider orbit together with any additional territories that might be conquered in the west, east, north and south. Italy's place would materially be not very much different. It is within these lands where according to the "Schwarze Korps" the romantic dreams and yearnings of anyone possessing pioneering faculties would find ample scope for laying the foundations for a greater Germanic future.

The third set of German acquisitions would be colonies proper. Colonies in Africa, Asia and wherever else would not be used as supplementary territories where the workers might settle and live, but as mass productive areas of raw materials which would assure a higher standard of living for the millions of Germans working in the Reich. "The work done in the colonies," to quote the "Schwarze Korps," "must aim at attaining the greatest advantages for the Fatherland with the least possible expenditure of man-power. No German farmer, craftsman or colonist would be sent to the colonies, only administrators acting as organizers and symbolizing the Reich supremacy. The colonizers would organize colonial production but only the native population would work there for it could produce cheaply."

"Das Reich" hinted that moderation or mercy would not be the guiding spirit anywhere. "Our people are destined to be the pivot of the new order. They must always fight against the temptation to devote their energies to the good of others." Equally outspoken was Walter Darre, the Reich's Minister for Agriculture. "It will be our duty to organize the territories which will be gradually included in the Germanic area. Completely new methods will be introduced into our new Lebensraum. All soil and industrial property will be appropriated without exception and distributed primarily among the worthy members of the party, and soldiers who were accorded honors for bravery in the war. This new aristocracy will have slaves assigned to it as their property, consisting of landless non-German nationals. We actually have in mind a modern form of medieval slavery which we need if we are to fulfil our great tasks. The most important reason for slavery is the abolition of the gold standard and its replacement by work. The work done must be as cheaply as possible if our economic conquest is to spread extensively and rapidly."

By the beginning of 1942 Vichy gave the figure of foreign civilians working in Germany as 2,000,000, exclusive of any laborers from the conquered Soviet provinces. In addition 1,350,000 prisoners of war were employed chiefly in agriculture. Conquered and "collaborationist" Eastern Europe supplied by far the largest number: Poles 875,000, Czechs 150,000, Slovaks 80,000, Croats 40,000, Magyars 21,000, Bulgarians 5,000 and Rumanians 4,000. Among them were 25,000 women working in domestic services.

The human side of this transfer is revealed by the methods used in the recruitment of foreign labor. If a Czech student could not find employment at home within a certain period, he was conscripted for labor in the Reich. Similarly workers who had lost jobs in the industries in the occupied countries on account of lack of raw material or closing of factories would be sent to take up the posts vacated by the Germans mobilized for war. In Tarnov and other Polish towns men were simply rounded up in the streets. The German Press often admitted that resistance had to be overcome in summoning labor for the German war machine. Usually the workers were impressed by higher nominal wages, largely the result of the higher evaluation of the Mark as compared with their domestic currencies. The working hours range between 55 to 60 per week, but in some cases as much as 14 a day. The food is of the same standard as that of prisoners of war. Leaving jobs, changing occupation and freedom of movement is prohibited and punished. Workers are under the control of the employment exchange. Wages are partly deposited at the Reich Verrechnungsstelle, the clearing office, and sent to the families at home through the official channels. The German Press occasionally reveals what figures fail to express. Thus the use of foreigners for unskilled labor is regarded as advantageous on racial grounds, for "they should in all circumstances serve the workers of German stock in any given trade."

The foreign labor policy clearly indicates the degree to which the various territories under the new order are treated as inextricably intermixed. The Reich commands all the reserves of raw materials and manpower. The economy of the conquered countries has been mortgaged in favor of the Reich economy which will be the center consuming the agricultural produce and raw materials plus manpower of all Eastern Europe. The plan involves large movements of population and industries under coercion. In particular heavy industry, engineering works and chemical undertakings producing tools of war and, incidentally, also tools of revolt, are to be brought within zones of safety and in so far as political considerations do not stand in the way, to zones of economic advantage. Some three million Poles are reported to have been moved from industrial to agricultural regions and the total figure of such transfers can be counted as much higher. In order to meet the ultimate objectives something like twenty million people will have to be uprooted. For some time past, judging by the utterances of the Nazi spokesmen, the policy was devised to divert most, if not all, countries of the area to the intensification of agriculture and gradual restriction, if not elimination, of their industries. Rumania was to specialize in the cultivation under German control of soya beans, sunflower seeds and oats for German consumption, while Bulgaria and Greece would grow cotton.

In the latter part of 1941 this policy was somewhat modified and radical de-industrialization was no longer sought as feasible and advantageous. A desire was evinced to preserve and modernize Hungarian, Rumanian and Bulgarian industries with German money and under the supervision of German technicians. Light industries and such branches of production as enjoyed certain local advantages were to be left intact and even developed within the general industrial plan. This would in no way interfere with the long standing program of establishing German industrial hegemony in Europe. The master mind would be sitting in Berlin safely entrenched behind the military power recently rejuvenated in the field of victory and direct from the nerve center the whole system of the new economico-militarist civilization. With the tightening of political control over the surrounding areas there would be no longer ground for fear of economic competition. A measure of decentralization, limited to smaller and lighter industries, appeared more economical on account of the nearness of raw materials and abundance of cheap labor. To what extent this new policy was dictated by war stringency rather than by more long term considerations remains to be seen.

The biological fertility of non-Germanic races in Eastern Europe had always been regarded by the Nazi demographers as a menace to the German future. They calculated that in 2000 A.D. the post-Versailles Reich would have 47 million population instead of 68 million, so that it might become a space without people. During the two decades between 1890 and 1910 the population of Germany increased from 49 to 65 million, whereas between the two decades following 1919 it grew only from 63 to 68 million. The postwar increase amounted to 8 per cent as compared with the pre-World War I increase of 33 per cent. The Nazi population policy succeeded in slowing down the decline but not enough to procure an annual increment of 1,300,000 regarded as desirable if the German race were to maintain itself. There has also been a marked fall in the young age groups in contrast to a relative increase in the number of people above fifty years of age. The growth of the population of the non-Germanic peoples of Eastern Europe also slowed down but there was still an annual increase of one million, excluding Russia. The Poles for instance would number ten more million before reaching the stationary period.

There is a certain dilemma in the Nazi attitude towards this population phenomenon. On the one hand, it would seem advantageous to depopulate the non-Germans so as to insure the preponderance of Teutonic element. Artificial methods of depopulation, such as long separation of men from women, have been freely discussed by the racial experts. On the other hand, growing masses of politically subdued, socially degraded, and economically exploited aliens would provide the masters with cheap labor which would make it possible to compete with low cost industries overseas. Low incomes under the conditions of a monocultural rural economy would mean low living standards, however, with the result that Eastern Europe would offer only limited markets for German manufacture. Europe before the Nazi conquest was far from self-sufficiency. The same would hold for a Europe dominated by Germany. As Hitler extended his economic space from one conquered country to another he undoubtedly strengthened his war potential, but in the long run he did not solve the problem of insufficiency. Without trading with extra-European countries he could not satisfy the needs of his own nation and of his victims without running the risk of ending in economic stagnation. Thus expansion led to more expansion. It is flaws like these which make the new order a dubious proposition, quite apart from the experience that keeping 325 million foreign peoples in permanent dependence or subjection is in itself an uneconomical enterprise.

The integration of Eastern Europe in the *Grosswirtschaftsraum* is most marked in the field of financial and monetary policies. The German Mark has taken the place of the common standard. Through the adoption of a clearing system and large purchases of foodstuffs and raw materials from the dominated regions the banks have been constrained to accumulate large Mark reserves which serve as a note cover for local currencies. Technical arrangements vary from one country to another but the effect is pretty much the same everywhere. The arbitrary high evaluation of the Mark in terms of other currencies combined with the generally enforced price policy lowered the purchasing power of the dominated nations. Through rigid price fixing the evidence of inflation has been artificially concealed and the levelling down of living standards by means of an early adopted rationing system, discriminatory though it is, has produced the impression of economic equality in poverty. Eventually all transactions between the dominated countries, Italy included, have been done through the Berlin exchange clearing. The earlier trade-at-gun-point practices have thus been supplemented and sometimes replaced by a rigid totalitarian mechanism which no dominated nation is in a position to break because no alternative choice is left. The omnipresence of the German military force behind all these political and economic operations and experiments serves as the compelling factor of ultimate resort.

Summary

By the end of 1941 World War II was by no means approaching the point of contraction. On the contrary, it had already entered upon its oceanic phase. The conquest of Eastern Europe was consummated, however. In the great maelstrom that swept over it all the smaller nations were thrown back into subjection. While the war raged in Russia and Africa and the final Axis victory was anything but assured, preparations were nevertheless made in Berlin to stage another Congress of Vienna sometime early in 1942 to sanction the Nazi conquest and organize the new order. The reverses of the Russian campaign interfered with these plans. Despite the retreat from Moscow Germany was still the dominating military power in Eastern Europe at the turn of the year.

Surprising as the sudden emergence of such a colossus appeared to be, the path of its advance could clearly be traced to a series of preventible factors had the world made a more accurate and timely analysis of the trends of the time and had the great powers as well as the small ones acted in concert. The isolationist policy of the United States had been an important minus agent in the failure to give the world, of which America is as much a component part as Europe, a more solid basis for a healthier organization. More consequential, however, was the failure to distinguish between the primary and the secondary issues on the part of the European great powers. What was in the back of the great upheaval? Was it really another profound revolution aiming at liberating humanity from the unbearable chains of the past that had exhausted its vitality, or was it simply another attempt of a militaristic people that had refused to accept an earlier defeat as the final word of history and resumed its march once its potential rivals were caught napping? Assuming that both factors played a part in the cataclysm, which one was to receive major attention, or what means were to be employed to meet the dual challenge? Were the two isolated phenomena or was there deeper causation between them? Was it not that totalitarian suppression of human liberties was deliberately chosen as a prerequisite of territorial conquests through total warfare? To what extent did the fear of bolshevism and of the revolutionary character of economic and social changes inherent in it cause the capitalistic democracies to fraternize, temporarily but at a very critical moment, with fascism as the alleged conservator of old virtues? Or was it not the continuation of a century long struggle between England and Germany for supremacy? If so, how came it about that Stalin was at one time more feared in the west than Hitler? For several years prior to the ascendency of Nazi Germany and even during the first years of her rule a good many westerners were offering Eastern Europe as a plausible area for German expansion. On what grounds did they assume that Hitler of 1933 or 1936 was different from Hitler of 1938 or 1939? Was it not until March 1939 before the acknowledged democratic leaders began to realize the full implications of the facts that had in the meantime been established? Did not the European powers have among themselves enough resources to check the avalanche at its source? Was it the inept leadership or the inarticulateness and debility of the masses that was more responsible for the failure of a united action whether through collective security, effective peaceful change, or concerted military intervention? At the time when Mussolini and Hitler preached and practiced the spirit of military conquests the democracies were committing themselves to practicing the policy of the will to peace. When the totalitarian powers in Asia, Europe and Africa were changing the life of millions of peoples, the democracies were arguing that war did not change anything. Was it higher ethics or selfish convenience that made people believe they were saving themselves behind the shelter of such inadequate formulas as isolation, neutrality or non-interference?

One by one the component parts of the fabric are being brought within place and in due course the details behind the individual moves will be detected and given proper value. In the meantime Eastern Europe had to bear the brunt of the impact. Temporary and incomplete though this conquest is, it serves the purpose of reminding the people everywhere of certain fundamentals to be borne in mind if a better international community is to emerge from the present struggle. One of these fundamentals is that the differentiation between remote and nearby nations has lost much of its meaning, and that the old distinction between the so-called general and the so-called specific national interests is no longer valid. Another of these fundamentals is that human dignity, a moral code, the four freedoms and elementary decency presuppose a general and common application and cannot be enjoyed in the long run by anyone if they are to be enjoyed only by a few. The avalanche started to slide in Eastern Europe from which it has now spread to all the oceans. When the wreckage it caused is in process of being mended, and when new pillars are raised where the old ones crashed, it will be the task of wise statesmen-ship to trace the disaster to the point where it started in order to build anew soundly. Eastern Europe will have to be organized not in the spirit of the past but to hold firm in the future.

Part Six

The Future of Eastern Europe

V for Victory

What will happen to Eastern Europe is an issue of more than local European significance. The establishment at the center of unrest of such conditions as would prevent another tornado of war from running wild is one of the primary prerequisites of international peace. Eastern Europe, i.e., the zone of small and medium sized nations between the Baltic, Adriatic and Black Seas, and between Germany and Italy in the west and the Soviet Union in the east, must be organized politically and economically if the world is to be spared being dragged into incalculable conflicts every generation. It is not that the people living in this zone are any worse or different from the rest of humanity, or that they are possessed of some particularly evil characteristics. It is the accumulation and combination of geographical, historical, strategic, cultural and ethnic factors that attach to this area more than ordinary importance and make it a vulnerable spot of the continent. No doubt the various divisions referred to in the first part of this volume lie at the root of the precarious situations which the individual nations had to grapple with at each turning point of their history. Yet there are in many parts of the world divisions more profound and frontiers less logical without neces-

sarily giving rise to analogous troubles. What has made Eastern
Europe lately especially vulnerable was the rise in its immediate
neighborhood of the dynamic impact of Germanism which under
Hitler cast off all pretenses of limited purposes and peaceful economic penetration in preference to military conquest and total
control. If this single outstanding fact and its far-reaching implications had been intelligently appreciated much of the loose talk
about the fiasco of postwar Central and Eastern Europe could
have been dispensed with.

Ever since the middle of the nineteenth century the notion was
being drilled into the German mind by the pangermanists and
the ruling Prussian junkers that in order to live more abundantly
the Germans must unite and expand, reach imperial status, acquire colonies, dependencies and protectorates from which to
draw all the good things of life so far denied to them because of
retarded development and the meanness of rival powers. In the
Nazi terminology, Lebensraum was substituted for pangermanism
and the procurement of it became synonymous with the manifest destiny of a vigorous people filled with the will to expand.
Postwar insistence on equal status, rearmament, self-determination, a term the real meaning of which was entirely alien
to German thought, and constant evocations of the have-not
formula, were tactical stages in German diplomacy calculated to
arouse the people at home and to manipulate public opinion in
democratic, and often gullible, nations abroad. Nazi counter-
revolution found its task comparatively easy of attainment because it was practiced upon a docile people, imbued with military tradition, humiliated by a recent defeat, drained economically,
and despairing at the inability of inexperienced so-called democratic governments to solve the country's problems.

The essentials of Hitler's new order were canvassed already at
the beginning of the World War I under the slogan of Mitteleuropa. Central Europe was to be a blockade-proof union of
Eastern European lands under Prussian command, a customs

union serving German heavy industries, not as an end but a stepping stone for further expansion beyond its confines. The inhabitants of the controlled territories were to be denied equal rights, for nothing could sound stranger to Prussian ears than a concept of some universal organization in which weaker nations would unite for the purpose of upholding their rights. The very notion of universal peace through arbitration and disarmament provoked the anger of men around the ex-Kaiser as well as of those forming the inner Nazi circle. Mitteleuropa appealed to the junkers as much as to men like Stinnes and Krupp. It also appealed to Stresemann, the clever Realpolitiker, whose foreign policy was not fundamentally different in ultimate objectives from that promulgated by his more oratorical and more radical opponents like Hugenberg or Hitler himself. Like Hugenberg's nationalists and Hitler's national socialists Stresemann, too, attributed the German collapse in 1918 not to military defeat but to diplomatic debility which had not prevented Germany's encirclement. In the most truly Teutonic tradition he regarded it as a tragedy that he did not have at his disposal the Prussian army that once supported Frederick the Great.

Hitler's deeds could indeed be illustrated by the words that were current in Germany decades earlier. To quote Paul Rohrbach in 1916, Germany had to find a way to be one of the races owning the world. Then as now Eastern Europe was to be the nucleus of a new imperium, reaching through Austria-Hungary, Bulgaria and Turkey to the Gulf of Persia. To have freedom of the seas, the real bone of contention with England, Germany had to acquire Egypt, seize Belgium, the French Channel coast and Denmark, as the keeper of the entrance to the Baltic sea. The absorption of Scandinavia and of Holland, "soaked in German blood," and the establishment of naval and air stations at Dover, Malta and Suez, were parts of the scheme. Paul de Lagarde in his writings drove the Russians out of the Black Sea and the Slavs out of central and southeastern Europe and visualized immense lands at eastern frontiers for colonization. Others saw in the east the only continent offering a splendid field for expansion if Germany only knew how to exploit the opportunity and take the lands before the Cossacks seized them. The German Emperor would then have it in his power to direct the destinies of Asia Minor, and a few hundred or thousand armed colonists would rebuild the beautiful plains and make him the peacemaker of all Asia. The writers in "Weltpolitik" sounded a similar tune by emphasizing that Germany must absorb all the lands between the east and the west, from the Baltic to the Near East, wherefrom all foreign influence must be removed.

In Africa a nucleus of another empire was envisaged taking in the Cameroons, Southeast Africa, the Belgian and French Congo. "In case there should be no Central Europe we would certainly still have Central Africa," wrote Paul Leutwein, "although we could not for one moment think of a Central Europe without a Central Africa." Maximillian Harden joined the exalted chorus in his "Zukunft" by adding a few more territories to the empire of the future. "Morocco entirely in the hands of Germans, German guns aimed at the roads to Egypt and India, German troops at the borders of Algeria, this aim would certainly be worth its great sacrifice." And furthermore: "To raise the storm flag of the Empire in the English Channel which opens and shuts the thoroughfare to the ocean, never has there been a more justifiable war." A victorious war was expected to give Germany the chain of colonial possessions stretching from Egypt and the Indian ocean to the Atlantic ocean and including the Portuguese colonies along the African coast. Holland was expected to be joined to this Empire as a federal state, retaining her royal house and her South American and Pacific islands. Still another empire to which Germany saw herself entitled, according to Tannenberg, lay in Asia. It would include a generous piece of the basin of the Chinese rivers, the Malayan peninsula, Syria, Mesopotamia and British India. In his work "Grossdeutschland" the same writer regretted that the Germans had missed the opportunity to take possession of Cuba and he suggested that it would be a blessing for the peoples of the South American republics if they came under German protective administration. The southern half of South America was specifically mentioned as suitable for seizure. Argentina and Brazil were described as states from which all signs of life had disappeared. In Lange's "Reines Deutschtum," "the somewhat miserable little states in South America must be brought to listen to reason by force or otherwise." By other writers a note of melancholy was registered at the fact that neither Paraguay nor Argentina did not up to then belong at least partially to Germany.

The turn of luck on the First World War battlefields placed these ambitions temporarily in abeyance. The dissolution of Austria-Hungary removed the bridge which was to link up the European nucleus of the German imperium with all the subsidiary empires in Asia, Africa and the Western Hemisphere. At first the German nationalists received the collapse of the Habsburg monarchy as a setback. Soon, however, the National Socialists began to glorify the disappearance of the monarchy as a triumph for the pangerman cause. Purified from their association with the Slavs and Magyars, the Austrians were supposed to have finally found the road clear to the union with the Reich. Small Austria was raised in the eyes of Hitler, himself an Austrian with a Prussian complex, to the pivotal role of the key to the gates of Central and Eastern Europe. The expansion eastwards was to be realized piecemeal. The Anschluss was to bring Mitteleuropa to fruition. That was the reason why the Anschluss had been opposed by the nations that feared that the disappearance of Austria would put their own existence in jeopardy.

The idea of Mitteleuropa was tactically held in suspense during the intermezzo between the wars, and instead the more limited objective of a "natural" union of two Germanic peoples became the motto of German propaganda and diplomacy. At the same

time nothing was permitted to occur that would tend to consolidate the postwar system. In particular Eastern Europe was
to be prevented from organizing itself into a larger union. Not
all the people saw through this game. Men in high positions of
responsibility, both inside and outside the area, in their gullibility accepted the Nazi propaganda without sifting through the
evidence. Ignorant of the role which a Nazi controlled Eastern
Europe would play in the scheme of world domination, or bored
with the recurrence of problems they wished to ignore, many
statesmen sought the easiest escape in lamenting the loss of the
good old times and secretly wishing that the small nations had
never been brought to light from the state of submerged obscurity.
Widely circulated organs of public opinion in England, France
and the United States indulged in superficial simplification of
the Eastern European issues and not a few counsels recommended that Germany be given a free hand to "organize" the apparently incorrigible little peoples.

Amidst the confusing attitudes toward Eastern Europe, Hitler
prepared himself to act. As probably the only head of a great
power, who besides Mussolini, knew exactly what he really
wanted, he resumed the struggle where it had been left off in
1918. Anxious to avoid fighting on two fronts, he secured alliance with Italy, forming the Axis, tried to buy off Great Britain before invading Poland, eliminated temporarily the Soviet
Union, and by the Tripartite Pact brought in Japan as a counterpoise against the United States. At the same time Mussolini and
Japan were entrusted with the task of building up in Africa and
Asia the two subsidiary empires, the Italian one and the "co-
prosperity order in Eastern Asia," both of which would eventually
fall into Germany's grasp one way or another. Even totalitarian
diplomacy cannot have everything its own way, however, and its
success depends on what the other party, or parties, do or decline
to do. Germany did succeed in avoiding a two-front continental
war for the time being, but the same technical advances of mod-

ern total warfare by the use of which she subdued Europe made it possible for Great Britain, the Soviet Union, the United States, China and the Allied powers to cut short the distances and force her to fight a multi-front battle that in the long run defies the conventional assumptions.

Nowhere is victory over the Axis hoped for more wholesouledly than in Eastern Europe. Were Germany to win the war, all the smaller nations of the zone would be exposed to losing all the four freedoms and the Slavs among them would in particular be literally suppressed. Many of them would be done away with in the truest meaning of that term. This is commonly felt even by the overwhelming majority of peoples whose rulers have aligned them with the Axis out of treachery, incompetence, considerations of private gains, misconception of true national interests, or the weight of circumstances beyond their control. The broad masses of Slovakia, Croatia, Rumania, Bulgaria or Hungary had little constitutional or any other opportunity to influence the course of foreign policy when the diplomatic situation was being created to involve them in the war on the side of Germany. They had no say when the decision was actually made. Slovakia was separated from Czechoslovakia and opened as a convenient supply route for German invasion of Poland under the Nazi pressure and with the help of men of no truly representative character. The Croatians should not be identified with their self-imposed leader Pavelitch who in 1929 fled abroad and organized in Italy the terrorist group, the Oustachis. Had it not been for the support extended to him by Mussolini and Hitler, Pavelitch would have never been brought back. As elsewhere in the occupied territories, the Quislings of his type are isolated from the masses and maintain themselves in power only as Axis instruments to share the responsibility for the acts of violence perpetrated by the occupying powers.

Rumania is another example of a country whose people are anti-Nazi but whose rulers have forced them by acts of omission and commission into the Axis arms. In the November plebiscite of 1941 General Antonescu asked for approval of his policy of collaboration with Germany. Considering the presence of the German army of occupation, the outstanding fact of the plebiscite was not that 872,000 approved and only 17 disapproved Antonescu's policy but that 90 per cent of population abstained from voting. The pro-Russian Bulgarians would have hardly consented to serve Hitler's cause had it not been for the dictatorial activities of King Boris and his pro-Nazi military clique which ever since 1935 had ruled by decrees and deprived the people of any chance, short of civil rebellion, of reversing the course of official diplomacy. Hungarian Prime Minister Bardossy assured the readers of the "Leipziger Neueste Nachrichten" in July 1941, that Hungary had flung herself with enthusiasm into the war against Moscow for the liberation of Europe and that she was fighting in traditional friendship side by side with Germany for the extermination of the focus of war in the east. To understand the statement, it is necessary to recall that it was made to a Nazi paper at a time when Hungary was under virtual Nazi occupation, and that the spokesman represented the very fascist and feudal class of a country whose land-owning gentry families have for centuries placed their clan interests above those of the broad masses. Under Horthy's rule reforms were spoken of and some limited measures for improvement were occasionally passed but substantially the social structure underwent no change. The same elements have been the mainstay of Horthy's anti-democratic régime and have been supporters of collaboration with the Axis. As for Finland certain allowances should be made for her grievances against the Soviets because of earlier aggression, but the wisdom of her government in allowing the country to become the base for the Nazi attack on Russia will hardly stand the test of history.

In the meantime the people of Eastern Europe had been given the opportunity to taste Mitteleuropa at close quarters and to find through intimate experience the true nature of the Nazi solution. The victory over the Axis will inevitably lead to a parallel victory of the people against the rulers who failed. Internal coups and revolutionary acts are likely to accompany the change. By one of the frequent paradoxes of history both groups of nations of Eastern Europe may in the end be saved, i.e., those standing in the Axis camp and those opposing it. In that way good may eventually be wrested from evil and Eastern Europe may be ready for a healthier settlement.

The Atlantic Charter

The joint Anglo-American declaration of August 14, 1941, bearing the official signatures of President Roosevelt and Prime Mininster Churchill, and agreed upon during a meeting on the "calm and blue seas" somewhere in the Atlantic, may well mark the beginning of the course towards a reasonable peace settlement. Well-meant and high-sounding statements of principles had unfortunately been so frequently offered during the two decades between the wars by both the totalitarian and the democratic leaders that they fell flat on people's ears. The cause of international morality requires therefore the restoration of the dignity of words as much as it needs the restoration of the decency of deeds.

Of the eight points of the declaration it is particularly the second and the third that have most direct bearing upon Eastern Europe. Point two says that Great Britain and the United States "desire to see no territorial changes that do not accord with the freely expressed wishes of the people concerned." Point three runs as follows: the two powers "respect the right of all peoples to choose the form of government under which they will live, and they wish to see sovereign rights and self-government restored to those who have been forcibly deprived of them." Together with point one, assuring that neither England nor the United States seeks any aggrandizement, territorial or other, the Atlantic Charter suggests in principle the broad political aspect of the future status of the countries of Eastern Europe. In substance, if not by definition, the declaration re-introduces the World War I recognition of the right of self-determination of nations. National self-government is an element of democracy projected into the field of international relations. It implies that right is not an issue that can be settled exclusively between the great powers to which smaller nations should simply submit.

In 1918 and afterwards much ink was spent on what self-determination exactly meant and at what stage a social group feeling and calling itself a nation was to be accorded the right to political self-expression. The issue has not been closed. To-day the question of applying the right of self-determination to the peoples of Eastern Europe presents itself in a form which in one way is more simple than in 1918. Nations which to many outside people seemed obscure or ignorant at the time of World War I have in the meantime impressed themselves upon the body politic of Europe. If the two points of the Atlantic Charter mean anything concrete, they mean that national independence and freedom to choose their own government should be restored to the Finns, Estonians, Latvians, Lithuanians, Poles, Czechs and Slovaks, Austrians, Magyars, Rumanians, Yugoslavs, Albanians, Bulgarians and Greeks, as well as to such nationality groups as might claim and receive national status. Other than strictly ethnic reasons will have to be considered again, however, if the anomaly is to be prevented of sacrificing the interests of majorities to those of minorities. As far as is known, no secret agreement exists between the great powers which would commit them to a violation of the self-determination right such as had existed prior to the entry of the United States in World War I, and especially before the declaration of Wilson's fourteen points in January 1918. In that direction the ground is clearer. Yet problems such as frontiers, minorities, sovereignty, etc., will again attract the attention of the theoretician and of the statesman.

With regard to the future frontiers no surprise should be caused by stating that they need not necessarily differ very much from those of 1919. It is almost certain that most of them will undergo another careful scrutiny, however. The British government declared, for instance, that it is not bound by any frontier in the area. As to the Soviet Union, Stalin referred to war aims in the speech of November 6, 1941. He said that Russia's first aim was to free her own territory, and the second aim was to free "the enslaved peoples of Europe and then allow them to decide their own fate without any outside interference in their internal affairs." Earlier on September 24, Soviet Ambassador Ivan Maisky informed the Inter-Allied Government Council in London that his government "proclaimed its agreement with the fundamental principles of the eight point declaration," and added that "consistent application of these principles will secure the most energetic support on the part of the government and peoples of the Soviet Union." The question of frontiers was mentioned more specifically in the Polish-Soviet treaty of July 30, 1941. The treaty invalidated the German-Soviet agreement on territorial partition of Poland in 1939, without giving the Poles a positive guarantee of their pre-partition frontiers. The Soviet official newspaper "Izvestia" commented on the 1920 frontiers as ones that should not be regarded as immutable. The British government at the same time emphasized in a note to the Polish government in London that it did not recognize any territorial changes which had taken place in Poland since August 1939. Thus both Moscow and London repudiated the changes brought about by violent action without assuming any positive guarantee as to the previous boundaries. In line with its general policy of avoiding explicit commitments in regard to problems to be worked out directly by the parties concerned, the British government affirmed the same attitude in connection with the future boundary between Yugoslavia and Italy and between Czechoslovakia and Germany.

In a federal structure the boundary functions would be limited largely to administrative purposes with the exception of the international frontiers of the whole federation. The outer frontiers could not be drawn without regard to strategic necessities. Should Eastern Europe be restored intact in its prewar system of absolutely sovereign states, an eventuality which seems to have very few advocates, all frontiers would have to be considered in the light of their military and economico-military functions unless an effective universal system of security were established which would relieve individual states from the burden of seeking safety separately or through alliances. Most serious endeavor should be made to restore the freedom of the smaller nations in such a manner as to render them as homogeneous as possible so as to eliminate potential zones of friction on minority grounds. In a recent comment Dr. Beneš formulated the Czechoslovak point of view: "This war is at the same time a revolution and Europe will issue from it much changed. While refusing a priori to accept any dictate of any kind we wish to agree on our frontiers with our neighbors in a friendly fashion, and in this the ethnographic, economic, as well as strategic integrity of our state territory must be maintained. Changes in detail are possible, as it will certainly be possible to obtain frontiers corresponding to our requirements and to those of our neighbors."

The place of Austria in Central Europe deserves more serious attention than it has lately been receiving. It should not be forgotten that it was only after the annexation of Austria that the strategic position of Czechoslovakia became untenable just as the destruction of Czechoslovakia rendered weak the position of Poland. The way in which "Austria ceased to exist as an independent state," the phraseology used by the British Foreign Office in acquiescing in the accomplished fact, did not materially differ from the way in which all the subsequent victims of aggression passed away. The last Austrian Chancellor is still held in Nazi captivity, and the Austrian people have not yet had the opportunity to decide upon their fate. That chance should not be denied them at the postwar settlement. This is a gigantic war, and small patterns in its fabric are liable to be overlooked unless it is realized that it is the small fractions that make up the aggregate. The Anschluss should not be the only alternative to separate existence. No nation can in the future be really free, independent and secure by relying on its own resources. This is doubly true of small nations cut off from the seas and having as neighbors powerful states imbued with the will to expand. Should the Austrians prefer to join a democratic union of small Central and Eastern European nations as equal partners nothing should be allowed to stand in their way.

The Sudeten German problem which furnished Hitler with a technical pretext for truncating Czechoslovakia first in order to destroy her afterwards, received prominence largely owing to the abortive attempt of the democracies to buy the peace of the world by handing over a vital strategic area to the aggressor. Since then it has been proved that the separation of the territory inhabited by the Sudeten Germans from Czechoslovakia deprived the country of sound economic existence and fatally compromised her security. The natural economic unity of Czechoslovakia had been freely admitted by German spokesmen before and after the war. Last year the Nazi official organ "Die Zeit" brought out several examples of the economic ties existing between the amputated Sudeten region, the Protectorate and Slovakia. A satisfactory status acceptable to both the Czechs and the Germans will have to be worked out with regard to the Sudeten Germans. Rectifications of boundaries combined with an exchange of population and decentralization within the framework of democratic constitutions offer ample opportunities for a truly humane solution of all nationality problems in Eastern Europe.

If we believe as we should that democracy and self-government offer a basis for the improvement of human relationships the world need not necessarily be worse off if it consists of one hundred states instead of eighty. In other words, the restoration of independence to those small nations which were deprived of it during the period of great aggressions need not alarm the supporters of international cooperation. It was among the small nations that such cooperation received often more genuine support than among the great powers. One might even go as far as to insist that it was largely because of the inability of great powers to agree that the cause of international collaboration received so many setbacks. International economic cooperation immediately after World War I failed because Great Britain and the United States either made so many reservations as to render it nugatory, or simply did not wish it. The League of Nations failed not because the small nations were uncooperative, but because the governments of great powers wanted it to fail. Great powers derive certain advantages from their greatness. They must also assume greater responsibilities which go with it.

The Atlantic Charter, accepted by Great Britain, the United States, the Soviet Union and their allies, does not offer a card index of remedies to be automatically applied to cure specific diseases. But it points out the way. If it postulates the restoration of sovereign rights it does not imply that nations should not unite in wider organizations where conditions are favorable for larger unions. The restored freedom must be used intelligently. Sovereignty as a practical doctrine took five centuries to develop. It grew out of the political, economic and cultural conditions existing at the end of the Middle Ages. It can hardly be undone by a single penstroke. It is not certain that powerful nations would scrap their sovereignty by a legislative act or otherwise and submit to a united and institutionalized conduct of their political, economic and military diplomacy. It is more likely that long term alliances will be formed between some of them after the war for the purpose of maintaining peace through concerted policies. A new federal world order, comprising the great powers, will certainly come in a somewhat more distant future. Highly desirable as it is, such a new system of federated peoples among the great powers will more likely emerge from a sufficiently long practice of gradually widening concerted action in political and economic fields rather than from any pre-arranged hard and fast scheme.

In Eastern Europe conditions are somewhat different. There the idea of a union is more deeply rooted than in the west, and should be brought to fruition regardless of what the great powers choose to do. As shown in the second part of this volume, local tendencies toward unification made themselves more manifest in Eastern Europe than elsewhere. More farsighted statesmen realized that with divided economy, divided diplomacy, divided strategy all the separately spent energies, investments and labors would melt into thin air in the wake of economic depression and panzer divisions. The obstacles to unification lay both with the small nations of the area and the outside great powers. Local diversities which handicapped unification could be converted into an asset if through union cultural characteristics and group traditions were safeguarded within and without. Multi-national union accepting cultural plurality without trying to forge artificial and oppressive uniformity seems to be the common ground for understanding provided that the great powers do not hinder but encourage the process of transformation. The argument against conceiving Eastern Europe as a potential unit was based on the assumption that Greece, for instance, was too far away from Poland to feel equally endangered from the same direction. The war proved the falseness of any such assumption. Ever since the liberation of the Greeks and even before there had been an inner logic in the series of advances and reverses in the fate of all the small nations situated between Germany, Italy and Russia. Each thrust by Germany eastwards led to a counter westward movement by Russia, embroiling the Baltic region as well as the Balkans. Italy marching side by side with Germany only intensified the two movements. In post-Versailles Europe the small nations shied from uniting to meet the outside threats in common because they did not want to anger the great powers or because they regarded such threats as remote. Consequently they limited their cooperation to cover smaller risks closer to home. Efforts to please the aggressors, and to buy their friendship by concessions at the expense of solidarity among themselves, left the disunited small peoples at great disadvantage. Germany and Italy marched in and Russia took her own precautions dictated by strategy. To Great Britain the nations of Eastern Europe meant little more than "the eastern fringe" of European continent. The Chamberlain government treated it as a distant land "about which we know very little." In the United States up to recently many people refused to admit that the march to Prague in 1939 was a link in the same chain of fateful events that led to the unprecedented attack upon Hawaii in December 1941.

The union of small nations would hardly enjoy long life if Germany, Italy or Russia were included. What Eastern Europe would look like under Germany has been plainly demonstrated by the "new order." It would be Mitteleuropa under exclusive German domination. It is reasonable to expect that Italian Lebensraum in the Balkans would definitely fall under the iron fist of German economic and political strategy. Victory over the Axis must be complete enough to disillusion Germany from attempting to reconquer her small neighbors again. Otherwise the war will have been fought in vain. Italy will have to be brought down to the understanding that her interests, too, can best be served by cooperation instead of domination. Such combinations as an Adriatic union including the small Balkan States under Italian leadership would not mean building for the future. Unfortunately there are many people in England and the United States who still cannot free themselves from the traditional bondage of visualizing Eastern Europe as inevitably dominated by a great power. Down to the outbreak of the war the inevitable solution was seen in German domination. Germany was said to possess the genius of organization which in addition to her undeniably real economic interests made her the natural organizer of the smaller peoples. Only after it had become clear that the control of 120,000,000 Eastern Europeans increased her base for even more formidable domination of the world did the advocates of giving her a free hand to "organize" begin to see the light.

With Russia's entry in the war the adherents of the domination theory switched over to the inevitability of Russian hegemony. The participation of Russia in the war means also her participation in the peace settlement, an event the great importance of which will be properly estimated in view of the disastrous consequences of her absence from the Peace Conference in 1919. Russia is as much in Europe as Germany, Italy, France, Great Britain or Spain, for she takes in almost one half of that continent's territory. The attempts of the Axis and its satellites to place her outside European civilization are as futile as they are in disagreement with geographical and political facts. It is in the interest of the Soviets to have along their western borders an orderly bloc of small nations economically sound and politically free and strong. The Polish-Soviet pact concluded in July 1941 and reaffirmed in December of the same year was a sign in the right direction. If it means the end of the ancient Polish-Russian feud no better testimony to the wisdom of the two governments could be wished for. Ambassador Maisky's promise to build up a new Europe after this war on the principle of self-determination of nations struck a similarly encouraging tune. Russia's declared respect for Turkish integrity including the Straits should further strengthen the hope of those who wish to see the Eastern European zone established and developed in its own right. It should not be forgotten that efforts towards building up collective security coincided with and were directly linked to Russia's re-entry into prominence as a European great power. Neither could it be gainsaid that the Moscow record pertinent to the period down to Munich was good. British isolation from Eastern Europe contributed to Hitler's expansion in that area and encouraged the forces which eventually led to the war. American isolation from Europe had a similarly negative effect. An agreed policy on the part of the Soviet Union, Great Britain and the United States to assist the peoples of Eastern Europe to consolidate their area politically and rebuild it economically could not fail to introduce the element of stability that was lacking in the past. An agreement of such kind presupposes a reorientation of the policies of the great powers in the sense that they look towards international collaboration as the best safeguard of their vital interests.

A fatalistic view of German, Russian or any other domination of Eastern Europe is one of the most unfortunate political assumptions. The Poles, Czechs, Slovaks, Serbs, Slovenes, Croats and Bulgarians, altogether some sixty million people, are Slavs. The rest of the Eastern Europeans, i.e., the Finns, the Baltic peoples, the Austrians, Magyars, Rumanians, Albanians, Turks and Greeks belong to other ethnic groups. Supposing that, having no other choice, the majority of Slavs should prefer Russian protection to that of Germany, inevitably the non-Slav groups would be drawn within the German or other power-political orbit. The division would inevitably go on with the same undesirable consequences as in the past decades. The old bogey of panslavism, so skillfully exploited by the pangermanists of Vienna and Berlin as well as by Mussolini, would reappear to cast its shadow. In this connection the all-Slav congress held in Moscow in August 1941 was an event of considerable interest. The assembled representatives of the Russians, Ukrainians, White Russians, Poles, Czechs, Slovaks, Serbs, Croats, Macedonians, Montenegrins, Bulgarians, Slovenes and Ruthenians rejected the panslav program of the pre-World War I coinage as "a reactionary movement." The Soviet representative Alexis Tolstoy refuted any desire "to attempt to assume leadership or play the role of guide." "The hour has struck for the entire Slav world to unite for the speedy and final rout of German fascism. We unite as equals. Amongst us there must be no seniors and no juniors. We have one burning, all-embracing urge: that the Slavs, as all our neighbors and all other peoples, should be able peacefully and undisturbedly to develop within their frontiers."

There is no doubt that, to quote Jan Masaryk, "Hitler's murderous pangermanism is stirring up a self-protecting panslavism even in Russia." However, the romanticism of the nineteenth century panslavs, never a vital doctrine, is as little realistic to-day as ever. The vision of a great Slav empire embracing all the three hundred million Slavs in a single state under the scepter of the Tsar expressed the reaction to the Germanizing and Magyarizing policies in the Habsburg monarchy. Restricted as it was to small circles inside and outside the Russian empire, the panslav ideology lost its ground with the fall of Austria-Hungary and the rise of the Soviet state. The Slavs of Eastern Europe feel that their life and future are inseparably knitted with the life and future of the non-Slav Austrians, Magyars, and Rumanians, and that given the proper understanding of their position on the part of the rest of Europe they will be able to create a prosperous community.

The Governments in Exile

Some economists have been inclined in the past twenty years to explain the political collapse of the world in general and of Eastern Europe in particular chiefly by the ignorance or disregard of economic factors. In so far as the assumption is not made that political problems would look after themselves once the primacy of economics is recognized, the economic argument is very strong indeed. The accumulation of vast international war debts unpayable without dislocating the economy of the creditor nations, especially the United States, America's high tariffs, unregulated foreign lending little concerned with inevitable consequences, the abandonment of equal treatment of international trade, hoarding and subsequent destruction of supplies of commodities badly needed in other parts of the world, and, more specifically, the failure to understand Eastern Europe as an area possessing a high degree of economic unity, and the even more regrettable postwar policy of the industrial powers of refusing to tackle seriously the question of the Eastern European agricultural surpluses and thus unwittingly playing into the hands of rising dictators and aggressors, were without the least doubt contributory factors of the war. At the same time economic devices alone would not have been sufficient in the absence of enough political security and peace in which to operate. It can not be repeated enough that it was not until after the great powers permitted the League of Nations to fall into desuetude and the French security system collapsed that the Axis launched its offensive against the smaller states. Political settlement is therefore the major prerequisite of both peace and economic prosperity.

The need of the organization of Eastern Europe into a union has grown into an almost vital issue of the war. Whether the union is conceived as a United States of Eastern Europe, a confederation or a federation of states, a democratic union, a commonwealth of the small nations, a system of blocs in the Baltic area, the Danubian basin and the Balkans, or a regional union merged into an all-European confederation, all these concepts derive their inspirations from one and the same realization that political safety and freedom from economic want can better be obtained in unison than from division. The governments in exile of Poland, Czechoslovakia, Yugoslavia and Greece have been discussing postwar organization among themselves and with the British government, and Austrian, Hungarian, Rumanian and other privately constituted committees of the exiles from the Axis-controlled nations have been stressing the issue in appeals to their own nationals in the English speaking countries as well as to public opinion at large. The impossibility of escape from the occupied countries explains why some of the exiled groups may not be as fully representative of all the political shades of the population at home. But in each case they do represent the spirit of freedom and interpret the wishes of the peoples who had been deprived of the means of free expression. The Czechoslovak Government in London, for instance, includes recognized political leaders of all major groups of Czechs and Slovaks. Similarly the Croats fill important positions in the Yugoslav Government alongside of the Serbs. The way in which individual members of these governments managed to slip through the Axis fingers, and the fact of their functioning belong to the memorable annals of this war. The individual exploits of soldiers and pilots who under most harrowing conditions travelled or flew many thousand miles to join their colors in the far-flung battlefields make glorious one-man-anabases which will not be lost on future generations. And is it too much to expect that the unique experience of direct and continued contacts between twenty-six United Nations may eventually bring us nearer to the realization of a new kind of diplomacy by unintermitting consultation, seeking broad and lasting solutions instead of short-lived formulas?

The joint Polish-Czechoslovak declaration of November 11, 1940, was one of the first indications of the new Eastern Europe that will emerge out of the war. The two governments declared their determination, at the conclusion of the war, to enter as independent and sovereign states into a closer political and economic association, which would become the basis of a new order in Eastern Europe and a guarantee of its stability. Both governments realized that the declaration marks only a beginning and that in order to be developed into a durable working instrument it must rest on mutual confidence, good faith and reciprocity, good faith and confidence being subtle values which cannot be created by declarations alone but must grow out of constantly repeated experience. The examination of the political, economic and military policies which would fall under united control is carried on between expert joint committees. United diplomacy and defense, customs, transportation and monetary union are likely to form the basis of the confederation. Search for the framework of a structure of such scope necessarily involves a variety of points of view. Some people would favor retention of separate national parliaments, presidents and armies with a confederal general staff, pooling of armaments, a supra-national council including cabinet ministers, a common economic council and parliamentary delegations. Others want to see a united Polish-Czechoslovak state grow out of the initial agreement with common government for the control of foreign affairs, defense, trade and finance. In each eventuality the Polish-Czechoslovak declaration envisages the extension of the unifying tendency so as to cover other smaller states and become a nucleus for the organization of all Eastern Europe.

On January 5, 1942, the Kings of Yugoslavia and Greece signed in London an agreement uniting their two countries for common defense, foreign policy and international trade. Expert committees have been set up to study and prepare the practical ways of giving effect to the agreement. The two nuclei of confederation, the Polish-Czechoslovak and the Greek-Yugoslav, work in close union with a view to organize Eastern Europe as a whole for unity.

What are the minimum requirements for such an organization to rest on solid foundations? Which should be the maximum objectives to make it a more perfect union? In other words, what are the aims it is desirable to pursue, and what are the possibilities lying within the limits of practicability? How much of that which is undesirable could and should be avoided? What can be done that one would like to do and what must one do because it is necessary? It is between these two poles that the bases of a union will have to be laid down.

Enough was said in the previous chapters about the various divisions existing between the peoples of Eastern Europe. Hitler in a sense united most of the people in a front of resistance. It must not be overlooked, however, that Hitler has also sown new seeds of discord in pursuing the diplomacy of conquest through division. By skillfully manipulating the centrifugal elements among the Slovaks and Croats, and by playing on the expansionist ambitions of the Bulgars and Magyars, he added to the already existing difficulties. His structure will fall to pieces once his grip over the smaller peoples is gone. Nevertheless, some of the factors which permitted his rise may need to be coped with in a more constructive spirit.

A certain minimum of common political, cultural and economic traits are a condition of the successful working of a union. No one realistically versed in Eastern European affairs will underestimate the complexity of the issues involved. The establishment in all countries of democratic methods of government, insuring freedom of speech and of the Press, freedom of assembly, faith and movement, and safeguarding the integrity of the individual, are indispensable prerequisites of a free union. The exterior form of government need not be uniform. Czechoslovak republicanism could accommodate itself easily to Yugoslav monarchism, for instance. The symbols of tradition may vary, but the substance of each régime, the basic notion of the relationship between the governing and the governed would have to be substantially democratic. Any tendency towards the democratization of political and social structure will be conducive to serving the cause of unity. The reorganization by General Sikorski of the Polish parliament in exile so as to make it correspond to the traditional political and social life of Poland may become an element of strength. The semi-authoritarian period between the military putsch in 1926 and 1939 was not a happy one for the Polish people and for the cause of solidarity among the small nations. The Nazi doctrine of the master race and the semi-feudal outlook of the Magyar ruling class, to mention only the two most obstructionist attitudes, could under no circumstances work for harmony. In so far as such differences as these are the result of long developments in the past, the adaptation to the required minimum of community of outlook can hardly occur without profound social changes. The democratic victory will have to remove the militaristic caste as well as political and social despots and racists. The leveling process will be thus encouraged, but only through genuine democratic institutions can it lead to permanent victory. It is important that great powers discontinue rendering official and unofficial assistance to reactionary tendencies.

"The free Hungarian" movement has been in existence for some time past in pre-Vichy France, England and the United States. Composed of exiles or old residents in the democratic countries the movement, comprising several thousand, stands in sharp opposition to the present Hungarian government and its supporters. The aims of the movement, as defined by the London office, are to play an active part in the fight for freedom against totalitarianism and German expansion, for free elections and land reform along the lines undertaken in Czechoslovakia before this war, for the pacification of Central Europe by collaboration between Hungary and her neighbors, and for opening the Danubian region to western democratic influences. Committees with similar programs have been formed by Hungarians in the United States. They should be distinguished from the activities of individuals who behind the prominence of their names camouflage themselves as democrats while actually acting in the interests of the oppressive régime at home.

Like the democratic Hungarians, the Austrian exiles share the disadvantage of limited numbers, the lack of a government abroad that would be representative of the majority opinion of the population, and in the case of the Austrians, the unity of purpose and of strategy. To some extent this may be explained by the noncommittal attitude of the great powers with regard to the general organization of Eastern Europe, and more specifically to the future of Austria. All the Austrian exiles are staunchly anti-Nazi. A good many of them, however, would favor union with a democratic Germany particularly if the Reich were transformed into a federation of autonomous lands. The legitimists propagate the restoration of the Habsburgs in Austria and Hungary and link it with a plan of creating a Danubian federation. A monarch, the legitimists say, could form the bridge between the socialists of Vienna and the conservative peasants of the Austrian provinces. Moreover, he could also be a symbol of unity between the different nations of a Danubian federation, including, above all, the Austrians, Czechs and Magyars. An analogy is drawn, rather ineptly, to the symbolic position of the British throne in the Empire.

In the minds of most Eastern Europeans Austria-Hungary proved faithless to her mission. By attacking Serbia in 1914 she signed her doom. The Habsburg dynasty is associated with centuries long misrule. Except for the small legitimist group, the idea of restoration commands no popular support in any country, Austria included. After the defeat of the Axis the trend will be towards political, economic and social democracy to which the restorationists have little to contribute. Whatever merits the Habsburg monarchy may have had in a Europe of dynasties in the centuries gone by, the new Eastern Europe will not return to the year of 1526, nor to 1867, and not even to 1919 or 1938.

The Austrian socialists in exile, many of whom were driven out of their native land as far back as the authoritarian régime of Dollfuss, are equally strong in denouncing the Anschluss imposed by force. They stand for a solution of the Austrian problem "whereby the vital interests of the Austrian people shall be put in accord with the vital interests of all their neighbors." The socialists strive for a "democratic and socialist development of Austria within a democratic federation of all Central European countries and all Europe." There is another group, Catholic Austrians, supporting the idea of Small Austria in contradistinction to the Greater Austria that looms behind the program of the legitimists and to some degree also behind the socialist concept. The Catholics refuse to become "a satellite of Germany, a policy pursued by the late Austro-Hungarian monarchy since 1867," and "look towards a federative union of all the smaller nations between Germany, Italy and Russia." The question of the Habsburgs is according to this group not limited to Austria alone but concerns all the so-called succession states of the Austro-Hungarian monarchy. "The main problem for the Austrian people is to be liberated from Germany and from any German dominated or pro-German European scheme." "The future Austria should not be based upon the exclusive ideology of traditionalism or revolution, as implied in the principle of legitimism or revolutionary socialism, but upon the idea of democracy combining both conservative, progressive and social elements of industrial and agricultural classes."

The Free Rumanian movement in London has undertaken the task of coordinating the activities of similar Rumanian organizations for the purpose of stirring the Rumanian people into action to resist Nazi domination. Its spokesmen believe that their efforts will be shared by an overwhelming popular support at home. The British government has taken official notice of the Committee's work and permitted it to function. Otherwise Great Britain has been at war with official Rumania since December 1941.

With regard to the status of the governments in exile those of Poland, Czechoslovakia, Greece and Yugoslavia enjoy full recognition by Great Britain, the Soviet Union, the United States, and by other governments residing in London, i.e., Belgian, Norwegian, Dutch, Luxemburg and the de facto Free French cabinet. The military units of the governments in exile take part in the prosecution of the war, and their diplomatic activity is coordinated with that of the great powers through the Inter-Allied Council in London. Their ultimate objective is the liberation of their peoples from the Axis occupation and the restoration of their independence. A complete victory over Germany, Italy and their junior partners is the principal prerequisite of the attainment of that goal. However, the attitude of the great powers towards the specific problems entering into the compass of the restoration will play a determinative role when it comes to the definitive settlement. In the same way the strategy of the governments in exile acting jointly or severally may have an important bearing on the course of the formative stage of the process out of which the new Eastern Europe will emerge. Lastly, no less important will be the lineaments of the economic and social structure as well as the psychological frame of mind of the people at home. It is they who bore directly the brunt of the assault and who have had personal experience of the Axis rule.

With regard to this last point evidence is plentiful of the spirit of defiance. Resistance to the new masters reasserts itself in most varied ways and intensity and takes on most incalculable forms. Among the Poles, Czechs, Serbs, and to a lesser degree among the other conquered peoples there is none of the willingly given cooperation which the Nazis expected and of which they boasted in their propaganda. In some parts of Eastern Europe administration is functioning thanks to the local Quislings but the people have nothing to do with it. The Germans have had no success in capturing the sympathies of the masses which almost without exception look forward to the Axis defeat. At the same time there is a general feeling that this war transcends the limits of habitual warfare, that more than frontiers are at stake, and that the world faces one of its most profound social transformations which will change both the status of individuals and of nations. The opposition to the Nazi rule derives its sustained strength not only from the determination of the subject nations to prevent their national spirit being crushed but also out of the awareness of the material consequences which would result from the Axis victory. The "Deutsche Allgemeine Zeitung" of October 6, 1940, dispelled any doubts in that respect by saying that "the revenues from taxation alone which may be expected from the new parts of the Reich under normal conditions will be sufficient for the service and amortization of the armaments debt incurred by the Reich during the war."

The Poles, Czechs and Serbs are among the most victimized of all the Nazi victims. The terror reached its limits when whole-

sale preventive shootings were ordered of members of the intelligentsia, as well as of the key men in labor and cooperative groups.
The discontent is general throughout Eastern Europe, and as the
chances of the Axis victory grow slimmer and the process of the
dissolution deepens the situation on Hitler's third front, the home
front, will become more and more untenable. Passive resistance,
the slow-down in production, secret and open sabotage, boycott
of Nazi propaganda, the determination not to give up the spirit
of resistance regardless of the time element, these are only the first
stages of the war on the inner front. In Serbian mountains, aided
by nature, organized military revolt has been going on ever since
the occupation of Yugoslavia, and this despite the fact that whole
towns were razed and large communities were summarily dealt
with. There is an inexhaustible reservoir of courageous men and
women preferring to die standing than on their knees. The third
front will play an ever increasing part in the total war. Half of
European production could eventually be wrecked and the Axis
power thus undermined at the source. The military defeat of the
Nazi army must come first, however. Disarmed populations cannot fight against tanks with bare hands. The interconnection between all the fronts should therefore be kept constantly in mind,
and the potentialities of the home front weighed in their due
proportions.

Toward a More Perfect Union

As remarked in the previous section, the idea of grouping various states and nations into a federation of one kind or another has
developed into one of the issues of the war. It has taken hold of
both the realist and the doctrinaire, the practical statesman and
the theoretical planner. So far most energy has been spent where
it can produce no harm but little practical good, i.e., on drafting
federal and similar constitutions. Fascinating though such activity
may be, the unreality of it becomes apparent once it is found that
much of it moves in a vacuum. The propaganda value of federal

projects should not be underestimated, however. People are led to think in terms of unity rather than diversity and the power of aroused public opinion may eventually become the deciding factor.

The principal point to be fully realized concerns the state of affairs which will exist in Eastern Europe at the close of the war. The area does not represent and never represented a political unit. Even during its most simplified aspect in 1900 it was shared by several political entities such as Russia, Germany, Austria-Hungary, Rumania, Serbia, Bulgaria, Montenegro, Greece and Turkey. The present war divided the individual nations again into several camps. Hungary and Bulgaria side with Germany as in 1914. Rumania which in World War I fought against the Central Powers, was maneuvred by Hitler and Mussolini to fight for their cause. The Axis-created puppet states of Croatia and Slovakia are allied against the nations with whom they united in 1918, and whose independence has been suppressed. Finland fights Britain's ally—the Soviet Union. The Baltic states which emerged from World War I and the Russian Revolution as independent units, lost their independence to the Soviet Union in 1939, and in 1941 were in turn submerged in the Greater Reich. The Poles and Czechs were swallowed by Hitler, the Slovenes by Hitler plus Mussolini, and a more or less similar fate befell the Serbs, Albanians and Greeks. Turkey alone at the beginning of 1942 maintained fragile neutrality between the two principal belligerents.

In addition to and underneath these arbitrary carvings millions of peoples were shifted within their territorial habitats from one sovereignty to another. Thus the Ruthenians became a new minority in Hungary together with Rumanians and other Slavs. Hungary and Germany included within their frontiers millions of non-Germans and non-Magyars. Italy increased her non-Italian population. Bulgaria received many Serbs and Greeks. Whole nations such as Poles and Czechs were reduced to minority nationalities. Moreover, millions of people have been earmarked for transplantation, or have actually been uprooted. Rumanians of former Rumania were given to Hungary, and Hungary in turn was made into a German vassal state. In each country the German groups were raised to a privileged status and above all these confused gradations and degradations the emblem of the swastika was hoisted as the symbol of Nazi supremacy. The famed German sense of organization ran amok.

Unnatural as the present situation is, it is reasonable to expect that the Axis defeat will automatically lead to a series of disentanglements which will facilitate a more salutory political organization. The pro-Axis governments will drop out of the picture or will have to be removed. Most of this work will be done by the people themselves. Where force will be necessary, force must be applied fairly but resolutely. The situation in Eastern Europe will not be substantially different from the general situation in Europe as a whole. A degree of chaos seems to be unavoidable. The intensity and duration of the malaise will depend upon the amount of effective assistance the great powers will be willing to render and upon the measure of collaboration offered by the local constructive statesmanship. The fact that the Nazi pattern is only an imposed surface will reduce the transitional difficulties. On the other hand, there may occur local disturbances of a social nature. Attempts may be made, as after World War I, to retain other people's lands, to seize more territory by putsches, and to place before the world accomplished facts. The restitution of the forcibly acquired territory by Germany, Italy, Hungary and Bulgaria must be a precondition of cessation of hostilities. There should be no disagreement on that account between the allied governments. The United States supplied long ago a moral precedent by its non-recognition doctrine. If international law is to be restored and lawlessness banned, seizures lawlessly committed must be annulled. Disputes over mixed border areas will reappear and must be dealt with on the basis of common agreements having behind them allied authority and enforcement. The diplomacy of give and take will have to receive ample play if the old controversies are to be eliminated and solid ground prepared for the peaceful coexistence of various groups that have been repeatedly kept apart by home-made and foreign-encouraged antagonisms.

The process of cleansing Eastern Europe of the Nazi surface will meet less obstruction than is sometimes assumed. The more important and temporarily more burning problem will be that of providing the impoverished and plundered population with foodstuffs, clothing and other necessities as well as medical supplies. Relief work if done fairly and expeditiously will introduce the element of comfort that may go a long way toward creating the psychological climate for a better political understanding. In executing the plan of a new Europe that would last "one thousand years," the German government employed a great deal of ingenuity to give it a basis of law, Nazi law. Hitler himself assumed power "legally," and every one of his subsequent conquests was accompanied by a display of legality, Nazi legality. The results of the Nazi law will have to be done away with.

The recovery of freedom will release new strength of faith among the occupied nations and regenerate their creative capabilities. The local nuclei of reconstruction will have to be aided from outside until the somewhat molten transitional period yields to a more solid situation. It is therefore vital that Great Britain, the Soviet Union, the United States come to a comprehensive unity of views as to the short and long-term organization of Eastern Europe. If under the stress of the long war the three countries retired to their own preoccupations, the consequences might be most undesirable. Even more calamitous would the political situation become if England and Russia failed to reach a clear understanding. The interests of the two powers are not necessarily contradictory and irreconcilable. The past few years have taught them both a useful lesson. The underlying note of their agreement must be full respect for the interests of the smaller peoples and renunciation of all attempts to infringe their rights or menace their development on the basis of their own proper institutions. The small nations on their part must free themselves from the archaic notion of constituting a barrier between the east and west. Eastern Europe is by geography a thoroughfare. In order to avoid becoming again the highway for tanks it must become a conveyor of goods. For that purpose all the important routes of communication inside and outside Eastern Europe must be under a united international management, must be Europeanized. The same principle will have to be applied to Germany. There is nothing more pernicious than for a nation to assume a mission of trying to prevent or hamper international exchange of goods, or to constitute itself a self-appointed missionary. Equality and freedom of trade and of communication will have to be exempted from limited national control and submitted to international cooperation. The highest purpose of existence of both great and small nations is to live decently and to allow others to live likewise. No one has a so-called special mission of doing this or preventing that. The world would indeed be better off without many such self-appointed crusaders.

The United States may not be interested in having a direct hand in the settlement of the details of the Eastern European organization. However, it cannot refuse to place behind it its moral authority and it must not confuse moral support with convenient do-nothingness. Its principal task as the leading world power must be to participate in shaping the broad and at the same time effective outlines of the world society in which the vast majority of decent people want to live. Equal opportunities for advancement of all nations in the field of economic and social progress and upholding international morality have become so intimately associated with the Roosevelt-Hull diplomacy that the world rightly expects American resources to be placed at the disposal of all humanity on an equitable basis. The Atlantic declaration pointed the road but much more will have to be undertaken concretely if that well phrased document is to be more than a diplomatic move made under the stress of war psychology.

The problem of Eastern Europe is as much and even more tied up with the future of Germany as any other European region, in fact as Europe in general. What will happen in and to Germany after the war will bear directly on what will happen in and to the smaller nations on her borders. The German speaking people make up about one-seventh of the total European population. With the exception of Russia they represent therefore the largest and most homogeneous group. Yet their relative strength gives them no title to the domination of the remaining six-sevenths of Europe's people. The German voice will and must be heard at the councils of Europe, but it must not be the voice of a military terrorist. Neither can it be the voice of an economic monopolist. International disarmament and control of the production of war material is practically possible. How to check German heavy industry is one question and how to prevent it from becoming once again the arsenal of aggression is another. Another way will be the development of the economic potentialities of the Eastern European peoples themselves. No opportunity or pretext should be left to Germany to make it possible for her to declare herself the sole protector of the semi-developed nations. International cartels will have to be placed under a united control of the producers, consumers, labor and governments so that they cannot become an instrument of German economic exploitation of temporarily weaker peoples.

The common problem of the Eastern European area is how to raise the standards of living and the level of purchasing power of a relatively overpopulated region under undeveloped agricultural conditions. The remedy points to more industrialization and labor-intensive farming. This does not mean that preponderantly agrarian communities will have to be transformed into unbalanced industrial regions. Neither should such a policy be regarded as economic nationalism provided that nothing is done to seriously interfere with international division of labor and specialization. Without a degree of regional planning forming a part of international planning with government participation or the application of private common sense initiative, the task would prove almost impossible of achievement. On the other hand, given proper understanding of the essentials of the problem the increased purchasing power of more than one hundred million people would benefit world trade as much as it would accommodate a peaceful Germany. Once for all, the concept of treating the German people as a problem child should be abandoned. The idea has again become popular of trying to plan out for the Germans how they should live in the future. No self-respecting people will accept such an attitude. Let the Germans solve within their proper space their own internal affairs as best as they can. But make it clear to them, and insist on it by practical and effective policies, that through cooperation they can go much further than by unilateral action. Above all make it impossible for them to wage a third world war in the future. Do not sentimentalize on the fate of a race of eighty million people while forgetting that in its neighborhood over a hundred million people have an equal right to a decent life. Discard the myth of German organizational supremacy. This war has shown that the Russians or the Chinese are as good organizers as any if opportunities are not withdrawn from them.

The supreme war council and the inter-allied economic executives created during the war may provide the starting points for putting Eastern Europe along the peaceful road for the duration of the transitional period. More than one half of the Eastern European peoples are or should be indirectly represented on these councils through the exiled governments of Poland, Czechoslovakia, Yugoslavia and Greece. The remaining peoples will not consider it advantageous to obstruct the work, if the work is broadly conceived and fairly executed. Mobile military units placed in strategic centers of Eastern Europe will be sufficient to restore and maintain order to allow the postwar passions to quiet down and enable the war-weary peoples to settle down to peaceful

THE FUTURE OF EASTERN EUROPE

pursuits. Efficiently managed international controlling bodies having charge of shipping, raw material supplies and necessary finished goods should not be unable to handle the economic side of the transitional period. It was done before and it could be done again, and better. In the meantime the true political and social realities will emerge from the chaos brought about by the Axis arbitrary machinations. Then it will be the task of wise statesmanship to embody these true realities into a constitutional framework.

The technical aspects of Eastern European union present certain practical difficulties but they should not be regarded as insurmountable or serious. The moral and factual demobilization will open ways and means toward dealing with them in a rational manner. More vitally important are certain fundamental principles the observance of which will be necessary. One of them, i.e., the minimum of unity of moral, political, economic and social outlook, has already been referred to. Only sheer optimism would maintain that such a unity already exists. It does not. But the majority of people desire it and should be able to give it concrete forms of expression. There will always be recalcitrant elements but they will be kept in check and must not be allowed to reverse the course of events. It is also unlikely that all the nations will join the unifying movement at the very start. The Hungarians for instance may find it hard to relinquish some of the advantages which they wrested from their neighbors due to the Axis conjecture. There must be no excessive zeal in forcing union on any one who is not ready for it. The growth should be empirical rather than categorical. If union is made worthwhile the ranks of the recalcitrants will automatically grow thinner. The ideal of having all the nations between Germany, Russia and Italy under one roof may take a long time to materialize. Individual groups may eventually never belong to it and seek their future elsewhere. Yet it can be soundly assumed that for the majority a union represents the most advantageous if not the only course.

The essential point of the union, or whatever alternative plan may take its place, will be the Eastern Europeanization of the military and economic power. So long as power is compartmentalized, a united policy of defense and broad economic control is unthinkable. The constitutional forms in which the regionalization of power will be integrated may vary. A sui generis form of multilateral alliances of eternal validity would represent the weakest though not necessarily an entirely ineffective arrangement. A hastily concocted union might prove as ineffectual at the time of crisis as a system of alliances. In the end it will not be the form but the realization of common interest that will make the union strong or effete. On the other hand it is the form backed by the agencies of enforcement which may act as an ever present and compelling reminder of the community of interest. In any case the maximalization of sovereign rights and minimization of common duties will have to be eliminated and sovereignty as such will have to be re-interpreted in a thoroughly new and unorthodox light. No member state will be the sole and ultimate judge of its action in the field of international and economic policies. Its rights and duties will be controlled by special organs possessing the enforcing authority. A return to anything that had existed before 1938 must not take place. Old traditions cannot be left out of account entirely, and where possible and serviceable, new institutions will be grafted upon healthy tradition.

Equally essential will be the re-interpretation of the status of the individual citizen with regard to the state and the union. The safeguard of individual freedoms will be the basis of all intercourse. The people must be more concerned with the dignity of human personality than with so-called national prestige which in many ways is nothing else but the vulgar deification of vested prerogatives and selfish ambitions of unscrupulous groups of oligarchs. The establishment of a society in which all peoples would enjoy equality of economic opportunities and social security without distinction of language, race, religion and birth must be made into the organic law of the new Eastern Europe. The generalization of the conception of human integrity will solve more than half of the minority problems and may be found more practicable than any transfers of large masses of people from their ancestral homes. Within the union protection of remaining minorities would be equally generalized and no single state could pass legislation that would be discriminatory and opposed to the organic law. Eastern Europe would thus be a region where people can move freely without being molested by reasons of their nationality.

Since the small nations are not equal in size, economic development and political maturity, care must be taken and proper institutional safeguards established, with force behind them, so that no single state or a combination of states could create within the union a preponderance of weight and use it for the domination of the rest. Eastern Europe must not allow itself to be degraded to the Reich where Prussia made herself through steel and fist the domineering factor. In a measure the existing national and cultural diversity of the component parts of the area will serve as an automatic barrier to such attempts. Due to their historical evolution and innate traditions the individual nations of the union would claim and retain a large measure of state rights compatible with the unity. In that respect no existing federation could be transplanted to Eastern Europe. The peoples must evolve a political system of their own. To some extent the experiences of the growth of the Swiss confederation may furnish guidance.

Lastly, the Eastern European system must not include any great power. Neither can it be directed against any great power except in self-defence. It must not be conceived as an autarchic system pursuing a restrictive economic policy. Considering the absence of many important raw materials, capital and geographical position there is little likelihood of such perversion. The ultimate security of the Eastern European peoples will depend upon the measure of universal security that the great and small powers will organize after the war. The same applies to the ultimate economic prosperity. Eastern Europe is not and never can be a world of its own. The delegates of the Polish, Czechoslovak, Yugoslav and Greek workers, employers and governments formulated their views and expectations in a joint declaration to the conference of the International Labor Organization held in November 1941 in New York: "We hope that the end of this war which was forced upon us will save a hundred million inhabitants of Central Europe and the Balkans from their present state of wretchedness by assuring them the possibility of stable employment, guaranteed by reconstruction and by the development of their industries, and that those peoples will be included within the sphere of international exchange of goods and services." A free Eastern Europe is a social, moral and political axiom. To prevent another enslavement of the small nations as a step towards the enslavement of the large ones is a vital concern of all.

Epilogue

On January 1, 1942, representatives of twenty-six nations fighting the Axis signed a declaration by which they pledged themselves to employ their full resources against the Axis powers with which they were at war and not to make a separate armistice or peace with the enemies. The declaration may be adhered to by other nations which are, or may be, rendering material assistance and contributions in the struggle for victory over Hitlerism. Among the United Nations are peoples of all continents and of every important region of the earth. There are four nations of Eastern Europe, Poland, Czechoslovakia, Yugoslavia and Greece, representing more than a half of the population of the area. The United Nations have in their hands a preponderance of physical and moral power which will make it possible for them to embody in concrete forms the principles of the Atlantic Charter and to establish the rule of law to preserve human rights and justice. Complete victory over their enemies will enable them to introduce and re-create such methods and organizations of international collaboration as will best meet the requirements of the new world that is painfully emerging from the present chaos and destruction. The instinct of survival is deeply ingrained in human nature, and before the last shot is fired on the battlefront the brains and the hands of men will already be deeply engaged in the work of postwar reconstruction.

The United Nations' declaration is of universal appeal. Other nations may join it. This openness is in fact one of its most meritorious aspects. As soon as the military situation permits it, many more nations will rally behind its support. There is a good chance that this time the world leadership will not fail, and that the peoples whose freedom shall be restored will use it wisely and constructively. The inability to learn from the past has always been one of the obstacles to wisdom and to progress. In the same way, unwillingness to share the benefits, the sacrifices and the responsibilities has always stood in the way of true democracy. Each nation will have to carry its share of responsibility. Each nation will also be entitled to its share of authority. It will be the task of the United Nations of to-day and those of to-morrow to plan continually and to cooperate permanently in order to discharge their responsibilities in an equitable manner. The nations of Eastern Europe will have their share of responsibilities. Their takings will to a large extent be dependent on their givings. Their specific task will be to convert their region, in cooperation with like-minded nations of the world, to a region of political stability, economic prosperity, social justice, national and individual freedom, and universal usefulness. They owe this to Europe, they owe this to themselves.

Bibliography

The author is indebted to the following sources of information, documents, books and periodicals, which were particularly useful and valuable in writing the volume:

BOOKS

ALBRECHT-CARRIÉ, RENÉ: *Italy at the Peace Conference*, Columbia University Press, 1938.

ANCEL, JACQUES: *L'Europe Centrale*, Paris, 1936.

ARMSTRONG, HAMILTON FISH: *Where There Is No Peace*, New York, 1939.

BALTIC INSTITUTE, THE, TORUN, 1935-1936: *Baltic Countries: A survey of the peoples and states of the Baltic with special regard to their history, geography and economics.*

Baltic States, the Royal Institute of International Affairs, London, 1938.

BASCH, ANTONIN: *The New Economic Warfare*, Columbia University Press, 1941.

BENEŠ, EDUARD: *Boj o bezpečnost státu*, Praha, 1934.

BENEŠ, EDUARD: *Germany and Czechoslovakia*, Praha, 1937.

BERBER, FRITZ: *Das Diktat von Versailles*, Essen, 1939.

BORKENAU, FRANZ: *The Communist International*, London, 1938.

British War Blue Book, 1939.

BUELL, RAYMOND LESLIE: *Poland, Key to Europe*, New York, 1939.

BULLOCK, MALCOLM: *Austria 1918-1938*, London, 1939.

CARNEGIE ENDOWMENT FOR INTERNATIONAL PEACE: *International Conciliation Documents,* New York, 1920-1941.

CHAMBERLAIN, NEVILLE: *In Search of Peace,* New York, 1939.

CHURCHILL, WINSTON: *Step by Step,* London, 1939.

CURREY, MURIEL: *Italian Foreign Policy 1918-1932,* London, 1932.

DYBOVSKI, ROMAN: *Outlines of Polish History,* London, 1931.

FIALA, VACLAV: *La Pologne d'aujourdhui,* Paris, 1936.

GEDYE, G. E. R.: *Betrayal in Central Europe. Austria and Czechoslovakia: The Fallen Bastions,* New York, 1939.

GENOV, S. P.: *Bulgaria and the Treaty of Neuilly,* Sofia, 1935.

GERMAN LIBRARY OF INFORMATION: *Documents on the Events Preceding the Outbreak of the War,* New York, 1941.

GESHKOFF, THEODOR I.: *Balkan Union in Southeastern Europe,* Columbia University Press, 1940.

GUETZÉVITCH, B. MIRKINE: *Les Constitutions de l'Europe Nouvelle,* Paris, 1938.

HASKINS, CHARLES HOMER, and LORD, ROBERT HOWARD: *Some Problems of the Peace Conference,* Cambridge, 1922.

HENDERSON, SIR NEVILLE: *Failure of a Mission,* New York, 1940.

HITCHCOCK, EDWARD B.: *I Built a Temple of Peace,* New York, 1940.

Hitler's Route to Bagdad, Fabian Society, London, 1939.

HUNGARIAN MINISTRY OF FOREIGN AFFAIRS: *Papers and Documents relating to the Foreign Policy of Hungary,* Budapest, 1939.

INSTITUT INTERNATIONAL DE COOPERATION INTELLECTUELLE: *Chronique des événements politiques et économiques,* 1918-1936.

International Security. Harris Foundation Lectures, the University of Chicago Press, 1939.

JACKSON, J. HAMPDEN: *The Baltic,* London, 1940.

JACKSON, J. HAMPDEN: *Estonia,* London, 1941.

JACKSON, J. HAMPDEN: *Finland,* London, 1938.

JÁSZI, OSCAR: *The Dissolution of the Habsburg Monarchy,* Chicago, 1929.

KERNER, R. J., and HOWARD, H. N.: *The Balkan Conferences and the Balkan Entente*, University of California Press, 1936.

KROFTA, KAMIL: *Z dob naší první republiky*, Praha, 1939.

LANGDON-DAVIES, JOHN: *Finland, the First Total War*, London, 1940.

Land of Socialism Today and Tomorrow, The, Moscow, 1939.

LAPRADELLE, A. G.: *La paix de Versailles*, Vol. X, Paris, 1939.

LAVERGNE, BERNARD: *Munich, défaite des democraties*, Paris, 1939.

LEAGUE OF NATIONS, CONFERENCE ON RURAL LIFE: *The Land Tenure System in Europe*, 1939.

LEAGUE OF NATIONS, CONFERENCE ON RURAL LIFE: *Population and Agriculture with Special Reference to Agricultural Overpopulation*, 1939.

Le Livre Jaune Français, Paris, 1940.

LENGYEL, EMIL: *The Danube*, New York, 1939.

LIAS, G.: *Beneš of Czechoslovakia*, London, 1938.

LLOYD GEORGE, DAVID: *Memoirs of the Peace Conference*, Yale University Press, 1939.

LUCKAU, ALMA: *The German Delegation at the Paris Peace Conference*, Columbia University Press, 1938.

MACARTNEY, C. A.: *Hungary and her Successors*, London, 1937.

MACARTNEY, C. A.: *National States and National Minorities*, the Royal Institute of International Affairs, 1934.

MACHRAY, ROBERT: *The Little Entente*, 1929.

MACHRAY, ROBERT: *Poland 1914-1931*, London, 1932.

MACHRAY, ROBERT: *The Struggle for the Danube*, London, 1938.

MARKOVITCH, LAZARE: *La politique extérieure de la Yougoslavie*, Paris, 1935.

MASARYK, T. G.: *The Making of a State*, London, 1927.

MASARYK, T. G.: *The New Europe*, 1918.

MINISTRY OF FOREIGN AFFAIRS OF FINLAND: *Finnish Blue Book*, New York, 1940.

MIRKOVICH, MILOSLAV: *Yugoslavia's Choice*, Foreign Affairs, 1941.

MORANT, G. M.: *The Races of Central Europe*, London, 1939.

MOURIN, M.: *Histoire des grandes puissances depuis la guerre,* Paris, 1939.

OPOČENSKÝ, JAN: *The Collapse of the Austro-Hungarian Monarchy,* Praha, 1928.

PADELFORD, NORMAN J.: *Peace in the Balkans,* New York, 1935.

PASCHA, CASI MUSTAFA KEMAL: *Der Weg zur Freiheit,* Leipzig, 1928.

PASVOLSKI, LEO: *Economic Nationalism of the Danubian States,* New York, 1928.

Peaceful Change, International Institute of Intellectual Cooperation, Paris, 1938.

POLISH MINISTRY OF FOREIGN AFFAIRS: *Official Documents Concerning Polish-German and Polish-Soviet Relations,* 1933-1939.

PRIBICHEVICH, STOYAN: *World Without End,* New York, 1939.

PROKOPOVIC, S. N.: *Le commerce international d'après guerre des Etats Danubiens,* Praha, 1936.

RAUSCHNING, HERMANN: *The Voice of Destruction,* New York, 1940.

RIEGER, BOHŬS: *Imperial History of Austria,* Praha, 1912.

RIPKA, HUBERT: *Munich Before and After,* London, 1939.

ROSE, ADAM: *La reconstruction économique de l'Europe Centrale et Orientale,* Politique Etrangère, 1940.

ROUČEK, JOSEPH: *The Politics of the Balkans,* New York, 1939.

ROYAL INSTITUTE OF INTERNATIONAL AFFAIRS: *Europe Under Hitler,* 1941.

ROYAL INSTITUTE OF INTERNATIONAL AFFAIRS: *Nationalism,* 1939.

ROYAL INSTITUTE OF INTERNATIONAL AFFAIRS: *South-Eastern Europe,* London, 1939.

SCHACHER, GUSTAV: *Germany Pushes South-East,* London, 1937.

SCHUSCHNIGG, KURT: *My Austria,* New York, 1938.

SETON-WATSON, R. W.: *A History of the Roumanians,* Cambridge, 1934.

SETON-WATSON, R. W.: *Racial Problems in Hungary,* London, 1908.

SFORZA, CARLO: *Fifty Years of War and Diplomacy in the Balkans,* New York, 1940.

SMORGORZENSKI, CASIMIR: *Poland's Access to the Sea,* London, 1934.

SOFRONIE, GEORGE: *La politique internationale de la Roumanie,* Bucharest, 1938.

Statistical Baltic Yearbook, the Baltic Institute, 1936.

Statistical Yearbook of the League of Nations, The.

TAYLOR, R. P. D. STEPHEN: *Handbook of Central and Eastern Europe,* Zurich, 1932.

TOYNBEE, ARNOLD J.: *Survey of International Affairs,* the Royal Institute of International Affairs, 1920-1938.

VONDRÁČEK, FELIX JOHN: *The Foreign Policy of Czechoslovakia,* Columbia University Press, 1937.

WAGEMANN, ERNST: *Der Neue Balkan,* Hamburg, 1939.

WEIGNER, KAREL: *L'égalité des races européennes,* Bruxelles, 1935.

WENDEL, HERMANN: *Der Kampf der Südslawen um Freiheit und Einheit,* Frankfort, 1925.

WISKEMANN, ELIZABETH: *Czechs and Germans,* the Royal Institute of International Affairs, London, 1938.

WISKEMANN, ELIZABETH: *Undeclared War,* London, 1939.

WOLFERS, ARNOLD: *Britain and France Between Two Wars,* New York, 1938.

WRIGHT, F. CH.: *Population and Peace,* International Institute of Intellectual Cooperation, Paris, 1939.

PERIODICALS

The American Review on the Soviet Union: The American-Russian Institute, New York, 1940-1941.

The Bulletin of International Affairs: The Royal Institute of International Affairs, 1938-1941.

The Central European Observer. A Fortnightly Review: Prague, 1920-1938, London, 1940-1942.

Czechoslovak Sources and Documents: Orbis, Praha, 1931-1938.

The Economist: London, 1940-1941.

Foreign Affairs: Hopper, Bruce, "The War for Eastern Europe," 1941.

Foreign Affairs: Mosely, Philip E., "Transylvania Partitioned," 1940.

Foreign Policy Reports: Foreign Policy Association, New York, Vol. XV: Nos. 5, 19, and 24; Vol. XVI: Nos. 15, 1939-1940.

The Journal of Central European Affairs: University of Colorado, 1940-1941. (The parts dealing with the period of appeasement and the outbreak of World War II appeared in slightly modified form in the Journal in April and October, 1941.)

The Review of Politics: Fraenkel, Ernst, "German-Russian Relations Since 1918," the University of Notre Dame, 1940.

La revue de France: Ionesco, Take, "La Petite Entente," 1921.

Revue International des Etudes Balcaniques: Beograd, 1934-1935.

The Slavonic and East European Review: School of Slavonic Studies, King's College, London, 1921-1939.

Yale Review: Seymour, Charles, "Czechoslovak Frontier," 1939.

Index